STUDIES
IN GDR
CULTURE
AND
SOCIETY 7

Selected Papers from the Twelfth New Hampshire Symposium on the German Democratic Republic

Editorial Board:
Margy Gerber, Chief Editor
Christine Cosentino
Volker Gransow
Nancy A. Lauckner
Christiane Lemke
Arthur A. Stahnke
Alexander Stephan
W. Christoph Schmauch

UNIVERSITY
PRESS OF
AMERICA

Lanham • New York • London

Copyright © 1987 by

University Press of America,® Inc.

4720 Boston Way
Lanham, MD 20706

3 Henrietta Street
London WC2E 8LU England

British Cataloging in Publication Information Available

Co-published by arrangement with the
International Symposium of the
German Democratic Republic

"Homosexuality and the Situation of Homosexuals in the GDR"
© 1987 by Rudiger Pieper

"Fortschritt im real existierenden Sozialismus"
© 1987 by Fred Klinger

ISBN: 0-8191-6486-0 (pbk. : alk. paper)
ISBN: 0-8191-6485-2 (alk. paper)

All University Press of America books are produced on acid-free
paper which exceeds the minimum standards set by the National
Historical Publication and Records Commission.

Table of Contents

Acknowledgments

The editors wish to express their thanks to Kinderbuch-verlag and Verlag Junge Welt in Berlin for their permission to use photographs of three children's books they published. The photographs, taken by Gail Hueting, appear as illustrations in her article on children's literature.

Preface

The eighteen papers collected here are revised versions of papers presented at the Twelfth New Hampshire Symposium on the German Democratic Republic, which took place at the World Fellowship Center near Conway, New Hampshire from June 20-27, 1986. This interdisciplinary conference on the GDR has been held annually since 1975.

The 1986 Symposium was attended by approximately sixty GDR specialists from the United States, the Federal Republic, the GDR, and other European countries. The general theme of the Symposium was "The GDR Today and Tomorrow." With the exception of two sections dealing specifically with literary and aesthetic subjects, the seminars were interdisciplinary; topics included the ambivalence of progress, the situation of minorities, nation building and national identity, and methods and goals of socialization. Papers on these subjects, and others, were given by sociologists, political scientists, Germanists, historians, etc. in combined sections, the goal being to broaden the perspective by illuminating the issues from various sides.

The Symposium is pluralistic in its philosophy. It has no particular political stance and welcomes well-argued and well-documented views from all sides. With the increased participation of specialists and authors from the GDR in recent years, the Symposium has come to be a meeting place between East and West.

In this volume of the series, there are for the first time several contributions from GDR participants: the author and screen writer Wolfgang Kohlhaase, known especially for his collaboration with the film director Konrad Wolf; Lothar Bisky, cultural sociologist and *Rektor* of the Hochschule für Film und Fernsehen of the GDR; Alfred Loesdau, historian at the Akademie für Gesellschaftswissenschaften beim ZK der

SED; and Rainer Saupe, economist at Humboldt University in Berlin. Although the members of the Editorial Board are not necessarily in agreement with the views presented in these papers, they consider it highly desirable - and in keeping with the spirit of the Symposium - that GDR scholars be given the opportunity to contribute to Western study of the GDR, and that Western GDR specialists be familiar with GDR positions and research.

With this volume, as with the first six volumes of the series, we would make research results conveyed at the Symposium available to a wider audience and thus promote both research and teaching about the GDR.

Margy Gerber
Chief Editor

Some Remarks about GDR Cinema

Wolfgang Kohlhaase

Don't expect to get a complete survey from me - a sort of "State of the Union in the Movies" address. I'll just give you some information, and talk about some ideas that occurred to me as someone who works as a filmmaker in the GDR.

Let me give you the information first, for maybe this or that intellectual or moral question will be better understood when you know the mechanics of GDR filmmaking. DEFA, the GDR film concern, was founded in 1946. It was the first film company in postwar Germany. Let me remind you of such films as *Die Mörder sind unter uns* (*The Murderers Are among Us*) by Wolfgang Staudte, *Ehe im Schatten* (*Marriage in the Shadow*) by Kurt Maetzig, and *Unser täglich Brot* (*Our Daily Bread*) by the important director Slatan Dudow. Before 1933 Dudow had made the film *Kuhle Wampe* with Brecht and Eisler; thus when looking for a left-wing proletarian tradition in German film, one must include Dudow.

These first films were a response to Nazism. They and others contributed to the consciousness being developed in the part of Germany which later became the GDR. With the help of such films, feeling ashamed and acknowledging one's guilt became a sort of public process. The films attempted to communicate a new view of history.

The motif of antifascism with which DEFA started has remained a crucial element of our film industry. While it was vital immediately after the war to reflect anew on the role of the Germans in this century, today's concern is to see to it that the memories of fascism do not fade. Living experience dies with the people who took part in it. What is written in textbooks easily turns into abstraction. When one looks back to the past, the complex character of that time gets lost and its most unbelievable details disappear. A film such as *Die Verlobte* (*The Financée*), for instance, reminds us of the price paid in the resistance movement, of the certainty and despair, of all the blood and courage it cost.

DEFA has been in existence for forty years now. During this time it has made some eight hundred films, including some bad ones. Its annual output of fifteen to twenty films is based on its technical rather than its artistic capacity. I am referring to feature films now. In addition, there is a studio for documentary films and one for animated films. And DEFA makes a lot of television films as well.

The studio for feature films works on a budget basis. That means that it gets a certain amount of money, say fifty million Marks, from the state budget, and with this money the annual production, say eighteen films, has to be financed. It is up to the studio to decide how it allocates the money. The completed films go to another state organization, the Progress-Film-Verleih, which distributes the films, getting them into the movie theaters and taking charge of their marketing.

The studio gets its budget independent of the profit made. For the filmmaker this means that money is not the first thing to be discussed when a new film is planned. How much you can make with a movie is not a priority, although it is taken into consideration since there is a certain relationship between the number of people who see a movie and the effect the movie has on the public. The financial failure of a film - I myself have made both movies which were popular and movies which were regrettably poorly attended - does not endanger the next project of those involved. However, if a film hasn't reached many people, its maker will probably sit down and think about its problems before beginning his next film.

Sociologists have known for a long time that the good old reliable type of moviegoer does not exist anymore, not in the GDR nor anywhere else, and there are many reasons for this. As in other countries, we too are witnessing a decrease in movie attendance. Today we are as glad when one million people go to see a movie in its first year as we were ten years ago about an attendance of two million. The average attendance is below half a million. This is quite acceptable for a country of our size; we are not more unfortunate than others in this regard. Still, when you go to a theater with thirty rows of seats to see a movie you made and find only five other people there, you have the awkward feeling that something must have gone wrong. There is nothing more pathetic than two filmmakers arguing about for which better reasons people stayed away from whose film.

Approximately 120 films are shown in the GDR each year. A third of these films come from socialist countries; two thirds, from Western countries - and about half of these from the United States. This is the sort of competition our films face in the movie theaters, and, in addition to this, they also have to compete with five TV channels, two of our own and three from the Federal Republic. All five channels together show about thirty films per week. Thus our filmgoers need an additional reason to go to the movies - or another kind of reason. There is also the problem of a change in pastimes. Nowadays many people leave the city for the weekend. Friday is no longer a preferred day for going to the movies; formerly less popular days such as Tuesday, Wednesday, and Thursday are now gaining ground.

Again and again the question arises - and it is not an easy one: what should the profile of our films be like, under the circumstances I have just described? How can our films attract attention amidst the colorful variety of hundreds and hundreds of others? One formula, I'm sure, won't work: if you are interested in tender feelings, go to the French; if you want to watch cars chasing each other, go to the Americans; if you like the Mafia, glory, and misery under a southern sun, go to the Italians; if you want to learn something, come and see our films. If we followed such a concept we would quickly lose our audience, for people do not want to learn something at the movies. They want to find out, to experience, but that is something different. They want to participate in all sorts of human fate, and, in this mediated way, they want to educate their emotions and even their minds, but by means of play and pleasure.

The movie which reaches too few people costs too much in intellectual and material terms. On the other hand, the movie industry now has to take minorities into account to a greater extent than before. And it is important to have films which set new aesthetic courses, thus opening doors for different films and a changing audience. A GDR film critic once made the telling observation that cinema is more than film. What she meant was that one should not speak only of film as art in an elitist sense when talking about the cinema. The cinema is a strange meeting place of reality and the imagination, a place of this century's mass culture. Because it is such a social meeting place, it must not be lost to a society.

At the beginning of this talk, I mentioned that soon after the war was over our films contributed to developing a critical understanding of the terrible things in which most of the Germans had been involved. The Germans were not only sitting in real rubble, there was also rubble in their minds, in their emotional patterns left behind by Nazism. These films, which concerned nearly everybody, thus referred to burning contemporary issues. It seldom happens that emotions are stirred up in such a way and that there are so many questions of general interest.

But even today the movie industry lives from finding the magical point, those real and imagined stories which express the attitude to life that people have in a given decade, or even only in a certain year. Like any other art form, film is a sensitive instrument for measuring how human beings feel. To a greater extent than the classical arts it is linked to current issues, issues of fashion, from the length of skirts to the type of hair style, and, because it communicates by means of pictures which look like life itself, it more easily takes on the function of serving as an example. With this in mind one should not be surprised that a didactic view about the social role of art - which has a certain tradition in the GDR - was applied first and foremost to film.

It was often as a result of their political activities that people from the labor movement came by books, pictures, and songs, but they spent more time in prison than in libraries. They were looking for action and guidance for action - and, strangely enough, they sought guidance in the field of art. Upton Sinclair, for instance, was extremely well-known in the German labor movement of the 1930s. And Brecht, you will remember, for some time wrote plays which he called *Lehrstücke* (didactic plays).

Thus the love of the useful example has a history, and we have to do justice to it. At the same time, we need to clarify the issue. Socialism sees itself as a society which enlightens, and it hopes that the arts, too, will contribute to the general emancipation of man. A very important part of this emancipation is precisely the aesthetic one: the ability to approach

4

art - art as not simply a reflection of reality, but a playful way of using its possibilities - in a sensual, meaningful way. "L'education sentimentale," said Flaubert. That could be right for education and art.

A planned society has a rational idea of its organization; it feels a public responsibility. Of its problems it prefers to mention the soluble ones. But art always has to do with the ambiguous circumstances, the uncertainties of life, the shortcomings of the world. As for me, I do not deliberately write in a critical or uncritical way. I write from a sense of personal concern, from the sum of my experience in life and art. The political viewpoint does not dominate the poetic one; it is part of it.

A long, never-ending discussion about these issues is going on in the GDR - but not with the artists sitting on one side and the politicians on the other, practice here and theory there, here the administered and there the administrators. It is not that easy to put professions and views in their proper place. The artistic sense of a society is linked to political, philosophical, economic, and social developments; it is not permanently fixed. By being realistic, combining a sense of reality and the imagination, art may influence the very conditions of its existence. Film - finally I have come back to it - may do this in a popular place, the movie theater.

Ninety percent of the GDR movie audience is under thirty years of age. It views our films differently than films from other countries: more critically, more politically, more expectantly. It is looking for truth, not simply as a platitude but as an adventure in unknown proximity: the uncomfortable question, the suppressed problem, tragedy and comedy, the socialization of feeling. When films produce such encounters, the theaters are full; praise is voiced, but also opposition and argument, and disputes rage in the newspapers for weeks. Once in a while we make such films.

It goes without saying that young people do not want to only see films about young people. But, when planning its topics and genres, a film studio must consider the average age of the audience. The studio's plan takes political and cultural aspects into consideration, but it reflects primarily the declared intentions of directors and authors. Normally you make films that you yourself would like to see. You cannot cater to an audience; you cannot disguise your voice; you can show the world only as you yourself experience and understand it. Therefore we must see to it that budding filmmakers shoot their first films while they are still young. The feature film studio has decided to produce one film by a newcomer every year. One out of every fifteen films must be made by a beginner. This is a step in the right direction.

With this I come to another institution of our film scene: the Hochschule für Film und Fernsehen (Academy for Film and Television). It trains directors, cameramen, and producers, and provides an academic background in cinema. All graduates get a job. Before studying, the young people work as trainees in the film industry or in television, and after completing their studies they return. That makes sense but also creates conflicts, for during their studies they not only learn a lot, they also get older. Their views of reality and maybe even their ideas about their future place of work change; the place waiting for them may no longer live up to the ideas they have about themselves.

Let me now briefly address the quality of film education in the GDR. Music and the fine arts - but not literature, mind you - have known the principle of schooling for a long time. A student assigns himself to a master and learns what can be taught: the craft and a fundamental attitude. In synthetic arts such as film or television, this direct personal relationship between student and teacher is often impossible. Frequently the teacher has no practical experience, not to mention a reputation. Here in America I heard a phrase which sums up the situation: If you can, do. If you can't, teach! Talent, they say, attends to its craft, but craft doesn't automatically lead to talent. How does one recognize talent? Who recognizes it? How does it reveal itself in an exam? How can a difficult and stubborn talent find its way to and through a school?

I will stop here and take your questions. Perhaps I have given you the impression anyway that there are more questions than answers. That is not completely wrong! But, for writing and making films, it is not the worst situation.

Mass Media and the Socialization of Young People in the GDR

Lothar Bisky

This theme has been the subject of a wide range of sociological, psychological, and educational studies in the GDR. Representative surveys, interval studies, and a host of case studies have been carried out investigating the uses young people make of the media. Relevant research findings have been published and need not be repeated in detail here.[1] I will therefore concentrate on trends that are apparent in the mid-1980s.

Media Use in the 1980s

To start with, one can take as a given that the widespread use of all media (TV, radio, tapes, cassettes, newspapers, magazines) has become a permanent cultural behavior pattern among young people in the GDR. They spend, on the average, two hours of their daily leisure time using the media;[2] media use as a secondary or simultaneous activity (primarily listening to music) accounts for another two hours or more. The reception of information, knowledge, art, and entertainment through the media has assumed stable proportions. Particularly wide use is made of films (both cinema and TV films) and popular music. Differences in the available media notwithstanding, this pattern of media use is consistent with international trends. In spite of this stable situation, however, it would be wrong to conclude that there have been no

---

[1] Cf. inter alia *Zur Psychologie der 12- bis 22jährigen*, ed. Walter Friedrich and Harry Müller (Berlin: Deutscher Verlag der Wissenschaften, 1980); *Jugend konkret*, ed. Walter Friedrich and Werner Gerth (Berlin: Neues Leben, 1984), pp. 159 ff; and Lothar Bisky and Dieter Wiedemann, *Der Spielfilm - Rezeption und Wirkung* (Berlin: Henschel, 1985).

[2] *Die Freizeit der Jugend*, ed. Peter Voß (Berlin: Dietz, 1981), pp. 88 ff.

changes over the years. Four developments can be ascertained:

1. Compared with the 1970s, the media today play a more important role, especially in regard to the aesthetic and cultural experience of the younger generation. Households are equipped with radios and TVs to an extent that one can assume that all people have access to these media in their homes. The audiences of the various media have tended to become younger; the young generation comes into contact with the media as a continuous source of "secondary experience" at a very early age today. Their parents also grew up having a wide variety of media at their disposal. The media are thus making a growing impact on the social and cultural context in which socialization takes place.

2. Remarkably enough, studies undertaken in 1979 and 1982 by the Zentralinstitut für Jugendforschung in Leipzig show that reading, in contrast to international trends, has lost none of its popularity among young people in the GDR. The press has enjoyed a growing readership since the early 1980s; and fiction has likewise maintained its position as one of the top leisure time activities of young people. Although listening to popular music has been on the increase (mainly as a simultaneous activity) and TV viewing has remained relatively stable, reading has not in general declined.

3. There is a growing demand for interpersonal communication, for collective or communal cultural experiences. Demand in this field cannot yet fully be met despite the fact that statistics record an increase in the number of youth clubs and discotheques as well as a growing range of cultural activities for young people in the cities, towns, and villages.

4. As far as media content is concerned, the interests of the young generation have undergone substantial change in the mid-1980s. What stands out is the interest in peace, disarmament, and international understanding. This is by no means limited to popular songs by GDR rock groups or major events such as Rock for Peace and the Political Song Festival and their coverage in the media. Interest is directed towards journalism and the arts - news and discussion - as well. Young people today expect the media to focus more strongly on science and technology, and, parallel to this, on the cultural heritage. Interest in discussion of the assets and values of socialism and the socialist way of life is more widespread. And

8

last but not least, major current affairs programs and programs dedicated to the arts have aroused more extensive discussion than was the case in the past.

Film Reception among Young People

Within this framework of general trends, there are numerous differences in the way the media are used. These include a number of new phenomena that need to be studied in greater detail. One example is film reception: adolescents tend - although the trend is not dramatic - to watch fewer films on TV than young people did in the past; they show a lukewarm response to certain kinds of films that recorded high attendance figures not so long ago; and they respond more enthusiastically to films with high artistic standards than was the case previously.[3]

Film reception by young people today manifests what we call "functional differentiation."[4] This means that, in choosing the films they see, young people distinguish between the function the films are to serve, for example, pure entertainment or intellectual/artistic stimulation. A marked increase can be discerned in the number of young people who enjoy both light entertainment films and, in a different situation, films of high artistic quality, on which they place high demands. The same young people enjoy films like *Asterix* and *Mephisto* or *Fanny and Alexander*.

Striking here is that GDR feature films are judged by more critical standards than imported ones. Recent studies have shown that young workers in particular want to see their social experience reflected in GDR film production.[5] And an increasing need is being felt to develop social and cultural identity as a GDR citizen, a need which finds expression in the expectations people place in film and TV.

---

[3] Cf. inter alia Dieter Wiedemann, *Von der Unterhaltsamkeit des Unterhaltungsfilms*, Arbeitshefte der Akademie der Künste der DDR, No. 38 (Berlin, 1986), pp. 57 ff; Dieter Wiedemann and Hans-Jörg Stiehler, "Auf der Suche nach Kommunikation," *Beiträge zur Film- und Fernsehwissenschaft*, 25, No. 4 (1984), pp. 142 ff.

[4] For more information, see Bisky and Wiedemann, pp. 146 ff.

[5] See *Soziale Triebkräfte ökonomischen Wachstums. Materialien des 4. Kongresses der marxistisch-leninistischen Soziologie in der DDR, 26. bis 28. März 1985* (Berlin: Dietz, 1986), p. 218.

To put it in a different way, GDR film production is confronted with a great challenge which derives from the discriminating expectations of the young audience. This is connected with the continuing internationalization of viewing and listening experiences. It is a matter of record that the GDR, within the framework of the CSCE process, has markedly increased the proportion of film imports from the participating states. A UNESCO study on the exchange of TV programming shows that during the period under consideration (1983) imports from non-socialist countries accounted for 58% of the programming shown on GDR television during peak viewing hours.[6] Over and beyond this, numerous West German radio stations and three TV stations beam into the GDR and can be received by the bulk of the population.

The Socializing Impact of the Media

In view of the qualitatively new role the media play in the aesthetic and cultural experiences of the younger generation, their growing influence on the process of socialization is of particular interest. For quite some time now research on socialization has seen a considerable shift in emphasis. While in the early 1970s empirical research focused on the effects of individual media,[7] interest is currently being directed toward the long-term effects of media use and especially the interplay between the media and other factors contributing to socialization. A number of studies have been conducted which deal with the mode of reception and impact of media experiences.[8]

The media do not operate in a vacuum - neither in the short nor in the long run. There is always a social and cultural backdrop which influences media experiences; and other factors involved in socialization play a role as well. The social and cultural factors conditioning the reception of a film such as *Towering Inferno* by young people in the GDR are quite different from those influencing its reception by young people in the United States, for example.

---

[6] Bisky and Wiedemann, p. 143.

[7] See, for example, Lothar Bisky and Walter Friedrich, *Massenkommunikation und Jugend* (Berlin: Deutscher Verlag der Wissenschaften, 1971), pp. 112 ff.

[8] See Wiedemann and Stiehler, pp. 142 ff.

Culture of Communication

We find it useful therefore to study the socializing impact of the media from the viewpoint of what might be called the culture of communication. The term "culture of communication" is taken to denote the connections and interrelations between the cultural communication that takes place via the media and the various forms of interpersonal communication. Among young people - and other people, for that matter, as well - media communication is integrated into the various processes of direct communication within the family, at school or work, among friends, in the youth organization, in local cultural life, etc. One of the reasons why the media play a greater role in socialization today is because they are having a stronger impact on direct cultural communication within the family, in the cultural life of the community, etc. At the same time, this impact is filtered, modified, and complemented by the network of direct cultural communication.

Today hardly anyone underrates the long-term impact of the media on mass psychology, on opinion, persuasions and values, and on everyday consciousness and moral guidelines for daily behavior. These long-term influences take effect, however, only in constant interaction and interrelation with other forms of communication. Research findings have established, for example, that young people who are especially involved in social activities use the media in different ways and with different results than others who are less active.[9] The large-scale involvement of young people in economic, political, social, and cultural activities - one of the aims of socialist youth policy - clearly affects the way people use the media and the influence the media have on them. Primary social experience gathered through social activity alters the reception of social experience conveyed through the media. Extensive efforts to impart political education to young people, be it at school, in the youth organization, at work, or in a vocational training program, have been shown to influence the reception of political information, its integration into broader contexts, the assessment of information, etc.[10]

[9] *Massenmedien und ideologische Erziehung der Jugend*, ed. Lothar Bisky (Berlin: Deutscher Verlag der Wissenschaften, 1976), pp. 52 ff.

[10] *Jugend - Weltanschauung - Aktivität*, ed. Peter Förster (Berlin: Neues Leben, 1980), pp. 130 ff.

Our research and experience indicate that, when combined with social activity, lively political debate, and other forms of cultural life, the media can be employed productively. For this reason, GDR theorists do not subscribe to the views expressed by some cultural critics as to the inevitability of media influence; nor do they succumb to the widespread media pessimism. Instead we view the media as an enriching element and indispensable part of cultural advancement. This approach has been supported by the emergence of new creative elements in the way young people perceive the media in the GDR.

This is not to say that the media cannot have a deleterious effect in the GDR! Excessive TV viewing, for example, produces one-sided cultural needs and interests among a certain portion of children and young people in the GDR, too. Sociological studies have shown, however, that, as a rule, TV as such is not the main reason for such one-sidedness, that excessive TV viewing occurs only in combination with other factors, especially those relating to the family (such as lack of interests within the family, excessive TV viewing by the parents, lack of conversation with the children), and that excessive TV viewing leads to one-sidedness only under these conditions.[11]

For quite some time now a discussion has been underway on media education. Although the discussion is far from over, there is widespread agreement that it should not be a special subject but should draw instead on the wide range of possibilities offered by the education system and intellectual and cultural life in general with the goal of promoting meaningful and discriminating use of the media. Given the fact that the GDR is virtually bombarded by radio and TV programming from the Federal Republic and West Berlin, special importance is attached to active and independent media reception, to developing a critical approach to the information offered. The more this ability is developed and the stronger the impact made by the GDR media, the more the media will help advance the culture of communication, impart information and knowledge, and promote the pleasure evoked by art and entertainment in the broadest sense of the word.

---

[11] See *Zur Psychologie der 12- bis 22jährigen*, pp. 168 ff.

Media Offerings for Young People

To render the media more effective as a means of socialization, greater efforts are being made to improve the quality of radio and TV programming and films for children and adolescents. Here there are valuable traditions (such as children's TV programming and the radio program DT 64) which can be drawn upon and furthered in keeping with the conditions that have arisen in the 1980s. In March 1986 a special radio channel for young people (Jugendradio DT 64) was put in operation, broadcasting eleven hours daily. *Junge Welt*, a newspaper for young people published by the FDJ, and youth magazines enjoy wide popularity: *Junge Welt* has a daily edition of two million copies - the highest of any paper in the GDR; and youth magazines such as *Trommel* and *Neues Leben* have doubled their editions in the last twenty years to 708,000 and 541,000 respectively.[12] The range of popular music, especially rock music, has been expanded considerably, although supply is still behind demand. An extensive range of international music is available, a development which is in keeping with GDR cultural policy. In the GDR, exposed as it is to all kinds of international influences, it is important that the domestic media provide young people with programming that appeals to them. On the other hand, one must not lose sight of the fact that the GDR's annual output of fifteen to seventeen feature films cannot satisfy the need for films, nor can domestically produced rock music, etc. suffice. Cooperation with the socialist countries and cultural exchange in general thus acquire significance.

Conclusion

Despite all the contradictions and problems involved, the GDR media have a quite productive influence on young people's socialization, promoting their development as individuals and their entry into socialist society. The GDR is seeking to achieve a high cultural standard for the media in the context of culture as a whole. Thus it is an important fact that young people in the GDR do not use the media to the exclusion of other cultural activities. Hence the term "culture of communication," which includes media culture as one part. The media recipient who acts as a communicator in the various other forms of communication is an indispensable

---

[12] Edeltraud Peschel, "Journalismus als kulturelle Institution in der entwickelten sozialistischen Gesellschaft," *Theorie und Praxis des sozialistischen Journalismus*, No. 3 (1986), p. 157.

element in the culture of communication. This implies the development of communicative abilities and skills in a way that is conducive to lively cultural communication within the family, in the neighborhood, at work, etc. Cooperation between educational institutions, the media, and local cultural facilities is of great importance from this point of view as well.

The higher the educational and cultural standards the more able people are to use the media in a productive and critical manner. Conversely, the media give considerable stimulation to cultural life as a whole, since they represent a productive challenge to local cultural facilities to improve their offerings and thus win the attention of young people whose expectations and needs have been informed by the national and international media content.

Various fears as to possible negative effects of media use have proven to be unfounded. Those who believed, for example, that rock music would focus the attention of young people exclusively on the latest trends were mistaken. And extensive use of the media does not keep a large number of young people from actively fostering their cultural heritage. Thus there is no reason to take a pessimistic view of the media. The role the media play in the socialization of young people rests however on interaction with other socialization processes; it is largely dependent on the degree to which young people become involved in public life, on the level of social relations, on educational and cultural standards, and on the development of the culture of communication in general.

Literature for Tomorrow's Citizens:
Children's Books in the German Democratic Republic

Gail P. Hueting

The German Democratic Republic takes literature for children and young adults seriously and accords it as much importance as it does literature for adults.[1] Children's literature is a significant area of GDR book production. Six of the eighty GDR publishing houses specialize in children's books, and approximately twelve percent of the titles published each year are meant for children and young adults - in 1983, 802 titles out of a total of 6,175.[2] Another quantitative indication of the significance of children's books is that large numbers of copies are printed - an average of 37,000 copies of each title.[3] Although some of the titles published each year are new editions of old favorites, such as fairy tales of the Brothers Grimm, and others are translations, especially of Soviet children's books, authors and artists living in the GDR write and illustrate many of them.

This paper first discusses several aspects of GDR children's literature: its general importance; its role in the socialization of children; GDR publications that offer criticism of children's literature; characteristics of authors who write for children; and the GDR publishing houses that specialize in children's books. It then describes six recent children's books in more detail.

---

[1] "Children" and "young people" are specific concepts in GDR law and cultural policy. Children are boys and girls up to age fourteen; young people (*Jugend*) are those between the ages of fifteen and twenty-four. "Jugend," *DDR Handbuch*, ed. Hartmut Zimmermann, 3rd ed. (Cologne: Wissenschaft und Politik, 1985), I, 683.

[2] Unesco, *Statistical Yearbook* (Paris: Unesco, 1985), pp. VII-48, VII-106.

[3] Unesco, *Statistical Yearbook*, p. VII-106.

Role of Children's Literature in the GDR

In the GDR, children's literature is expected to treat serious themes and to challenge its readers. The West German critic Konrad Franke summarized its role concisely:

> Völlig der literarischen Konfektion entwachsen ist dagegen die Kinder- und Jugendliteratur der DDR, weil diese Literatur konsequent ernst genommen wird, von den Kulturpolitikern, von den Verlegern - vor allem aber von den Autoren. . . . Die Lust, Kinderbücher zu schreiben, vergrößerte sich, als es zur erklärten Absicht der DDR-Kulturpolitik wurde, nicht mehr rein kindliche, nur in Kindergesellschaften spielende Geschichten zu schreiben, sondern literarisch die Welt der Kinder an die Welt der Erwachsenen heranzuführen. Nicht mehr nur "Tier"- und "Abenteuer"-Bücher wurden jetzt von den Autoren erwartet, sondern auch biographisch bestimmte Erzählungen, realistische Berichte aus dem antifaschistischen Widerstandskampf, aus der Arbeitergeschichte.[4]

Children's literature is one of the means of socializing and educating children in the GDR. The goal of all socialization there is to develop the "socialist personality," which Hannes Hüttner, a GDR sociologist and children's book author, defines as follows:

> Wir suchen in sozialistischen Gesellschaften einen bestimmten Persönlichkeitstyp zu erziehen: Menschen, die hochgebildet, aber keine engstirnigen Spezialisten sind, Menschen, die Genuß an geistigen und materiellen Werten finden und besonderen Genuß darin, solche Werte zu schaffen, Menschen, denen die sozialistische Ideologie selbstverständlich ist, was heißt, daß sie unsere sozialen Ziele übernehmen, aber nicht darauf verzichten, die Realität des Sozialismus unseren Idealen anzunähern, Menschen, die stolz sind auf ihr Land

---

[4] Konrad Franke, *Die Literatur der Deutschen Demokratischen Republik*, 2nd ed. (Munich: Kindler, 1973), p. 384.

und sich deshalb respektvoll und neugierig zu
anderen Völkern verhalten.[5]

Obviously, institutions like the child-care and school systems
and the youth organizations (the Pioneers and the Freie
Deutsche Jugend) dominate among the means of developing
such a personality. They emphasize the collective. Children's
literature in the GDR shares with these institutions the goals
that Hüttner lists but can instill them more subtly and engage
the individual child.

Children's books can have an impact on their readers in
several ways. Books can open their minds to limitless
possibilities. How children and adults are depicted in books
will influence children's perceptions and attitudes. Literature
for children, like any form of literature, can impart information, often in an absorbing and entertaining way. Good
children's books can also lead readers to an appreciation of
literature later in life, and fostering such an appreciation is a
major goal of GDR cultural policy.

Reviews and Criticism of Children's Books

Criticism and commentary on children's literature are no
longer mainly the concern of teachers and librarians, although professionals in these fields naturally write about it.
Reviews of children's books appear in the literary sections of
GDR newspapers, in journals like *Neue Deutsche Literatur*
and in anthologies of criticism such as *Kritik in der Zeit* and
DDR-Literatur im Gespräch.[6] The *Börsenblatt für den Deutschen Buchhandel*, the weekly journal of the GDR book trade,

---

[5] Hannes Hüttner, "Zur Spezifik der Kinderliteratur," as quoted in *Das
Kinderbuch: Gedanken und Ansichten*, ed. Renate Gollmitz (Berlin: Kinderbuchverlag, 1983), p. 206.

[6] *Kritik in der Zeit: Literaturkritik in der DDR 1945-1975*, ed. Klaus
Jarmatz, Christel Berger, and Renate Drenkow (Halle: Mitteldeutscher Verlag, 1978); Karin Richter, "Kindliche Erwartungen und literarische Angebote:
Zu Neuerscheinungen des Kinderbuchverlages Berlin," in *DDR-Literatur '83
im Gespräch*, ed. Siegfried Rönisch (Berlin/Weimar: Aufbau, 1984), pp. 91-
110; Christian Emmerich, "Bewährungsort Familie: Gedanken zu Jürgen
Leskiens Erzählung 'Georg,'" in *DDR-Literatur '84 im Gespräch*, ed. Siegfried
Rönisch (Berlin/Weimar: Aufbau, 1985), pp. 210-15. Reviews of children's
books are also included in *Kritik 75: Rezensionen zur DDR-Literatur*, ed.
Eberhard Günther, Werner Liersch, and Klaus Walther (Halle: Mitteldeutscher Verlag, 1976) and in *Kritik 82: Rezensionen zur DDR-Literatur*, ed.
Eberhard Günther, Werner Liersch, and Klaus Walther (Halle: Mitteldeut-
scher Verlag, 1983).

carries many articles about children's literature. The Kinder-buchverlag, the largest publisher of children's books, itself sponsors theoretical and historical research on children's literature. It issues three series: Beiträge zur Kinder- und Jugendliteratur, an annual collection of critical essays; Resultate: Theoretische Schriften zur Kinder- und Jugendliteratur, a monographic series; and Studien zur Geschichte der deutschen Kinder- und Jugendliteratur, treatments of specific periods and genres. The Kinderbuchverlag also published, in 1981, a book entitled *Literatur für Kinder und Jugendliche in der DDR*. Intended primarily for future teachers, it is useful for anyone interested in GDR children's literature; it is probably the most comprehensive and readable survey of the field.

Children's Book Authors

A growing number of prominent GDR writers have tried their hand at children's books. Stephan Hermlin and Stefan Heym have retold legends and fairy tales for children; Helmut Baierl, best known as a dramatist, ventured into children's literature with *Polly erzählt*.[7] Kito Lorenc has written poems for children as well as for adults. Peter Hacks, Werner Heiduczek, Franz Fühmann, and Erwin Strittmatter are known both for their children's books, published by the Kinderbuchverlag, and for their adult writing.[8] Johannes Bobrowski was a children's book editor for the privately owned Altberliner Verlag and wrote, in addition to his poems and fiction for adults, *Hans Clauert, der märkische Eulenspiegel*.[9] Many other authors have concentrated mainly on children's books, such as Gerhard Holtz-Baumert, Hannes Hüttner, and Götz R. Richter, to name only a few. The former director of the Kinderbuchverlag, Fred Rodrian, the present acting director, Katrin Pieper, and the editor-in-chief of the Altberliner Verlag, Alfred Könner, are also authors of children's books.[10]

---

[7] Stephan Hermlin, *Die Argonauten* (Berlin: Kinderbuchverlag, 1974); Stefan Heym, *Casimir und Cymbelinchen: 2 Märchen* (Berlin: Kinderbuchverlag, 1966); Helmut Baierl, *Polly erzählt* (Berlin: Kinderbuchverlag, 1983).

[8] Many of the children's books by these five authors are listed in Kinderbuchverlag, *Verlagsverzeichnis 1949-1979* (Berlin: Kinderbuchverlag, 1980).

[9] Johannes Bobrowski, *Hans Clauert, der märkische Eulenspiegel*, ill. Werner Klemke (Berlin: Altberliner Verlag, 1956).

[10] Some of the children's books by these writers are listed in Kinderbuchverlag, *Verlagsverzeichnis*.

GDR Children's Book Publishing

Children's book publishing is a specialized field in the GDR. Unlike the major publishing houses in the United States, which may have a trade (fiction and general) book line, a textbook line, and a children's book line, most publishing houses in the GDR have well-defined areas of specialization. Except for Verlag für Lehrmittel, the publishing houses that concentrate on children's books do not publish other types of material, and even within the field of publishing for children, they have developed distinct profiles (the term used in the GDR book trade).

After World War II a number of private firms continued to publish children's books alongside the state-owned giants; there were more private publishing houses in this field than in other areas of publishing. While there was no doubt about their relative importance, they had a respected place and were able to print and sell an average of 10,000 to 12,000 copies of each title they issued. These firms were active in the first years after 1945, when the need for new children's books was especially acute. The Abel & Müller Verlag, Altberliner Verlag, Verlag Rudolf Arnold, Alfred Holz Verlag, Gebr. Knabe Verlag, and Karl Nitschke continued to exist into the 1980s. The Rudolf Arnold Verlag and Altberliner Verlag are still active, but the Abel & Müller Verlag has not advertised its picture books since 1982, and the programs and imprints of the others have been taken over by the state-owned publishing houses. Karl Nitschke in Niederwiesa is a "production group" within the Kinderbuchverlag, and Alfred Holz is an imprint used by the Kinderbuchverlag on some of its books. Knabes Jugendbücherei, the series issued by Gebr. Knabe Verlag, was incorporated into a new series with the title Kleine Jugendbücherei by Postreiter-Verlag in 1985.[11]

The Altberliner Verlag Lucie Groszer is still publishing its high-quality picture books, along with a few titles for older children, and its books are much admired. In 1945 Lucie Groszer was running a bookstore, the Altberliner Bücherstube, on Neue Schönhauser Straße in Berlin (in a Rococo building where her publishing house is still located). Wanting to turn to publishing instead, she planned to issue books about the literary heritage and history of Berlin, but she was

[11] Christel Foerster, "Neuer Name, bewährtes Profil: 'Kleine Jugendbücherei' des VEB Postreiter Verlag Halle," *Börsenblatt für den Deutschen Buchhandel* (Leipzig), 152 (1985), 172-73.

asked to publish three pamphlets for children for Christmas, 1945. These were a coloring book, *Schneeweißchen und Rosenrot* from Grimms' fairy tales, and *Ringel-Ringel-Rosenkranz*, a collection of rhymes. She continued to publish children's books, although a few Berlin books, such as *Altberliner Bilderbogen* by Hans Ludwig, came out later.[12] In the first few years nonfiction, biographies, and legends predominated. The most successful title was *Die Söhne der großen Bärin*, Liselotte Welskopf-Henrich's Indian book, originally published in 1951. (It was the first in a series that was promoted as a substitute for the very popular Karl May books, which were no longer being issued in the GDR.)[13] Picture books have made up the largest part of the program for many years. These include the series Bunte Kiste, Ein Tag im Leben eines Tieres, focusing on animals ranging from an ant to a lion, and Schlüsselbücher. Fairy tales are still important, including the collection *Kostbarkeiten aus dem deutschen Märchenschatz*,[14] as well as single illustrated tales.[15]

The other private publishing house that is still active, the Rudolf Arnold Verlag, began publishing in 1945. It now issues eight to ten titles each year - board books, hobby books, and illustrated nature books. The books are advertised as a group in the Leipzig Book Fair catalog, and the individual titles are included in *Nova*, the classified listing of forthcoming GDR books, but there is no general information available about the firm and its work.

---

12 Hans Ludwig, *Altberliner Bilderbogen*, ill. Klaus Ensikat (Berlin: Altberliner Verlag, 1965).

13 Liselotte Welskopf-Henrich, *Die Söhne der großen Bärin* (Berlin: Altberliner Verlag, 1951). A revised version, under the title *Der Häuptling*, became the third volume of a trilogy; the other two volumes were *Harka, der Sohn des Häuptlings* (1962) and *Top und Harry* (1963). Later editions were published by the Kinderbuchverlag in 1966 (in three volumes) and in 1971 (in six volumes, same contents). On the publication and reception of Karl May's books in the GDR, see Margy Gerber, "Old Shatterhand Rides Again! The Rehabilitation of Karl May in the GDR," in *Studies in GDR Culture and Society* 5, ed. Margy Gerber et al. (Lanham/New York/London: University Press of America, 1985), 237-50.

14 *Kostbarkeiten aus dem deutschen Märchenschatz*, ed. Elisabeth Hering (Berlin: Altberliner Verlag, 1964).

15 The history of the Altberliner Verlag is given in Werner Knibbe, "Editionen, die zum Bücherschatz der Kinder gehören: 35 Jahre Altberliner Verlag," *Börsenblatt für den Deutschen Buchhandel* (Leipzig), 147 (1980), 476-78.

Postreiter-Verlag in Halle became a state-owned firm in 1972. Founded in 1947, it has specialized in children's books only since the early 1960s. Before that a few picture books were published each year along with mundane printed goods like price lists, forms, stamp albums, and calendars. It now publishes fifteen new titles each year plus forty to fifty reprint editions. Most of the books, such as *Leporellos* (accordion-folded books) made of plastic and board books, are for very young children. There are also pop-up books and coloring books. A new development in recent years is a series of picture books illustrated with photographs, under the general title Kleine Fotoreihe, a pioneer effort in children's books; this concept is especially good for nature books.[16] In 1985, as previously mentioned, Postreiter-Verlag expanded its program to include the Kleine Jugendbücherei, which consists of classic and contemporary fiction for readers from eight to fourteen years old.

Another publishing house, Verlag für Lehrmittel, in Pössneck, should be mentioned briefly. Founded in 1946 by Rudolf Forkel, it has had its present name since the early 1970s. Its profile mainly calls for instructional aids, children's card games, hobby books, and educational games, but it also publishes eight to ten picture books a year.

Verlag Junge Welt and Kinderbuchverlag

The three publishing houses that dominate the area of books for children and young adults belong to the Freie Deutsche Jugend: Verlag Neues Leben, Verlag Junge Welt, and the Kinderbuchverlag. Verlag Neues Leben, founded in 1946, concentrates on books for young adults - with titles intended for teenagers as well as titles for a more general adult audience. It will not be discussed further here. Verlag Junge Welt was established at the end of 1951 to publish the magazines and the daily newspaper of the children's and youth organizations, a large volume of material in itself. In 1968, however, a book department was added, with the primary responsibility of developing nonfiction for children.[17] Of course many of these publications, especially the ones for

---

[16] Rolf Rohleder, "Für Vorschulkinder - hierzulande und anderswo," *Börsenblatt für den Deutschen Buchhandel* (Leipzig), 149 (1982), 875-78.

[17] Irene Kahlau, "Eine Anerkennung und neue Anforderungen: Buchredaktion des Verlages Junge Welt hat sich dem Kinderbuch aller Genres verschrieben," *Börsenblatt für den Deutschen Buchhandel* (Leipzig), 144 (1977), 827.

young children, are in picture book or narrative form. Some of the books have supplementary models or toys, such as a cut-out project or a hand puppet. This ties in with another major area of materials they publish: crafts instructions and paper models to cut out and assemble. Among the innovative books published by Verlag Junge Welt are a series of volumes entitled *Warum? Weshalb? Wieso?* and several "modern fairy tales," featuring wonders of science and technology.[18]

The Kinderbuchverlag was founded in June 1949. The very first book it published was *Der verwundete Sokrates*, by Bertolt Brecht. Today it publishes 450 titles a year, of which 150 are first editions; this makes it one of the largest publishing houses in the GDR. The Kinderbuchverlag has eight editorial departments: picture books, books for beginning readers, classics (including fairy tales and legends), contemporary literature, translations, historical literature and biographies, popular science, and theory and history of children's books. Two of the most successful titles published by the Kinderbuchverlag are *Timur und sein Trupp*, by Arkadii Gaidar, a translation from Russian, with 840,000 copies printed up to 1980, and *Alfons Zitterbacke*, by Gerhard Holtz-Baumert, with 835,000 copies.[19] The Kinderbuchverlag issues many of its books in series aimed at particular age groups. The ones for beginning readers are ABC - ich kann lesen, Die kleinen Trompeterbücher, and Buchfink-Bücher; for older children there are Abenteuer rund um die Welt, Alex-Taschenbücher, Die goldene Reihe, and Robinsons bil-

---

[18] *Warum? Weshalb? Wieso?* ed. Carola Hendel, 4 vols. (1980-85). Some of the modern fairy tales are: Lilo Hardel, *Mariechens Apfelbaum erzählt aus seinem Leben* (1979); Hannes Hüttner, *Hinter den grünen Bergen* (1981); Rainer Kirsch, *Die Perlen der grünen Nixe: Ein mathematisches Märchen* (1975).

[19] Fred Rodrian, "Tradition plus Neugier auf Neues, *Börsenblatt für den Deutschen Buchhandel* (Frankfurt am Main), 12 (1980), 285-87. Kinderbuchverlag, *Verlagsverzeichnis* shows the history of the two bestsellers. Arkadii Gaidar, *Timur und sein Trupp* has gone through many editions. In the translation by L. Klementinovskaia, it was first published by Verlag Neues Leben in 1950. The Kinderbuchverlag took it over with the 5th ed. in 1955. A new translation by Max Hummeltenberg was first published by the Kinderbuchverlag in 1977. Gaidar's book forms the basis for the Timur movement in the Pioneer organization, in which children volunteer to help people who need it, such as retirees and families of soldiers, with errands and chores on a regular basis. The second bestseller is Gerhard Holtz-Baumert, *Adolf Zitterbacke: Die heiteren Geschichten eines Pechvogels* (Berlin: Kinderbuchverlag, 1958). Editions published after 1977 included the sequel, *Alfons Zitterbacke hat wieder Ärger* (it first appeared separately in 1962).

lige Bücher. Mein kleines Lexikon and Regenbogenreihe are nonfiction series.[20]

Six children's books published in the GDR since 1982 will now be considered. These are books dealing with contemporary GDR themes in each of three categories: picture books, illustrated books for beginning readers (*Bilderbucherzählungen*), and fiction for older children.

Picture Books in the 1980s

GDR publishers are justifiably proud of their picture books. They are all printed in full color on sturdy cardboard, and many are published for export as well as for the GDR market, some with the minimal texts translated into English or French. One of the most unusual picture books that has appeared is *Ein wunderbunter Schmetterling*, by Gottfried Herold and Hajo Blanck, published by Verlag Junge Welt in 1985. Herold, who wrote the poem that forms the text, has written many verses for children, notably the collection *Die himmelblaue Sommerbank*.[21] *Ein wunderbunter Schmetterling*, which is in the shape of a butterfly, is suggested for children from the age of four on. (Verlag Junge Welt and the Kinderbuchverlag regularly include the age level along with the publication information.) Printed on the back cover, the text describes a butterfly's life cycle; it is presumably meant to be read to children. Since the entire poem is on the back cover, an adult reading it aloud can show a group of children the illustrations without having to turn the book around. In addition to the bright yellow brimstone butterfly on the cover, three butterflies and one moth are illustrated on the inside pages. Their wings are pictured accurately enough that they could be found in a butterfly book, but the heads and bodies are drawn in a distinctly anthropomorphic style. Perhaps the purpose of giving the butterflies faces is to make them seem less strange to children and to suggest to them that butterflies have feelings too. Thus the purpose of this book is different from that of the very good nature books (with color photographs) for young children that have been published in the GDR. *Ein wunderbunter Schmetterling* is imaginative rather than strictly realistic. Certainly it would draw young

---

20 Kinderbuchverlag, *Verlagsverzeichnis*, pp. 415-46.
21 Gottfried Herold, *Die himmelblaue Sommerbank* (Berlin: Kinderbuchverlag, 1973).

viewers' attention to butterflies outdoors and illustrates the sentiment that ends the poem:

Doch Schönheit macht die Welt ein wenig wärmer und wohnlicher und wunderbarer auch.

The second picture book to be discussed here is *Der Herbstwind bläst*, by Alfred Könner, with illustrations by Jutta Mirtschin, published by Altberliner Verlag in 1982. Könner, who is the present editor-in-chief of this publishing house, has written the text for many picture books issued by both his own house and the Kinderbuchverlag. Mirtschin has illustrated several picture books published since 1977. The pictures here are wonderfully evocative of a windy fall day with its changing skies. The scene is an area paved with small stones - perhaps a city street or a park. A small girl, Anne, has swept the leaves into a pile that is bigger than she is. Then, one after the other, a dog, some chickens, a cat with three kittens, and even a hedgehog walk through the pile of leaves. A girl rides through it on a scooter, and a boy jumps right into the middle of it. But the real culprit is the wind - it blows all the leaves back onto the path. Poor Anne, not so cheerful this time, begins sweeping them together again. Readers get a sense of how much fun it is to ride through a pile of leaves or to jump onto it, but they also realize Anne's predicament after her work is undone. Thus the message may be a little ambiguous.

Illustrated Stories on Contemporary Themes

Illustrated stories (*Bilderbucherzählungen*) are for slightly older children, beginning readers from six to nine years of age. They are not always illustrated in full color - many have very effective drawings in two or three colors. The stories have a definite plot and often include elements that are part of the daily lives of GDR children.

Ein Lächeln für Zacharias, written by Joachim Nowotny and illustrated by Horst Bartsch, was published by the Kinderbuchverlag in 1983. Nowotny has written many books of fiction for both children and adults. Bartsch was a student of Werner Klemke and is one of the most successful GDR children's book illustrators; one of his best known picture books is *Der kleine König und die Sonne*.[22] *Ein Lächeln für*

---

[22] Hoernle, Edwin, *Der kleine König und die Sonne: Ein Märchen* , ill. Horst Bartsch (Berlin: Kinderbuchverlag, 1976).

Two butterflies from *Ein wunderbunter Schmetterling*
Gottfried Herold and Hajo Blanck (Verlag Junge Welt)

Zacharias, suggested for children of six years and older, deals with smiles and the hunger for approval that everyone has. The situation narrated and pictured here is familiar to many schoolchildren. A five, a failing grade, in math leaves Zacharias feeling that nobody can approve of him. This feeling is mirrored in the illustrations. Hostile numbers with eyes seem to lurk in every corner - especially the giant pink number five, which has big teeth. Zacharias' parents and teacher are cross; a classmate is horrified. Zacharias cannot get a smile out of inanimate objects (the sun, a tree, an apartment building), and the smiles that people give him a little later, meant to be encouraging, seem condescending and frosty. His anguish lasts until he rides his bicycle out to visit his grandfather, who not only greets him as cordially as usual but also pretends not to hear about the bad grade. Having gotten his fill of smiles, Zacharias begins to feel better about himself and is even eager to tackle math problems. In the final picture the big number five is in pieces under his feet and the other numbers have shrunk to manageable size.

Eine Straßenbahn für Katharina, with text by Reiner Putzger and pictures by Hans-Eberhard Ernst, was published by Verlag Junge Welt in 1983. Putzger, born in 1940, has worked in radio and television and written children's programs, poems, and stories.[23] In this book Katharina has just moved to the city with her family and is fascinated by streetcars. She is caught riding without a ticket but then saves up her allowance to buy a monthly pass and rides everywhere after school. Next she turns her attention to getting her mother to go to work driving streetcars. At first the mother, who is staying home with her children, dismisses her daughter's obsession, but finally she does go to inquire about a job. Since drivers are badly needed, she can qualify in a short training course, work only day shifts, and get places in a kindergarten for Katharina's little twin brothers. The depiction of the family is rather traditional - Katharina's mother has stayed at home, and her father objects at first to his wife's working. But they do change: the mother takes advantage of the job opportunity; and the father adjusts (he even bakes a cake when the mother passes her licensing test). Katharina gets new responsibilities looking after her brothers, but she also gets a free streetcar pass.

---

[23] "Reiner Putzger," *Bestandsaufnahme: Literarische Steckbriefe,* ed. Brigitte Böthner (Halle: Mitteldeutscher Verlag, 1976), p. 82.

Cover of *Ein Lächeln für Zacharias*
Joachim Nowotny and Horst Bartsch (Kinderbuchverlag)

The book picks up on children's fascination with vehicles of all kinds; it gives a lot of information about how streetcars run and how one becomes qualified to drive them, and the last pages have streetcars to cut out and color. There are some rather obvious social lessons: riding on a streetcar without buying a ticket is bad for the collective; women, even those with young children, can and should contribute to society by going to work; and families can adjust with the support services available.

Trends in Children's Fiction: Modern Fairy Tales and Girls' Books

The next category, fiction for older children, is the traditional form of children's literature. Here one finds longer, sustained stories for readers who are beyond the beginning stages. They often have a few illustrations, but the pictures are clearly secondary to the narrative. There is great variety in the themes - psychological, social, historical - and settings - family, school, local, rural, foreign. These books are important as the bridge to adult reading.

Zumzuckel der Flaschengeist: Ein Robotermärchen, written by Helga Talke and illustrated in full color by Elinor Wiese, was published by Verlag Junge Welt in 1983. Its suggested audience is readers from age eight up. The many illustrations almost put this into the category of *Bilderbucherzählungen*, but the text is extensive, and the story predominates. This book is one of the modern fairy tales with which the publishing house attempts to provide new types of tales for an industrial, socialist society. Talke is the author of several children's books, including *Kurierpost für Berlin* and *Ein Schiff nach Tscheljabinsk*, two historical stories of the proletarian revolutionary past.[24] The title character in *Zumzuckel der Flaschengeist* is a genie who is released from an old bottle by a fisherman named Knautschke. Zumzuckel goes looking for another genie to take his place in the bottle so that he can be freed from the curse laid on him by Sultan Omar. The way to tell a genie, he says, is that it smells like rancid oil. He finds his way into a factory, where he encounters a "giraffe genie," called "Spuck Spritz" by the workers, which paints automobile bodies, and a "snake genie," nicknamed "Feuerschnauf," which welds metal. But he cannot

---

[24] Helga Talke, *Kurierpost für Berlin* (Berlin: Kinderbuchverlag, 1969); *Ein Schiff nach Tscheljabinsk* (Berlin: Kinderbuchverlag, 1983).

Katharina and her mother in the driver's compartment
Reiner Putzger and Hans-Eberhard Ernst,
Eine Straßenbahn für Katharina (Verlag Junge Welt)

communicate with them, much less lure them into his bottle. Deciding to take a nap, he goes into an empty apartment building. It catches fire, but Zumzuckel is rescued - or, as he thinks, eaten - by a "turtle genie" called "Rettefix." Knautschke, whom he encounters again, finally explains to him that all these creatures are machines, industrial robots that have been built to do dirty, repetitious, or dangerous tasks. Knautschke, being a rational person, breaks Zumzuckel's bottle and with it the spell. The story ends here, but there is another page of explanation of the three generations of industrial robots.

The idea of mixing fairy-tale elements like the genie and factual information about industrial inventions proves to be somewhat awkward in this story. The concept certainly has appeal; the other modern fairy tales may handle it more effectively. Here the author seems more comfortable with the rational and factual elements than with the fantastic ones. Something of the inner logic of fairy tales is missing. Zumzuckel, otherwise a resourceful character, does not realize that the society he has emerged into is completely different· from the sultan's court; this is almost the only motivation for the plot. Would a factual book on industrial robots have been more effective? Such a book might be less attractive to young readers who like fairy tales and a fast-moving plot.

The last book to be discussed is *Die Braut auf Rezept,* by Christamaria Fiedler (with black and white drawings by Fred Westphal). It was published by the Kinderbuchverlag in 1983; the second edition appeared in 1986. This is one of a growing number of "girls' books," a type that for many years was hardly published at all in the GDR. Sometimes it seems that all the best GDR fiction for children and young adults, from Erwin Strittmatter's *Tinko* to Günter Görlich's *Den Wolken ein Stück näher,*[25] features boys as the central figures; if there is a strong girl character, she still appears in conjunction with a male protagonist. One of the literary discussions of the 1950s centered on whether books for girls should be written. Some authors, such as Eva Strittmatter and Annemarie Reinhard, felt that children's literature should not be divided into girls' books and boys' books. Others, like Adolf Görtz and Alfred Könner, argued that girls' books could be useful if they gave a

---

[25] Erwin Strittmatter, *Tinko* (Berlin: Kinderbuchverlag, 1954); Günter Görlich, *Den Wolken ein Stück näher* (Berlin: Kinderbuchverlag, 1971).

positive picture of love and friendship and explored occupations that girls could follow. Alex Wedding suggested that girls' books would be needed only during a transitional stage.[26] Thirty years later they seem to be coming back.

Die Braut auf Rezept is most likely to appeal to girls eleven or twelve years old. It depicts, apparently accurately, things that would concern young girls growing up in the GDR: family, school, girlfriends, their own physical development, and their first acquaintance with boys. The added twist here is that the story takes place in a Kurort for respiratory disorders, to which children, like adults, are sent for six weeks of treatment. Much of the interest lies in the description of their treatment, living conditions, and schooling. Jola Mertens-Schmitt is a likable, spirited girl who tries to strike a balance between what she wants and what is good for the group. She is not above sneaking away to become better acquainted with Jens-Uwe Pohl, a boy from town who has trouble in school but dreams of working in the Antarctic someday. ,The relationship is completely (and believably) innocent; their only intimacy is kissing Eskimo fashion by rubbing noses. Ultimately their friendship leads to something beneficial to the collective: the local children are invited to a party by the group at the treatment center. There is much more, of course: the interaction among the girls in Jola's room, who are from various parts of the GDR; an understanding teacher and a sympathetic doctor; and Jens' neighbor and classmate Andrea. Jola, who maintains at the beginning that she positively will not go for treatment of her bronchitis, is just as reluctant to leave (especially before the final party).

At least two other well-known children's books seem to have influenced Die Braut auf Rezept. The episodic structure is much like that of Timur und sein Trupp , by Arkadii Gaidar. The understanding adult figures seem to be modeled in part on those in Den Wolken ein Stück näher, by Günter Görlich.

The children's books written and published in the GDR in recent years are characterized by variety and quality. The writing and the design of these books show many positive features and relatively little of the doctrinaire tone that many children's books had in the 1950s and 1960s. There are good

---

[26] Günter Ebert, Ansichten zur Entwicklung der epischen Kinder- und Jugendliteratur in der DDR, Studien zur Geschichte der deutschen Kinder- und Jugendliteratur (Berlin: Kinderbuchverlag, 1976), pp. 69-70.

reasons for some of our libraries to collect more of these books: they are a vital part of GDR literature; they are full of material for courses on the GDR; and selections from some of them - perhaps along with good children's books from the Federal Republic of Germany - might even be suitable material for language classes.

Socialization and Politics in the GDR: The Ambivalent Role of the Family

Christiane Lemke

In his *Kleine Literaturgeschichte der DDR*, the West German Germanist Wolfgang Emmerich points out that contemporary GDR literature dealing with the situation of children, youth, and young adults mirrors the search for identity presently to be found in the society as a whole.[1] The individual and his or her personal identity, on the one hand, and conflicts and alienation from society, on the other, portrayed from the perspective of those growing up, shed light on the process of socialization in GDR society. Some of the better known works Emmerich refers to are Ulrich Plenzdorf's *Die neuen Leiden des jungen W.*, Volker Braun's *Unvollendete Geschichte*, and Christa Wolf's *Kindheitsmuster*. The social relationships of children, in particular with parents, play a decisive role in this body of literature. The family appears as the first and most important emotional, social, and cultural agent of socialization - even in those works in which the failure of family socialization is described.

This is quite surprising given the fact that the GDR has long encouraged the collective care and raising of children in nursery schools, kindergartens, the youth groups of the Free German Youth (FDJ), and youth brigades, as a means of educating the new "socialist personality." Marxist-Leninist theory holds that traditional forms of socialization, in particular family socialization, will be replaced in socialist society by public means of child raising. The GDR has followed this ideological advice - with ambivalent results. Despite the strong support of public, collective child raising, the family

---

[1] Wolfgang Emmerich, *Kleine Literaturgeschichte der DDR* (Darmstadt/ Neuwied: Luchterhand, 1981), p. 198.

has maintained its great importance for children and youth. This is reflected not only in literature but in empirical findings and in family policy as well.

In the pages that follow I will take a closer look at the role of the family in the process of socialization from a sociological and political point of view. In the first part I will discuss research conducted by GDR social scientists in the 1970s and 1980s which clearly reevaluates the role of the family, and I will offer some explanations for why this is the case. In the second part I will try to assess the significance of socialization within the family, which from my point of view is bound between continuity or tradition, on the one hand, and change and reorientation, on the other. I will use two examples as illustrations: gender-specific role models; and what I call the authority syndrome. I will conclude with some thoughts on the relationship between socialization within the family and its significance for the political culture of the GDR.

Re-evaluating the Role of the Family

The family as a socialization agent has been widely discussed in Western political-science literature. In regard to the GDR, earlier Western scholarship ordinarily pointed out the decreased influence of the family. Thus in an article published in 1975, the American political scientist Arthur M. Hanhardt argued that the role of the family in shaping the attitudes and behavior of youth was declining in the GDR.[2] Sociological changes as well as the politics of child raising were promoting, as he wrote, a shift from socialization within the family towards socialization within the collectives of pre-school, school, and youth-group networks.

Hanhardt's double conclusion - declining role of the family, increasing role of public education and youth groups - reflects the fact that the role of the family as an agent of socialization has traditionally been downplayed both in GDR politics and in social research and theory. "Socialist family policy," as it was codified in the GDR Family Law of 1966,

---

[2] Arthur M. Hanhardt, "East Germany: From Goals to Realities," in *Political Socialization in Eastern Europe. A Comparative Framework*, ed. Ivan Volgyes (New York: Praeger, 1975), pp. 66-91. For more recent Western research on family socialization in the GDR, see Barbara Hille, *Familie und Sozialisation in der DDR* (Opladen: Leske und Budrich, 1985), and Gisela Helwig, *Jugend und Familie in der DDR. Leitbild und Alltag im Widerspruch*, Edition Deutschland Archiv (Cologne: Wissenschaft und Politik, 1984).

defined the family as "the smallest cell of society," in which the main task of society, i.e., educating the "socialist personality," was to be carried out.[3] Thus the role of family socialization was subordinated to state policy.

On a theoretical level, psychoanalytic theories of the significance of early childhood experience within the family were clearly rejected, and various theories of individual socialization were labeled as "bourgeois." It was argued that social conditions prevail over individual factors in child development and that the classic model of socialization in the family was based on wrong assumptions of bourgeois society about the relationship between the individual and society.[4]

Recent GDR studies have reversed this view, coming to the conclusion that the family does play a large role within the process of socialization after all. Several longitudinal studies conducted in the 1970s and 1980s by the Central Institute for Youth Research in Leipzig - one of the leading institutions for the study of youth in the GDR - found that parents are the most influential persons for children growing up in GDR society; parents serve as role models for behavior, as advisors in personal matters, and as generators of values and attitudes, including attitudes toward work, life style, and general ideological orientation ("Weltanschauung").[5] Of the 12 to 23 year olds surveyed in one of the studies, 90% had a positive emotional relationship with their parents; more than two-thirds of the 6th and 8th graders and over 50% of the 10th graders preferred their parents as advisors in all personal matters.[6] The attachment of students to the family remains strong as well: studies found a positive correlation between students' attitudes and those of their parents in respect to general attitudes and life style as well as to job choices.[7]

---

3 "Familiengesetzbuch der DDR," *Gesetzblatt der DDR I*, No. 1, 3 January 1966, p. 2.

4 This position is elaborated for example in the *Wörterbuch der marxistisch-leninistischen Soziologie*, ed. Georg Assmann et al. (Berlin: Dietz, 1977), pp. 569-70.

5 *Zur Psychologie der 12- bis 22jährigen*, ed. Walter Friedrich and Harry Müller (Berlin: Deutscher Verlag der Wissenschaften, 1980), p. 174.

6 Otmar Kabat vel Job and Arnold Pinther, *Jugend und Familie. Familiäre Faktoren der Persönlichkeitsentwicklung Jugendlicher* (Berlin: Deutscher Verlag der Wissenschaften, 1981), p. 33.

7 Kurt Starke, *Jugend im Studium* (Berlin: Deutscher Verlag der Wissenschaften, 1979), pp. 124-27.

Collective child raising has unquestionably changed the environment of children growing up in the GDR, compared to earlier periods of German history, but it has not replaced the the family as an influential socialization agent. It seems that this fact has caused a rediscovery of the family in social-science research as well as in theoretical approaches to the role of the family in society. Sociologists from the University at Leipzig maintain, for example, that the family - together with the workplace and the neighborhood - represents one of the most important environments for the "socialist way of life." On the basis of empirical surveys, the authors of the study, Alice Kahl, Steffen H. Wilsdorf, and Herbert F. Wolf, find that family life ranks among the most important values for GDR citizens and they assume that its significance will continue to grow in the near future.[8] The sociologist Irene Runge comes to similar conclusions in her description of family life and everyday culture in the GDR. She writes that the GDR is a "strongly family-oriented country."[9] Thus a process of re-evaluating the family is underway, filling the gap caused by ideological premises. This has produced some interesting new insights into family life in the GDR.

The new trend toward family-oriented research is prompted by several factors. The first and probably most simple explanation is that the development of empirical research methods has led to new findings about the process of socialization. Youth research, family sociology, and social psychology are new fields in the GDR, as compared with the United States and the Federal Republic. The improvement of empirical research methods as well as the number of projects on the subject of family socialization provide a better picture of how children grow up and how socialization is structured. Leading institutions in this respect are - in addition to the various university institutes - the Central Institute for Youth Research in Leipzig, whose research is for the most part commissioned and thus published only selectively, the Academy of Sciences, and the Academy of Pedagogical Sciences in Berlin.

Secondly, social-science research has been challenged by the sociological changes within the family which have

---

[8] Alice Kahl, Steffen H. Wilsdorf, and Herbert F. Wolf, *Kollektivbeziehungen und Lebensweise* (Berlin: Dietz, 1984), p. 84.

[9] Irene Runge, *Ganz in Familie* (Berlin: Dietz, 1985), p. 9. My translation here and throughout.

restructured social relationships and reshaped the conditions of socialization. One of the most significant changes is linked to the changing role of women and the fact that in the family both partners usually work. With about 87% of its women working, the GDR ranks internationally at the top of the scale of famale labor-force participation. The high employment rate of women resulted in a sharp decline in the birth rate in the late 1960s and early 1970s - a trend which caused the state to introduce a comprehensive program of benefits for working women. Working outside the home has changed women's self-perception and led to a search for new ways of living. As the director of the Scientific Council "The Woman in Socialist Society," Herta Kuhrig, has pointed out, the GDR is facing far-reaching changes in the relationship between men and women and between parents and children. A result of the equal rights policy of the GDR, the "liberation of the individual," as she puts it, has lead to a "new quality" of family relations.[10] The high divorce rate (3.0 per 10,000 inhabitants in 1985) and the growing number of children born out of wedlock (in 1978, 17.8% of all children; in 1983, 32%)[11] indicate that socialization in traditional "normal" families has been replaced by different forms of families. This has been shown most clearly by Jutta Gysi from the GDR Academy of Sciences in her work on family sociology and single parents. Gysi, who directs a recently initiated research project at the Institute for Sociology and Social Policy at the Academy, points out that young partners are searching for new life styles and maintains that these developments should be taken into account in housing and family policy.

The third factor leading to the renewed interest in the role of the family is that research on family socialization is often part of larger projects focusing on everyday life and culture, the so-called *Alltagskultur* and *sozialistische Lebensweise*. Beginning with Jürgen Kuczynski's multi-volumed work *Geschichte des Alltags des deutschen Volkes* (1980-85), everyday life and *Alltagskultur* have become popular subjects in GDR social-science research. The family is one of the most important networks in everyday life, a microcosm, in which the culture of everyday life is transferred from one

10 Herta Kuhrig, "Familie und Familienglück," *Einheit*, 40, No. 12 (1985), 1099-1105.
11 Jutta Gysi, "Frauen- und Familienentwicklung als Gegenstand sozialistischer Politik," *Jahrbuch für Soziologie und Sozialpolitik 1984* (Berlin: Akademie, 1984), p. 105.

generation to another. Thus the focus on the family and the role it plays in the shaping of atttitudes and behavior is encouraged by this new trend.

Fourth, and last, the trend toward family research has to do with the concept of socialist society and its development presently held by the political elite in the GDR. The so-called "intensified reproduction of society" ("intensive Reproduktion der Gesellschaft") calls for the intensive use of all resources of society, including the human one. In this concept, family socialization is upgraded because of its positive influence on human development: the family serves as a network for social and emotional security. Private niches are not only accepted but also encouraged, since psychology and youth research have demonstrated the positive and stabilizing effects of the family for young people, for example in preventing juvenile delinquency.

The Ambivalence of Change and Continuity

According to Anita Grandke, a leading scholar in the field of family research at Humboldt University, the "socialist family" preserves basic reproductive functions for the individual and society.[12] The core family, which she presents as the model for "socialist family relations," is important for social-relatedness, emotional security, and personal needs, both between partners and for children. Emphasis is put on a continuous, stable environment for children. Thus traditional functions of the family are preserved. On the other hand, socialist modernization, including sociological changes supported and initiated by the state and Party and political concepts to be carried out in education - visible in particular in the concept of the socialist personality, has changed the role and function of the family in regard to socialization. I would like to illustrate this ambivalence with two examples, the problem of gender-specific role models and the authority syndrome.

Family and social policy have encouraged the economic independence of partners and their right of equal opportunity in society as part of socialist modernization. But, as various studies have found, role-models within the family follow quite traditional male-female patterns. Sociological surveys have

---

[12] Anita Grandke, "Zur Entwicklung von Ehe und Familie," in *Zur gesellschaftlichen Stellung der Frau in der DDR*, ed. Herta Kuhrig and Wulfram Speigner (Leipzig: Verlag für die Frau, 1978), pp. 229-53.

found that the domestic division of labor is still very traditional; it is well-known that women do two-thirds to three-quarters of the housework and that women have about one-third less leisure time.[13]

In respect to the socialization process, studies undertaken by the Central Institute for Youth Research have pointed out, for example, that job preferences often reflect traditional gender distinctions, that girls have less leisure time than boys because girls are more often asked to help in the household, that leisure time activities follow gender-specific models, and that parents support gender-specific role models with their choice of toys and games, and the encouragement of certain behavior.[14] As the GDR cultural theorist Irene Dölling, who addresses the issue within the larger framework of GDR culture, has written, one might question whether this is only the result of "tradition" or whether these patterns of socialization are being reinforced by the social policy program, which, aimed at stopping the falling birth rate, encourages the idea of motherhood without strongly supporting new men's roles at the same time.[15] In the realm of "privacy" within the family, role models and socialization patterns seem to be quite resistant to change and here the ambivalent role of the family becomes obvious: the encouragement of continuity in (core) family socialization makes it very difficult to change gender-specific role-models.

The other example I will use here is that of the authority syndrome. As Theodor W. Adorno, Max Horkheimer, and other critical theorists of the Frankfurt School have argued, family socialization also transmits political attitudes and behaviors. In discussing the awakening of fascism in Germany, they criticized the "authoritarian character" produced in German families and held it partly responsible for the rise of fascism. As Gabriel A. Almond and Sidney Verba found in their famous cross-national political culture analysis *The Civic Culture* (1963), the West Germans - 30 years later - still sub-

---

[13] Irene Dölling, "Social and Cultural Changes in the Lives of GDR Women - Changes in their Self-Conception," in *Studies in GDR Culture and Society 6*, ed. Margy Gerber et al. (Lanham/New York/London: University Press of America, 1986), 86.

[14] Uta Bruhm-Schlegel and Otmar Kabat vel Job, "Exkurs: Geschlecht," in *Jugend konkret*, ed. Walter Friedrich and Werner Gerth (Berlin: Neues Leben, 1984), pp. 215-36.

[15] Dölling, "Social and Cultural Changes," p. 87; see also Irene Dölling, *Individuum und Kultur* (Berlin: Dietz, 1986), pp. 131-61.

ordinated themselves to the state and were less politically active than other populations despite the democratic structures of the political system. Be that as it may - Almond and Verba have been criticized in various publications[16] - the question is: What happened to this part of the German heritage in the GDR? Dietrich Staritz has recently maintained that authoritarian attitudes and behaviors (*Untertänigkeit*) not only survived in the GDR after the Second World War but were encouraged by a paternalistic state policy and the elite-recruitment policy of the SED.[17] Discipline, obedience, and subservience were encouraged while participation, critical awareness, activity, and individuality were discouraged.

One might argue that the family has also helped to preserve traditional patterns. As a consequence of the official GDR theory that fascism was basically a result of capitalism, subjective aspects of the political culture in Germany, of which family education is a substantial part, were denied. No effort was made to tackle the authority syndrome on the level of family socialization; no distinct re-education policy encouraged families to overcome the authority syndrome; socialist goals were to be realized instead.

Conclusion: Family Socialization and Political Culture

Family socialization plays an important role within the socialization process in the GDR. Despite the strong support for public child raising, families remain the first and most important socialization agent. There is evidence that this role is presently being recognized.

As a sociological phenomenon, family socialization is influenced by far-reaching sociological changes which have resulted from modernization and socialist family policy. Continuity and change are two - sometimes contradictory - characteristics of this development. Their effect on the socialization process, in particular the effect of single-parenting, and the role of "mixed" social standards, etc. needs to be further investigated.

---

[16] See David P. Conradt, "Changing German Political Culture," in *The Civic Culture Revisited*, ed. Gabriel A. Almond and Sidney Verba (Boston/Toronto: Little Brown and Company, 1980), pp. 212-72.

[17] Dietrich Staritz, "Untertänigkeit: Heritage and Tradition," in *Studies in GDR Culture and Society 6*, ed. Margy Gerber et al. (Lanham/New York/London: University Press of America, 1986), 37-48.

In everyday life, the family represents the most important informal institution for children and youth, which is the reason for its popularity. Like in other countries of the Soviet bloc - most notably in Poland - the family constitutes one of the most important aspects of everyday life; families are basic networks in society. They nurture what East European specialists have called the "second society" within state socialist societies. Thus they represent a microcosm of social and cultural patterns in which basic features of society are reflected and often refracted.

From a political point of view, family socialization should not be seen simply as the embodiment of privacy; due to the interrelationship between the public and the private, the interference of the political in all spheres of life, and the high degree of societal regulation, families are part of the political network set up to educate socialist personalities.

Therefore family socialization should be understood as part of the political culture of the GDR. Family socialization entails subjective perceptions, attitudes, and behaviors, and their transmission from one generation to the other; these include political attitudes and values as well as perceptions of self and social relations. Political-culture analysis which does not consider the role of the family will fail to explain basic political, social, and cultural mechanisms of the society.

Handicapped People in the GDR: Cooperation between Church and State

Gisela Helwig

About 1.2 million GDR adults are mildly, severely, or very severely handicapped;[1] and approximately 540,000 GDR children have physical and/or mental handicaps, including sensory deficiencies.[2] These numbers correspond percentagewise to statistics for the Federal Republic and other advanced industrial societies. The care of the handicapped and, increasingly, the effort to better integrate them into society are basic components of social, health, education, and employment policies in the GDR. Compared internationally, the GDR's achievements in this field are remarkable.

Since the mid-1970s social integration has received a higher priority than in earlier years. "These people have a right to be included in our lives as much as possible," Erich Honecker stated at the Ninth Party Congress in 1976.[3] The Party platform, adopted in 1976, calls for the integration of the handicapped by means of "appropriate education and working facilities, complex measures of rehabilitation as well as medical and social care."[4] In the same year the "Verordnung zur weiteren Verbesserung der gesellschaftlichen

---

[1] *Soziale Sicherheit für alle Bürger - Gesetz und Wirklichkeit in der DDR,* Panorama DDR (Berlin: Auslandspresseagentur GmbH, 1980), p. 12.

[2] Horst-Günter Kessler, "Die viel zitierte Integration ist noch nicht in Sicht," *Stuttgarter Zeitung,* 23 July 1983.

[3] "Bericht des Zentralkomitees der Sozialistischen Einheitspartei Deutschlands an den IX. Parteitag der SED. Berichterstatter: Genosse Erich Honecker," *Neues Deutschland,* 19 May 1976, p. 11. My translation here and throughout.

[4] "Das neue Programm der SED," *Deutschland Archiv,* 9, No. 7 (1976), 753.

Unterstützung schwerst- und schwergeschädigter Bürger" went into effect.[5] The problems of handicapped people have since become the subject of public discussion in the GDR. The media report on special schools and rehabilitation institutions and try to promote understanding for the handicapped and their families.

These developments stand in contrast to earlier years when the handicapped were a more or less taboo topic, a fact due primarily to the difficulty official policymakers had in reconciling physical and mental handicaps with the idea of the "allseitig entwickelte sozialistische Persönlichkeit."[6] In recent years experts such as Rolf Löther (Akademie für Ärztliche Fortbildung, Berlin), Susanne Hahn (an internist who in addition to practicing medicine concerns herself with questions of medical ethics), and Achim Thom (Karl-Marx-Universität Leipzig) have signalled a change in this thinking with their publications.

In an article published in 1981 Löther points out that the mentally and multiply handicapped are still frequently exposed to prejudice and often evoke questions about the "purpose of severely defective life and its preservation."[7] He sees in the situation of the handicapped an opportunity to demonstrate "the value of the principles and aims of socialist society," and in this context contends:

> Apart from the need to develop the material conditions for care, it is crucial to strengthen the ideological-ethical motivation to help the handicapped who require physical care and to raise the professional qualifications for this task. Security and well-being must also be granted those handicapped who until now have received inadequate care. (p. 144)

In his last sentence Löther is referring to the severely mentally handicapped who for a long time had been cared for

---

[5] *Gesetzblatt der DDR I*, No. 33, 9 September 1976.

[6] For this discussion, see Carol Poore, "Illness and the Socialist Personality," in *Studies in GDR Culture and Society 6*, ed. Margy Gerber (Lanham/New York/London: University Press of America, 1986), pp. 123 ff.

[7] Rolf Löther, "Eingliederung Geschädigter in die Gesellschaft. Weltanschaulich-philosophische Aspekte," *Wissenschaft und Fortschritt*, 31, No. 4 (1981), 144.

mainly by the churches without sufficient support by the state.

In a jointly written book Hahn and Thom likewise warn against "an undue devaluation" of people who do not fit the socialist ideal of personality; they point out that the emphasis placed on consciousness, activity, collectivity, and partisanship by this concept does not mean that the criteria for evaluating human life should be reduced to these attributes.[8] The "reduced capacity to be active" of the handicapped, the chronically ill, and old people need not result in the diminished social importance of their lives (pp. 30-31). Hahn and Thom consider in detail the writings of the Dutch moral theologian Paul Sporken, who emphatically rejects all speculation about "lebensunwertes Leben" and instead calls for cooperation between Christians and atheists to support a "humanizing process" for all humankind (p. 134).

The Background of Church/State Cooperation

The basis of GDR church/state cooperation in the field of public health and social welfare formulated in the following quotation can serve as a definition of this basis in regard to the care of the handicapped as well: recognition of the "common humanistic concern in spite of differing motivations and ideological positions."[9] This approach permits practical collaboration without basic ideological confrontation.

The churches' care of the sick and the handicapped has a long tradition in Germany; it dates back to the Middle Ages and has continued down through the centuries into modern times. After World War II the churches retained this function in all four occupation zones; and in 1949, when the Federal Republic and the GDR came into being, church/state cooperation in this field was continued in both German states. The cooperative arrangement is not the same however in the two Germanys. In the Federal Republic, the organizations referred to as "voluntary charitable care" (Freie Wohlfahrtspflege), of which the Protestant Diakonisches Werk and the Catholic Caritas are the largest, maintain altogether more than 60,000

---

[8] Susanne Hahn and Achim Thom, *Sinnvolle Lebensbewahrung - humanes Sterben* (Berlin: Deutscher Verlag der Wissenschaften, 1983), p. 30.

[9] Martin Ziegler, "Möglichkeiten diakonischer Aktivitäten in einem sozialistischen Umfeld," *Deutsches Pfarrerblatt*, 82, No. 9 (1982), 400.

institutions.[10] These facilities take precedence over state institutions in the health and social welfare sector; that is, additional state facilities are established only when the need exceeds the capacity of the voluntary charitable institutions.

In the GDR, the position of the church is less strong; the state has traditionally attempted to restrict its influence as much as possible. Church hospitals and facilities for the handicapped were initially allowed to continue their work because the state had no substitute for them, and because many religious facilities had resisted the fascist policy of euthanasia, a stance honored by the Soviet Military Administration and later by the GDR state. In the 1950s the state, disapproving of the connections between the West German and GDR Diakonisches Werk and Caritas, hindered the work of these organizations in the GDR.[11] That changed in 1958, following negotiations between the GDR government and the Protestant churches which culminated in the churches' acknowledgment of socialism. In a communiqué, dated July 21, 1958, church spokesmen declared: "In keeping with their belief, Christians fulfill their duties in accordance with the law. They respect the development of socialism and assist in the peaceful promotion of public life."[12]

Over the years church/state cooperation has grown until today the collaboration between church and state in health and social services has achieved a level which is without precedent in socialist countries. Public recognition of the churches' welfare activities has resulted in various concessions being made by the state, for example, the 1975 agreement whereby the training of medical personnel in church institutions received state recognition. The final examinations are taken at the appropriate state technical college.[13] Other milestones in church/state cooperation will be discussed below.

---

[10] The other organizations are: Arbeiterwohlfahrt, Deutscher Paritätischer Wohlfahrtsverband, Deutsches Rotes Kreuz, and the Zentralwohlfahrtsstelle der Juden in Deutschland. More than 45,000 of the 60,000 institutions are run by the Diakonisches Werk and Caritas.

[11] See Martin Reuer, "Diakonie als Faktor in Kirche und Gegenwart," in *Die evangelischen Kirchen in der DDR*, ed. Reinhard Henkys (Munich: Chr. Kaiser, 1982), pp. 216-17.

[12] As quoted in Reinhard Henkys, "Kirche - Staat - Gesellschaft," in *Die evangelischen Kirchen in der DDR*, p. 31.

[13] Reuer, p. 228.

Church Facilities for Health Care and Care of the Handicapped

Since central Germany is by tradition a Protestant area, the institutions of the Diakonisches Werk prevail: according to the latest published statistics (January 1983), the Protestant churches administer a total of 863 institutions with accommodations for 39,744 persons.[14] Among these are:

- 45 hospitals;
- 276 retirement homes and nursing-care centers;
- 120 recreation centers;
- 279 day nurseries;
- 16 institutions for the vocational training of medical staff personnel.
- 105 homes for the mentally and physically handicapped with facilities for 5,455 residents;
- special day-care centers for 509 mentally handicapped.

Caritas maintains eighteen homes for the mentally handicapped, thirty-three mostly smaller hospitals, numerous homes for the aged, nursing homes, and children's homes, as well as training institutions for nurses.[15] In Erfurt the churches together maintain an ecumenical day-care center for handicapped children.

The share of the total number of GDR hospital beds in church-run facilities is 7.25%; for senior citizen housing and care, 13%. Almost 50% of all severely mentally handicapped people are taken care of by the churches.

Outstanding facilities for the physically disabled are the three large *Diakonie* institutions with multifaceted rehabilitation programs: Oberlinhaus in Potsdam; Pfeiffersche Stiftungen in Magdeburg; and Marienstift in Arnstadt. Here physically disabled children and youths are educated, beginning with the first grade and ending with their graduation as skilled workers. Medical care is provided in specialized orthopaedic hospitals connected with the institutions. Both church personnel and state employees work in these hospitals.

---

[14] "Diakonie lobt Verhältnis zu DDR-Behörden. Petzold: Partnerschaftliche Zusammenarbeit mit dem Staat," epd *Landesdienst Berlin*, No. 99, 30 May 1985, p. 3.

[15] "Caritas in der DDR," *begegnung*, 26, No. 3 (1986), 27.

As a result of their experiences during fascism, the churches after the war focused their attention above all on the care of the mentally and multiply handicapped. There was a particularly great need in this area, as the state had long concentrated its efforts primarily on those handicapped who, after having attended special schools and/or rehabilitation programs, could be integrated into the labor force. Even today the most important institutions for the mentally handicapped - the Hoffnungsthaler Anstalten in Lobethal, the Neinstedter Anstalten near Thale, the Samariter Anstalten in Fürstenwalde - are owned by the Diakonisches Werk. The mentally handicapped are taught in keeping with their possibilities, the goal being to enable them to live meaningful lives within a community.[16] In the last few years there has been a tendency to intensify the cooperation with state institutions, e.g., in newly built special hospitals for the mentally ill.

The churches are committed to helping not only the handicapped themselves, but their families as well. Consultation hours, courses of instruction for parents, and recreation trips for them and their handicapped children are important aspects of their work. Moreover, churches promote better relations between the handicapped and the rest of society. They arrange sponsorships and meetings with individuals and organizations able to help the handicapped. Undoubtedly the GDR churches have made an important contribution to the heightening of social sensitivity towards the problems of the handicapped.

The financing of church activities in the health and social sector is in the main covered by the state. When a GDR resident is admitted to a hospital or other health or social welfare institution, payment is secured through the public health insurance plan. In principle, this applies to church institutions as well. They receive a cost-covering sum from the state, referred to as the "Pflegesatz," for each patient. Employees' wages are included in these "Pflegesätze." Personnel in religious institutions receive the same remuneration as their colleagues in state hospitals and homes, and they are included in the state-sponsored social security plan. Altogether the state transfers to the Diakonisches Werk and Caritas approximately 200 million Marks a year; funds for pastoral care, for cultural and social work, and, last but not least,

---

[16] Heinrich Behr, "Beispielhaft für Gesellschaft und Staat," *Kirche im Sozialismus*, 4, No. 2 (1977), 13.

for investments, are not included, however.[17] Therefore the churches are dependent on donations and the support of churches in Western countries, especially the Federal Republic.

Outcome 81

When comparative statistics on the care of the handicapped were published in 1981, the UN's Year of the Handicapped, the GDR was able to show impressive achievements in the following fields of care for the handicapped:

- early diagnosis of handicaps through a standardized program of medical check-ups designed to monitor the health of all children and youth;
- special education of handicapped children in kindergartens and schools with programs designed for their particular kind of handicap;
- occupational training of the handicapped and provision of special workshop positions for them;
- rehabilitation of adults who have become handicapped as a result of sickness or accident;
- legal protection and financial support of handicapped persons and their families.[18]

Deficits were found - as was the case almost everywhere in the world - in the field of social integration and in the creation of an environment oriented to the handicapped. Moreover, the Department of Health admitted that state support of the mentally handicapped and multi-handicapped had been neglected for a long time. While the number of places for non-educable children in daily, weekly, or permanent care centers was tripled in the decade from 1970 to 1980, one third of them still remained without care.[19]

On the other hand, the exemplary care of the very severely handicapped by the Diakonisches Werk and Caritas was officially commended in 1981. In an interview GDR Secretary

[17] "Dienst an vielen Kranken und Behinderten," *Neue Zeit,* 9 August 1983, p. 3.

[18] See Gisela Helwig, "Zum Jahr der Behinderten in der DDR," *Deutschland Archiv,* 14, No. 12 (1981), 1237-38.

[19] Gerald Götting, "Dienst am Nächsten - humanistische Tradition und schöpferische Verwirklichung in der sozialistischen Gesellschaft," in *Tradition und Verpflichtung,* ed. Sekretariat des Hauptvorstandes der Christlich-Demokratischen Union Deutschlands (Berlin, 1981), p. 13.

of Health Ludwig Mecklinger praised the following achievements of the churches:

- the program for reconstruction and building of nursing homes, institutions for mentally handicapped and multi-handicapped children and youths capable of learning, and of rooming houses for the severely psychically handicapped;
- the vacation care of severely and very severely handicapped children and the organization of vacations for the psychically handicapped in various holiday regions;
- active and creative participation in elaborating and testing the plan for training non-educable children and youths;
- cooperation in the vocational training of very severely handicapped at Marienstift in Arnstadt, in Oberlinhaus Potsdam, and the Pfeiffersche Stiftungen Magdeburg.[20]

As the Secretary stressed, all these activities had earned "unrestricted appreciation and official support" (pp. 71-72).

From Tolerance to Cooperation

On the side of the churches, 1981 was called the "Year of Stimulus" ("Jahr des Anstoßes").[21] While cooperation with public health institutions had been on the whole satisfactory even before, relations were greatly improved in 1981. The nomination of the director of the Diakonisches Werk, Ernst Petzold, to the governmental commission for the Year of the Handicapped, headed by Secretary of Health Mecklinger, was of special significance. It was the "green light" for all levels, and many joint actions were decided and coordinated. This process spread into all districts and regions; since the end of 1981 the Diakonisches Werk has been represented in all commissions and working groups dealing with rehabilitation.

Both the Diakonisches Werk and Caritas are now fully included in the planning for public health and social welfare in the GDR. In granting these church organizations a wide sphere of activity, the state shows its esteem for their efforts - despite ideological differences. The "principle of coopera-

---

[20] Ludwig Mecklinger, "Fortführung bewährter Zusammenarbeit," *Standpunkt*, 9, No. 3 (1981), 71.

[21] Heinrich Behr, "Jahr der Geschädigten 1981," *Standpunkt*, 9, No. 10 (1981), 255.

tion" has taken the place of the earlier "principle of tolerance," as Ernst Petzold put it in 1985.[22]

Heinrich Behr, director of Marienstift in Arnstadt since
1958, may be considered symbolic of the cooperation between state and religious institutions. Behr, who grew up in
this rehabilitation center for the physically disabled, which
was previously administered by his father, is a member both
of the general assembly of the Diakonisches Werk and the
state's Association for Rehabilitation. In addition he belongs to
the Conference of Directors of State and Religious Rehabilitation Centers and collaborates with state offices on the
"Physically Disabled Children" project in the Erfurt district.

The Pioneer Work of the Churches

Behr knows very well what he is talking about when he
states that numerous impulses for legislation have emanated
from the work of the churches. The "Verordnung zur weiteren Verbesserung der gesellschaftlichen Unterstützung
schwerst- und schwergeschädigter Bürger" of 1976 includes
for example several innovations based on initiatives of the
Diakonisches Werk. Behr mentions some examples:

- Training sessions for parents of handicapped children,
  recommended in the law, have taken place regularly in
  the Diakonisches Werk since 1965. A detailed report
  was sent to the Department of Health.
- Day-care centers for handicapped children were initially
  organized by the churches. The law requires an increasing number of public ones.
- The law attaches great importance to the organization of
  holiday camps for handicapped children. Since 1962
  handicapped children living in large institutions of the
  Diakonisches Werk have regularly spent one month a
  year at the seashore.
- The law also requires hospitals and homes to take care
  of handicapped children and youths for several weeks a
  year to enable their parents to go on vacation. Religious
  institutions have been doing that for a long time.[23]

Another example: the first "sheltered workshop" was organized by the Diakonisches Werk in 1962. In order to give it

[22] "Diakonie lobt Verhältnis zu DDR-Behörden," p. 3.
[23] Behr, "Beispielhaft für Gesellschaft und Staat," p. 14.

a legal basis it later was placed under the control of the Regional Council's Department of Health. Thus a model was created that became an orientation for other Regional Councils and supplied elements essential for a law concerning such workshops: "Anordnung zur Sicherheit des Rechts auf Arbeit für Rehabilitanden" (1969).[24] In keeping with this law, measures were taken to organize employment under sheltered conditions for disabled persons who would otherwise be incapable of working.

In 1983 the *Neue Zeit*, the daily paper of the CDU in the GDR, pointed out that the work of the Wichernheim in Frankfurt/Oder, which was founded in 1903 by the Protestant church, seemed to be exemplary in many respects. Two facilities, the paper wrote, deserve recognition for the "pioneer work" being done there: a "half-way-house" where old people who are confined to bed and who require constant care live together with severely disturbed persons who are often not open to any kind of therapy - thus closing a gap between a "normal" home and an "asylum"; and a house in which mentally handicapped men and women live together and are given the possibility of developing partnerships with one another. The binding character of these relationships is underlined by careful preparation in a "school for partnership" and by the attendance of all residents at the so-called "Wichern wedding." The article in *Neue Zeit* emphasizes the importance of this experiment and quotes Pastor Gehlsen, the director of Wichernheim: "Handicapped people must be enabled to live, to work, to love, to hope, to pray, and to spend their leisure time as normally as possible."[25]

The churches continue to improve their care of the mentally handicapped. Among other questions, the Advisory Board for Psychiatry of the Diakonisches Werk is now working on:

- problems of prenatal diagnosis;
- early registration of mentally handicapped children;
- cooperation with their families;
- housing programs for mentally handicapped adults;
- problems of partnership, marriage, and family planning

---

[24] *Gesetzblatt der DDR II*, No. 75, 5 September 1969.

[25] Joachim Winter, "Pionierdienste für Behinderte. Heute begeht das Wichernheim in Frankfurt(Oder) sein 80. Gründungsjubiläum," *Neue Zeit*, 15 February 1983, p. 3.

for mentally handicapped people.[26]

Conclusion

Work in institutions caring for the handicapped, especially for the severely handicapped, is difficult and emotionally taxing, as has often been recognized by representatives of the state. For example, in March 1986 Gerald Götting, chairman of the CDU in the GDR and member of the Staatsrat, said: "The church health and social welfare institutions in particular deserve gratitude and appreciation. The care being rendered there is often unusually hard. All the more, then, we must praise what is being done in those houses of charity." [27]

Press reports concerning the charitable activities of the churches often reflect open admiration. Apparently the mostly non-religious journalists are impressed by the exceptional commitment they see there.[28] In GDR literature as well, portrayals of a Christian life style increasingly occur. Thus Günter de Bruyn, for example, points out the difference in atmosphere between a state and a Catholic nursing home in his novel *Neue Herrlichkeit*.[29] That the Diakonisches Werk and Caritas have made their mark is expressed as well in the reflections of physicians, sociologists, and psychologists who have not only recognized the selfless commitment of many persons working in religious institutions, but have been motivated to give new thought to issues of human dignity and the right of old people, the handicapped, the seriously ill, and the dying to proper care. By and large, the discussion of ethical questions in medicine and social work has not been left uninfluenced by Christian ideas.[30] Ernst Petzold, in an interview in 1985, came to the following conclusion:

---

[26] *Jahresbericht 1984 des Diakonischen Werkes der Evangelischen Kirchen in der Deutschen Demokratischen Republik vom 5. März 1985*, manuscript.

[27] Gerald Götting, "Verantwortungsbewußte Hinwendung zum hilfsbedürftigen Mitmenschen," *Neue Zeit*, 22 March 1986, p. 3.

[28] See for example Ernst Beck, "Im Dienst am Nächsten. Karitative Arbeit im Eichsfeld," *Neue Zeit*, 2 March 1985, p. 4.

[29] Günter de Bruyn, *Neue Herrlichkeit* (Halle/Leipzig: Mitteldeutscher Verlag, 1984). West German edition: Frankfurt/M.: Fischer, 1984, pp. 155 ff.

[30] Cf. Rolf Löther, Susanne Hahn, and Achim Thom mentioned above. In addition, Ernst Luther, professor of philosophy at the University of Halle, has urged that Marxist philosophers collaborate with theologians and Christian physicians to work out new criteria for the goals and means of medical care (*IWE-Tagesdienst*, No. 78, 23 Mai 1986, p. 3).

Christian motivation, characteristics, and objectives are not only tolerated, but also respected in a spirit of partnership. Further: this independent character, marked by Christian belief, is recognized and honored as a prerequisite for committed and effective engagement.[31]

[31] "Ganzheitlich auf den Menschen gerichtetes Zeugnis. Gespräch Karl Hennigs mit Oberkirchenrat Dr. Ernst Petzold," *Standpunkt*, 13, No. 6 (1985), 157.

Homosexuality and the Situation of Homosexuals in the GDR

Rüdiger Pieper

"My son's class - he's just entered the 10th grade - took a trip during the vacation. Now he's told me about a classmate who acted strangely toward the other boys. One could almost think he's gay. . . . How can he be helped and . . . is it possible that he might seduce other boys to homosexuality with his approaches?"[1]

This letter, written by a worried mother, appeared in a 1984 number of "Unter vier Augen," a weekly column of the FDJ daily *Junge Welt* in which readers' questions about problems of partnership and sexuality are answered by a psychologist.[2] It was one of the first times that homosexuality had been treated in this popular column. Until the 1980s homosexuality was a taboo topic in GDR media; and, with very few exceptions,[3] it played no role in belletristic literature either.

This public stance on homosexuality seems to be changing. The column in *Junge Welt* is but one example of the breaking of the old taboo. In the last few years several articles on homosexuality have been published in popular magazines;[4]

---

[1] "Mit Verständnis gegenübertreten," *Junge Welt*, 24 October 1984, p. 5. This and other translations in the following are my own.

[2] See Rüdiger Pieper, "Official Policy and the Attitudes of GDR Youth towards Marriage and the Opposite Sex as Reflected in the Column 'Unter vier Augen,'" in *Studies in GDR Culture and Society 6*, ed. Margy Gerber (Lanham/New York/London: University Press of America, 1986), 109-21.

[3] For example, Beate Morgenstern, "Herr in Blaßblau," in her *Jenseits der Allee* (Berlin/Weimar: Aufbau, 1979), pp. 84-92.

[4] "Wie helfen, ohne zu schaden?"*Für Dich*, No.14, 1984, p. 41, and "Ganz unter uns gesagt: Gleichgeschlechtliche Liebe," *Für Dich*, No. 2, 1986, p. 46. Various articles dealing with homosexuality in the AIDS context will be cited below.

recently published books on sexuality have chapters on homosexuality;[5] and two collections of interviews with men include interviews with homosexuals.[6] Can this be regarded as a liberalization of the attitude toward homosexuality in the GDR?

In the following I will give an overview of the official GDR policy toward homosexuality and of the current situation of homosexuals there. Three topics are especially relevant - both for describing the life of homosexuals in the GDR and for a comparison with the conditions in Western countries: first, the legal situation; second, public opinion toward homosexuals; and third, their everyday living conditions. At the end of the paper, I will give some information on the AIDS problem in the GDR and its consequences for homosexuals there.

The Legal Situation

In postwar Germany, §175 of the penal code, the law against homosexuality which had been sharpened by the Nazis and used as a legal basis for imprisoning and persecuting tens of thousands of homosexuals, remained in effect - in the GDR as well as in the Federal Republic. In both German states homosexuals who had been imprisoned or otherwise persecuted by the Nazis were not, and still are not, regarded as victims of fascism, but rather as people punished according to the law and therefore not entitled to compensation.

In 1967, the GDR parliament passed a new penal code which not only abandoned §175 but did away with the section dealing with crimes of sexuality in general. Thus sexuality as such can no longer be treated as an offense, as was the case before. Sexuality figures in two parts of the penal code: rape and sexual harassment are included in the section "Crimes against the Person" - along with murder, battery, robbery, etc.; and incest and the sexual abuse of children and youth

[5] *Liebe und Sexualität bis 30*, ed. Kurt Starke and Walter Friedrich (Berlin: Deutscher Verlag der Wissenschaften, 1984); Igor Kon, *Einführung in die Sexuologie* (Berlin: Deutscher Verlag der Wissenschaften, 1985), a translation from the original Russian.

[6] Christine Müller, *Männerprotokolle* (Berlin: Der Morgen, 1985), pp. 56-69; West German edition, *James Dean lernt kochen* (Darmstadt/Neuwied: Luchterhand, 1986), pp. 56-69; and Christine Lambrecht, *Männerbekanntschaften* (Halle/Leipzig: Mitteldeutscher Verlag, 1986; Dortmund: Weltkreis, 1986), pp. 110-138.

under eighteen are part of the section "Crimes against Youth and the Family."[7]

In this latter section, a distinction is still made between homosexuality and heterosexuality. While heterosexual acts between adults and juveniles (ages fourteen to seventeen) are prosecuted only under certain circumstances - for example, if the adult is responsible for the education of the juvenile concerned, homosexual acts between adults and juveniles are an offense carrying a maximum penalty of three years prison. This legal situation can lead to absurd situations: for example, homosexual acts between two seventeen-year-olds are legal, but as soon as one of them turns eighteen, he may be prosecuted - until the other is eighteen as well. Although there are no current reports of criminal proceedings in cases like this, the different treatment of heterosexuals and homosexuals nevertheless represents a kind of discrimination. Interestingly, this discrimination involves lesbians as well. The new penal code, which meant a liberalization for homosexual men, was a step back for lesbians, since the old §175 applied only to men (as it still does in the Federal Republic, where the old law was modified at the beginning of the 1970s).

The reasons for abandoning §175 are clearly formulated in GDR publications (although no public discussion took place at the time, not even in juridical literature): as Siegfried Schnabl and Kurt Starke of the Zentralinstitut für Jugendforschung in Leipzig point out in their article on homosexuality, sex between consenting adult homosexuals does not harm society;[8] and criminality resulting from the prohibition of homosexuality, such as blackmail, could be prevented.[9] Reasons for the different treatment of homosexuals and heterosexuals are rarely given. Schnabl and Starke, who speak of the possible deleterious effects of homosexual activities on children and juveniles, are one exception:

> . . . it cannot be absolutely ruled out that in exceptional cases children and juveniles can be strongly influenced in their sexual orientation by massive and continuous homosexual activities

---

[7] *Strafgesetzbuch der DDR* (Berlin: Staatsverlag der DDR, 1984), esp. § 151.

[8] Siegfried Schnabl and Kurt Starke, "Homosexualität," in *Liebe und Sexualität bis 30*, p. 297.

[9] Kurt Richard Bach, *Geschlechtserziehung in der sozialistischen Oberschule* (Berlin: Deutscher Verlag der Wissenschaften, 1974), p. 256.

at an age where they are not fully developed psychosexually. Therefore young people under 18 are protected by law from homosexual activities with adults.[10]

This "exceptional case" is exactly what was worrying the mother who wrote the letter to *Junge Welt.* The answer given - and published in the column - differs from the view of Schnabl and Starke: "A young person can be seduced to commit homosexual acts, but not to homosexuality, if his character is not such that. . . . Parents need not be afraid that the homosexuality of a member of the collective is infectious."[11]

Changing Opinions about Homosexuality

These differing opinions reflect both the scientific discussion taking place in the GDR (and elsewhere) about the causes of homosexuality, and the attitudes within the population toward homosexuality. The various theories that are important for the scientific discussion can be classified into two opposing views: that homosexuality is caused by psychosocial influences - the theory of the dominant mother belongs to this group; and, secondly, that the causes are already present at birth - theories of genetic and hormonal influences belong to this second group.[12] Since Freud research has been undertaken, often with explicit political and moral implications, both to prove the inalterability of sexual orientation and the equality of homosexuals - or their inferiority - vis-á-vis heterosexuals, and to find ways to cure homosexuality.

In the 1970s, the GDR discussion was dominated by Günter Dörner and his research group at the Institut für experimentelle Endoktrinologie at the Charité in East Berlin. Dörner is an advocate of the hormone theory, the thesis that homosexuality is caused by hormonal changes in the mother during pregnancy. He has endeavored to develop a hormone therapy for homosexuals. Although Dörner no longer maintains that homosexuality is a disease, he retains his basic concept that homosexuality is "curable" and that it is better for the individuals involved to be cured. In an interview broadcast by Radio DDR in July 1985, Dörner said,

---

[10] Schnabl and Starke, p. 292.

[11] "Mit Verständnis gegenübertreten," p. 5.

[12] The most detailed discussion of this debate in a GDR publication is in Igor Kon, pp. 284 ff.

. . . homosexuality and bisexuality are not diseases. On the other hand, one has to admit that a large number of them [homosexuals and bisexuals] suffer during their personal development. And therefore, if one can prevent this, for example, then I would tend to say one should. But - I would like to emphasize - this is up to society to decide. In the end I personally am of the opinion that if a mother may decide whether she wants to give birth to a child or not, that she in the future then may decide as well whether she wants a heterosexual or even a homosexual child.[13]

Dörner's approach has come under attack - in the West for many years, in the GDR, publicly, since the 1980s. The Soviet expert Igor Kon, whose classic work on sexuology appeared in German translation in the GDR in 1985, comes to the conclusion that a biological explanation of homosexuality is impossible, that the roots lie in the personal development of the individual.[14] Schnabl and Starke, although conceding that Dörner made an interesting contribution to the search for the roots of homosexuality, call his work controversial. They represent the current GDR position, which is almost diametrically opposite to Dörner's:

No matter where the causes may lie, today we can be sure that homosexuality is as much a part of the personality of the person as heterosexuality is for the majority of the people, that they are neither responsible for their peculiarity nor can they or do they want to give it up. Just as heterosexuals do not wish to change places with homosexuals, there are homosexuals who would not like to change places with heterosexuals and are happy with their situation.[15]

Schnabl and Starke thus emphasize that homosexuals are neither sick nor to blame for their sexual orientation, nor necessarily unhappy because of it. They urge that homosexuals

[13] Interview broadcast by Radio DDR II, 17 July 1985 as part of the program "Studio 80 am Vormittag/PS zu einem Lebenslauf."

[14] Kon, p. 288.

[15] Schnabl and Starke, p. 293.

be treated as normal members of society, a position which stands in contrast to more conservative views that predominated in the 1970s. This change in attitude can also be demonstrated with the example of Kurt Richard Bach. In his 1974 schoolbook on sexual education, the educationist Bach headed his scant section on homosexuality "Abnormalities, Homosexuality" ("Abartigkeiten, Homosexualität") and maintained: ". . . the earlier a person notices his defect the better he can be cured."[16] Bach counseled: "One should not become friends with homosexuals or seek their company, although one should not scorn them either" (p. 256). It was Bach, on the other hand, who replied to the mother's letter about homosexuality in *Junge Welt*. The 1984 article was entitled "Mit Verständnis gegenübertreten" and he now wrote: "A person should refuse homosexual contacts if he does not want them without exposing and isolating the other person. Homosexuals are and remain precious members of the collective. They are colleagues and friends like all the others."[17]

The question arises about the attitude toward homosexuality within the population - whether or not the liberalization of the law and the change in the official attitude have influenced public attitudes. That prejudices against homosexuals still exist is explicitly stated by Siegfried Schnabl in an article that appeared in the women's magazine *Für Dich* in 1986.[18] In their 1984 article on homosexuality, Schnabl and Starke published the results of a survey which canvassed among other things the attitudes of GDR youth (16 to 30 years of age) toward homosexuality.[19] Fifty-two percent of those questioned agreed that homosexuals should not be discriminated against; the rate among women (55%) was considerably higher than among men (47%). Forty percent agreed, "with certain reservations"; and 8% opposed the view. The statement "I emotionally oppose homosexual contacts between men" was affirmed by 58%: 70% of the polled men, compared

---

[16] Bach, p. 256.

[17] "Mit Verständnis gegenübertreten," p. 5. This change of view took place, of course, not only in the GDR but in other countries as well. Books published in the United States and the Federal Republic in the 1960s and early 1970s tend to either pass over homosexuality entirely or to describe it as a crime or a disease.

[18] Siegfried Schnabl, "Ganz unter uns gesagt: Gleichgeschlechtliche Liebe," *Für Dich*, No. 2, 1986, p. 46.

[19] The survey was on sexuality in general; the results concerning homosexuality are to be found in Schnabl and Starke, pp. 299-305.

with 48% of the women. Only 22% of the young people questioned rejected the statement either totally or partially; 29% of the women and 14% of the men. Sexual contacts between women were emotionally opposed by 55% of those questioned; 22% accepted lesbian relationships, including 21% of the polled men. Schnabl and Starke add that people who have grown up in rural areas reject homosexuality more often than people living in big cities (pp. 301-02).

Everyday Life of Homosexuals

As is the case in the West, homosexuals tend to live in urban areas. A survey taken in 1979 shows that the percentage of young people with a homosexual orientation is higher in the big cities (5.3%).[20] Young gays and lesbians often try to find a job in Berlin or Leipzig, where homosexual subcultures exist. Here and in other big cities there are homosexual bars and other meeting places - in parks, for example - where it is easier to find a partner. And homosexuals enjoy greater anonymity there than in small towns and villages. In the big cities homosexuals ordinarily are not discriminated against when looking for an apartment (although problems can occur when a homosexual couple attempts to rent a flat together),[21] and reports about discrimination at work, worse career chances, for example, are relatively rare.

In regard to its homosexual subculture, East Berlin has achieved what the GDR is always striving for: international niveau. There are several homosexual bars and cafés, especially in the Prenzlauer Berg district; dance nights are held especially for homosexuals; there are gay groups and a predominantly gay beach at the Müggelsee. The parks and toilettes are frequented as often as they are in West Berlin - and that means they are crowded at times. The gay and lesbian scene is integrated, in contrast to the Federal Republic.

In the countryside and in provincial towns the situation is often quite different. Schnabl and Starke note various kinds of discrimination in the countryside: difficulties in getting a

---

20 Rolf Borrmann and Hans-Joachim Schille, *Vorbereitung der Jugend auf Liebe, Ehe und Familie* (Berlin: Deutscher Verlag der Wissenschaften, 1980), p. 87.
21 See for example the description in Christine Müller, *Männerprotokolle*, p. 63.

common flat - and sometimes even in getting a flat for a single person since families are favored when apartments are available; exclusion of homosexual couples from social events; rejection of advertisements for partners by local newspapers; and discrimination at work: "Thus many of them are always trying to keep from being discovered and therefore change their jobs and housing quite often."[22] Young homosexuals, especially, have difficulty finding a partner or even others with the same orientation. Many have little opportunity to develop their homosexuality, are frustrated, and sometimes opt for "normal family life," that is, marry and have children, because everyone gets married and has children. Others try to move to Berlin.

Coming-out Problems

One of the greatest problems for homosexuals in the GDR is that they receive almost no help during their coming-out. Young homosexuals in particular often have difficulties. As Schnabl wrote, "If they are not appreciated by their parents, teachers, and other people, or if they are disapproved of and avoided, they will feel like outsiders and face serious crises."[23] In contrast to Western countries, where books and magazines dealing with homosexual problems are widely sold and addresses of meeting places are published in gay newspapers and guides, little information of this kind is available in the GDR. The first widely available discussion of homosexuality in the GDR was the chapter by Friedrich and Starke in *Liebe und Sexualität bis 30*, which appeared in 1984. It included pictures of male and female homosexual couples for the first time as well. The only state institutions offering help for homosexuals are the family counseling centers. What young homosexuals are mainly looking for however, i.e., help from people who have had or are going through similar experiences, people with whom they can identify and groups of people who have the same orientation, does not exist in most cases.

The Role of the Church

Where homosexual groups do exist, they ordinarily meet in churches. Since the beginning of the 1980s such groups can be found in most big cities in the GDR. The Protestant

---

22 Schnabl and Starke, p. 298. See also "Ganz unter uns gesagt," p. 46.

23 Schnabl, "Ganz unter uns gesagt: Gleichgeschlechtliche Liebe," p. 46.

church seems to be the only organization that supports gay groups. But this is not the case in all areas, and support is often a source of controversy within local parishes. When, for example, a church paper in Berlin reported about the activities of a group of homosexuals that met in the church and asked its readers whether they would accept a gay or lesbian minister, most of the published responses were negative. Homosexuality was called a perversion, an offense, a sacrilege.[24] Discussions on the acceptability of homosexuality have also been held within the Federation of Evangelical Churches (Bund der Evangelischen Kirchen der DDR).[25] At least one conservative church organization has threatened to withdraw from the *Kirchenbund* because of church support of homosexuality.[26] In spite of this controversy, homosexual groups have had information desks at national church meetings in the last few years; church seminars on homosexuality have been held, and articles on homosexuality have been published in several national church newspapers.[27]

Still, the church groups do not reach all homosexuals. Not all GDR homosexuals feel at ease in a church setting. Those who do not accept the role of the church or who support the SED have the most problems. Since little help is available from state organizations, they face a conflict between their political convictions and their desire for contact with others who share their sexual orientation. If they attend homosexual meetings in a church, they encounter suspicion because of their Party affiliation, and at the same time they are regarded suspiciously by the Party because of their presumed relationship with the church.

Lack of Integration

A major problem of homosexuals in the GDR is the lack of integration in society. In spite of scholarly research findings that homosexuality is involuntary - that homosexuals neither choose nor are able to change their sexual orientation - and the official position of tolerance toward homosexuals, little

---

[24] Wolfgang Büscher and Peter Wensierski, *Aussteigerjugend im andern Deutschland* (Reinbek: Rowohlt, 1984), p. 121.
[25] Cf. Wolfgang Brinkel and Alwin Meyer, *Homosexuelle in der Kirche?* Aktion Sühnezeichen/Friedensdienste (Berlin: 1985).
[26] That is, the Landesbruderrat der Bekennenden Evangelisch-Lutherischen Kirche Sachsen. See Brinkel and Meyer, p. 4.
[27] See Brinkel and Meyer, pp. 4, 25-31.

has been undertaken to change public opinion and to integrate them better. Although the GDR abolished the law against homosexuality quite early, there has been almost no official action or campaign against the discrimination of homosexuals in everyday life. As Schnabl and Starke emphasize: "Beyond all doubt the legal step alone could not break down all the prejudices against homosexuals that were built up during the past."[28] If the GDR takes its official position seriously, it cannot confine itself to a few articles or book chapters, but must create institutions or groups that can help homosexuals. Why doesn't the FDJ have homosexual groups? Why doesn't the women's mass organization (Demokratischer Frauenbund Deutschlands) concern itself with lesbianism? As long as homosexuality is not accepted as a part of daily life in the GDR, many GDR homosexuals will try to move to the West, where they expect to find more acceptance. Interestingly, the AIDS issue seems to be leading to greater official efforts to integrate homosexuals into society, although the overall consequences may be ambivalent for GDR homosexuals and their situation.

AIDS

The outbreak of AIDS and the association of the disease with homosexuality have resulted in new suspicion toward homosexuals in the GDR, as elsewhere. The GDR was slow to admit the presence of the disease in the GDR and other socialist countries. In 1985 Niels Sönnichsen, director of the Dermatology Clinic at East Berlin's Charité and head of a special counseling group of the Ministry of Health, denied that there were cases of AIDS in the East bloc countries.[29] In February 1987, the first AIDS death was announced in the GDR; 14 other GDR citizens were reported to be infected by the virus.[30]

In spite of its initial reluctance to admit the presence of the disease, the GDR began quite early to take steps to combat its spreading. Blood tests have been imported from

---

[28] Schnabl and Starke, p. 298. The same position is taken by Schnabl in his article "Gleichgeschlechtliche Liebe," p. 46. See also Christine Müller, *Männerprotokolle*, pp. 66-67.

[29] "AIDS - eine neue Infektionskrankheit," *Wochenpost*, No. 40, 1985, p. 19. Also "Als Paar geschützt," *spectrum*, No. 16, 1985.

[30] Reported by the West German news agency Deutsche Presse-Agentur (dpa), 12 February 1987. See also Niels Sönnichsen, "Mit Strafen kann man nichts verhindern," *Der Spiegel*, 9 March 1987, p. 31.

the West (one million blood tests had been carried out by February 1987);[31] known virus carriers are registered by name; and GDR law provides for the quarantining of AIDS victims. Since1985, articles in the press have informed the population about the danger of AIDS.[32] Organizations such as Urania and the universities organize public lectures and discussions on the disease,[33] and juveniles are informed about AIDS in the schools. Special counseling groups have been formed since1985. The GDR has also started its own research program and participates in international conferences on the disease.

The fear of AIDS has affected the official policy toward homosexuals in two ways. First, efforts are being made to integrate homosexuals more effectively into society. As is stated in a recent article in the journal *Heilberufe*, when homosexuals are not integrated, subcultures arise which make the fight against sexually transmitted diseases more difficult.[34] Numerous articles urge more tolerance toward homosexuality, at the same time condemning promiscuity and acknowledging the need to reduce the danger of sexually transmitted diseases.[35] Secondly, steps have been taken to check the existing homosexual subculture. Police regularly patrol homosexual meeting points in East Berlin. And it has been rumored in the West that homosexuals are given preferential treatment in the granting of exit visas to the West.[36]

---

[31] Sönnichsen, "Mit Strafen kann man nichts verhindern," p. 31.

[32] In addition to the above mentioned articles in the *Wochenpost* and *spectrum*, an article appeared in *Junge Welt* on 3 October 1985.

[33] Most recently, for example, a "Sonntagsvorlesung" in the Großer Saal of the Dermatology Clinic of the Charité, as reported by the Deutsche Presse-Agentur, 24 February 1987 ("DDR: Großer Andrang in der Charité," *Der Tagesspiegel* [West Berlin], p. 13).

[34] Erwin Günther, "Homosexualität und ihre psychosozialen Probleme," *Heilberufe*, 38, No. 11 (1986), p. 425.

[35] Schnabl writes in "Ganz unter uns gesagt: Gleichgeschlechtliche Liebe": "Whoever for example exposes himself and others to the danger of sexually transmitted diseases by indiscriminate, constant partner-change and superficial intimate contacts, as is the case with a number of male homosexuals, must be requested to assume a more responsible behavior" (p. 46).

[36] In its article "Gestaffelte Abwehr" (15 September 1986, p. 148), *Der Spiegel* maintained that 10,000 emigration permits had been granted to homosexuals during the 1984 *Ausreisewelle* - a position from which it has since distanced itself ("Versteckspiel um Infizierte in der DDR," *Der Spiegel*, 16 February 1987, p. 148).

Whether AIDS will reinforce the process of liberalization and integration or force homosexuals back into their ghettos is an open question - not only in the GDR but around the world as well.

Use of Nature and Environmental Protection in the German Democratic Republic under Conditions of Continued Economic Growth

Rainer Saupe

In the 1980s questions of environmental protection have increasingly become central issues of public discussion. This has not occurred by accident. As a result of expanding industrialization, mankind is at present faced with numerous ecological problems which are still awaiting a solution.

Legislation and Institutions for Environmental Protection

In the GDR the protection of nature is anchored in the constitution as a mandate given to society and the state to safeguard the interests of the people. In contrast to numerous countries of Western Europe, where the maintenance and protection of the environment are not guaranteed by the constitution, the GDR codified requirements relating to landscape development and conservation as early as 1949, when the first constitution was adopted.[1] Since then the changing conditions of nature and resource conservation have been incorporated into numerous laws adopted by the Volkskammer, the country's parliament. In 1970 an overall environmental protection law (Landeskulturgesetz) was passed which regulates all matters relating to the maintenance, pro-

---

[1] Article 26 of the 1949 constitution reads: "Die Verteilung und Nutzung des Bodens wird überwacht und jeder Mißbrauch verhütet." Article 15 of the 1968 constitution, which replaced the first constitution, reads:
1. Der Boden der Deutschen Demokratischen Republik gehört zu ihren kostbarsten Naturreichtümern. Er muß geschützt und rationell genutzt werden....
2. Im Interesse des Wohlergehens der Bürger sorgen Staat und Gesellschaft für den Schütz der Natur. Die Reinhaltung der Gewässer und der Luft sowie der Schutz der Pflanzen- und Tierwelt und landwirtschaftlichen Schönheiten der Heimat sind durch die zuständigen Organe zu gewährleisten und sind darüber hinaus auch Sache jedes Bürgers.

tection, and development of the countryside, the establishment of nature conservation areas, wildlife reserves and national parks, recreation areas and resorts, the organization of coastal protection, and the protection of natural monuments and of flora and fauna.

The central administration and planning of nature development and protection in the GDR fall in the purview of the Council of Ministers. The responsible body is the Ministry of Environmental Protection and Water Resources, which was founded in 1971. All important long-term projects to be realized in these areas figure in the five-year and one-year plans for the national economy. After having been passed by the Volkskammer, these projects, like the other components of the plans, become law.

Much of the responsibility for environmental protection is vested in elected bodies of local government on the county, district, and municipal levels. They are obligated to coordinate and check on the measures taken by the state offices, combines, enterprises, and cooperatives to protect and efficiently use the national resources. The Local Authorities Act (Gesetz über die örtlichen Volksvertretungen), adopted in July 1985, provides the legal basis for this responsibility.

In order to further improve the integrated control of environmental conditions, a state-level Environmental Inspectorate (Staatliche Umweltinspektion) was established in September 1985 as a supplement to the State Water Authority (Staatliche Gewässeraufsicht). It is attached to the Ministry of Environmental Protection and Water Resources, with representation on the county councils. The function of this body is to monitor the observance of provisions and regulations concerning the reduction of air pollution and the safe disposal of wastes that cannot be recycled; it is empowered to impose fines (of up to 10,000 Marks) on enterprises or their responsible managers and staff for contravening relevant provisions.

In view of the varied problems to be solved in the protection and maintenance of nature and the environment, it has become necessary to mobilize the population to take active steps in the residential areas. Special activities are organized by the Nature and Environment Society (Gesellschaft für Natur und Umwelt), which was founded in 1980 within the framework of the Culture Union (Kulturbund). About 1,500 specialized teams and interest groups with more than 55,000 members undertake activities in many different fields of nature and landscape conservation. Together with local authorities, the Kulturbund organizes so-called landscape days, i.e., meetings devoted to special problems of environmental protection in selected types of nature, industrial districts, towns, and villages. Parliament members, government officeholders, workers from factories and cooperatives, scientists, and representatives of mass organizations discuss at these meetings problems relating to the efficient utilization of natural resources such as land, water, and forests, the protection of plants and wildlife, and the improvement of the recreational value of different types of landscape. The issues agreed upon by the participants are set down in plans of nature conservation to be approved and administered by the local councils.

Environmental Policy

A characteristic feature of environmental policy in the GDR is that it forms an integral part of the overall policy of the country. In contrast to Western countries the GDR views environmental protection not only as a technological problem but as part of the larger issue of international peace and disarmament, as it stressed in a study submitted to UNESCO in 1986. Environmental protection is a component part of the social and economic policies of the country, and, as such, is oriented toward two closely interrelated aims: the improvement of the living and working conditions of the population; and the increase of economic growth and efficiency. Contrary to the widespread opinion in Western countries that environmental protection and economic growth are conflicting aims, the GDR proceeds from the fundamental assumption that the the two cannot be separated. Economic growth and environmental protection are interdependent factors: continuous economic growth, comprehensive intensification, faster scientific-technological progress, and higher efficiency of labor are indispensable to the further development of the cultural and material standards of the population; at the same time, they require the efficient use of natural resources, their planned regeneration, and the elimination of damage to nature and the environment. Only substantial economic growth can provide sufficient material and financial means to plan and implement a far-sighted environmental policy.

Reducing Resource Depletion/Recycling

There are two basic ways of solving the problems which arise in connection with rapidly expanding industrial production. The first is to produce under conditions of minimal resource depletion. It is self-evident that lower raw material inputs reduce the burden on the environment since the quantity of waste products is thus decreased. For many years the GDR has aimed at reaching an annual GNP increment of about 5% with lower overall consumption figures for important energy and raw material sources as well as for material goods. Between 1980 and 1984 industrial production increased by 17%, while the consumption of energy, raw materials, and material goods went down by 22.5% over the same period.[2] While in 1980 only 8% of the GNP increase went hand in hand with a reduction in production inputs, this value had gone up to 40% by 1984.[3]

Production inputs can be reduced in several ways. The first aim should be to prevent unnecessary expenditures, e.g., to avoid losses during transportation. Secondly, structural changes in the national economy can help reduce production inputs, e.g., by shifting transportation from road to rail and waterways, which has been carried out in the GDR. These possibilities of input saving, though they always play an important role, are limited. The most significant input reductions will most likely result from switching over to new technologies and new production methods, or from introducing new types of products. In the GDR the main emphasis is therefore being placed on this latter method of input reduction.

The second way of solving the problems arising from growing industrial production is to develop and introduce technologies that increase the proportion of waste that can be recycled. At present, 43% of all waste is recycled in the GDR. As much as 12% of the required raw materials and material goods is met with recycled products; in 1985 six billion

---

[2] *Statistisches Jahrbuch der DDR 1985* (Berlin: Staatsverlag, 1985), pp. 140, 153. See also G. Friedrich, "Wie die Hauptkennziffern der Leistungsbewertung wirken," *Neues Deutschland*, 16-17 November 1985, p. 10.

[3] My own calculations based on figures taken from Otto Reinhold, "Sozialistische Planwirtschaft - Grundlage für die Politik der Hauptaufgabe," *Einheit*, 40, No. 11 (1985), 970; and Helmut Koziolek, "Organische Verbindung der wissenschaftlich-technischen Revolution mit den Vorzügen des Sozialismus," *Einheit*, 40, No. 11 (1985), 980.

Marks worth of raw materials could be replaced in this way.[4] There is still significant potential to be realized here, particularly in regard to ferrous and non-ferrous scrap, electronic scrap containing precious metals, and waste water, among other things. Recycling and reutilization technologies have been developed for about 80% of the industrial waste. The extent to which they will be put into practice depends mainly on the availability of funds. In order to achieve further progress in this area, a list of about 130 central research projects on waste recycling[5] has been drawn up, and approximately 150 additional topics have been included in the research and development plans of industrial combines.

Waste recycling is, however, not confined to industry alone. Domestic refuse - for example, used paper, plastics, and organic matter - is a potential source of raw materials as well. I would like to illustrate what is being done in this area in the GDR.

In 1984 the GDR population collected an average of twenty kilos of waste paper per household, which places the GDR third in the world after Japan and Taiwan; the GDR paper industry obtains about 50% of its raw material requirements from waste paper.[6] GDR specialists have developed technologies for producing different grades of paper from 100% waste paper input. The potential for collecting waste paper has not yet been realized in the GDR; domestic refuse still contains a significant proportion of crumpled paper. If every citizen in the GDR would collect one additional kilogram of waste paper per year, 160,000 seventy-year-old pine trees would not need to be felled, i.e., could be saved, per year.

---

[4] This figure and others in this paragraph are unpublished statistics prepared by the Zentrum für Umweltgestaltung der DDR. This is a research facility of the Ministry of Environmental Protection and Water Resources. It prepares analyses used in the planning of policies and measures in the area of environmental protection.

[5] Projects of the Ministry of Environmental Protection and Water Resources, the Ministry of Science and Technology, the Academy of Sciences, the Ministry of University and Technical Education, and various industrial ministries.

[6] This statistic and others in this paragraph are taken from the paper "Studie für die Internationale Gartenbauausstellung in Erfurt," prepared by Kombinat Zellstoff und Papier Heidenau, April 1986.

71

Of the some 33,000 tons of thermoplastic materials which enter GDR households as cases, packing materials, etc., each year, 10,000 tons - according to estimates - could be collected for recycling and reuse.[7] The refuse collection facilities available at present, however, cannot handle such a large quantity; in 1985 only 6,000 tons were channeled into recycling. The transformation of waste plastics into recycling granules and chips, which can be used for the production of a wide range of new plastic products, requires only 15% of the energy needed for the production of primary plastic material, thus this method offers the advantages of both environmental protection and increased efficiency of the national economy.

The question of how to utilize the remaining domestic refuse more efficiently still awaits an answer. The burning of domestic refuse obviously cannot be regarded as an ideal solution, since transportation and operation costs as well as the burden on the environment are great, and the heating value of such "fuel" is comparatively low. Research carried out in this field has shown that composting, i.e., decomposition, seems to be the most suitable method.[8] On the one hand, domestic refuse is present in large quantities (145-75 kilograms per person - as compared with 300-340 kilograms per person in Western countries) and has a high percentage of organic matter (50% and higher),[9] and, on the other hand, agriculture urgently needs these substances in order to increase soil fertility. In 1984 the first integrated treatment plant for domestic refuse began operating near Dresden; it has a mechanical treatment capacity of 30,000 tons per year, which means that one-third of Dresden's domestic refuse is prepared for further utilization or safe disposal at this facility. Five different types of such integrated treatment plants are being built. By 1990 the GDR expects to have built a total of 112 such units (38 are now completed). The result will be appreciable benefits for environmental protection: 1) 15% less nitrogen fertilizer will be needed in agriculture; 2) the chemical industry will be able to reduce its fertilizer production and thus decrease its energy use by approx. 10% and its annual output of sulphur dioxide by about 130,000 tons; 3) because of the decreased danger of water contamination,

---

[7] These and the following figures were provided by the Zentrum für Umweltgestaltung der DDR.

[8] Unpublished research conducted by the Institut für Forstwissenschaften Eberswalde.

[9] Figures provided by the Zentrum für Umweltgestaltung.

measures presently needed to eliminate nitrates from ground water become superfluous; and 4) with the reduction of the amount of waste to be deposited (down to 20-25%), communal dumping sites will fill less fast, resulting in considerable savings.[10]

In the GDR it is becoming increasingly clear that efficiency based on intensification is the best method of environmental protection: the more energy and raw materials saved, the fewer resources have to be depleted; the more efficient the use of secondary raw materials, the less waste and refuse; and the more machines operated on a three-shift basis, i.e., around the clock, the less necessary it will be to erect new plants and buildings and thus change the landscape.

Pollution and Protection of the Air

In the following, I will address problems the GDR faces in regard to air pollution. The Countryside Conservation Act, which went into effect in 1970, imposed on all factories emission limits for sulphur dioxide, nitrogen oxide, and other pollutants. In fixing such limits, standards of Western European countries served as guidelines. Practical experience has shown however that mere administrative regulations cannot produce satisfactory results. If such limits are to be observed, adequate scientific-technological and organizational solutions must be made available.

In the GDR, efforts to reduce air pollution are focused on three main goals: 1) the efficient use of energy and reduction of energy consumption; 2) the reduction of sulphur dioxide emissions, especially by the desulphurization of the flue gases generated in the burning of lignite coal (*Braunkohle*) - and administrative measures such as the distribution of less polluting grades of coal in the big cities and heavily industrialized areas; and 3) the reduction of nitrogen oxide emissions, mainly from car exhausts, by improving engine characteristics and traffic engineering.

Air quality largely depends on the energy sources employed, i.e., on the fuels used to fire power and heating stations and to drive car engines. In the future, too, the GDR will have to rely on its domestic lignite reserves. While lignite has the advantage of emitting relatively small amounts of

---

[10] Analyses prepared by the Zentrum für Umweltgestaltung.

nitrogen oxide, it contaminates the air with large amounts of sulphur dioxide and dust; and lignite mining, which is open-cast mining, has a long-term negative impact on agricultural and forest areas, and causes the ground-water table to fall.

As a way of coping with this situation, the GDR for many years has endeavored to use its energy sources as efficiently as possible. From 1970 to 1984 it was able to reduce lignite consumption to such an extent that the amount of sulphur dioxide emitted into the air went down by about 1.5 million tons.[11] This meant that sulphur dioxide emissions could be kept down to the levels of the early 1970s, while, over the same period, industrial output almost doubled. In some regions, particularly in areas of industrial concentration, sulphur dioxide emissions could be reduced considerably. Thus, in Berlin, for example, they have been almost halved over the last ten years, because heating stations switched from lignite to fuel oil and natural gas, and all gasworks in the city have been shut down. A further step toward the reduction of sulphur dioxide emissions was the freeze on building additional condensing power stations fired with fossil fuels. An alternative solution to the latter is offered by heating/power stations, i.e., power stations producing electrical energy and sending their steam into heat-supply networks. All future capacity extensions will be realized in the form of such combined heating/power plants and atomic power plants,[12] or achieved by other available means such as geothermal heat generation (in Waren-Müritz, Stralsund, Schwerin, and Neubrandenburg), biogas, wind power, and heat pumps.

----

[11] This statistic and the others in this section were provided by the Zentrum für Umweltgestaltung der DDR.

[12] Approx. 12% of the GDR's electricity is currently produced in atomic plants. In addition to the two existing atomic plants in Rheinsberg (70 megawatt) and Lubmin near Greifswald (4 times 440 megawatt), two 1000 megawatt reactors are to be built near Stendal by the mid-1990s. In connection with the construction of the Kernkraftwerk Nord near Greifswald, containments were developed and installed. In addition, GDR scientists have developed a diagnostic monitoring system for reactor cooling systems which has been recommended by the International Atomic Energy Commission as an international standard. At the beginning of the 1960s the Staatliches Amt für Atomsicherheit und Strahlenschutz, which is directly responsible to the Council of Ministers, was created. Its function is to monitor all safety and protective measures connected with the use of atomic energy. Regular measurements in Lubmin have shown that radiation levels are significantly below international limits. A law on atomic energy (Atomenergiegesetz) passed in 1983 places absolute priority on the protection of life and health over all economic and other considerations.

Since the main cause of sulphur dioxide pollution is lignite firing, desulphurization has become a central issue in the environmental program of the GDR. In the 1970s the so-called limestone additive drying method (*Kalkstein-Additiv-Trockenverfahren*) was developed. This new technology, in which ground limestone is added to fix the sulphur dioxide given off during the burning of lignite, thereby achieving a desulphurization rate of 60%, is employed in Vockerode, Karl-Marx-Stadt, Leipzig, and Freiberg, and will be introduced into more than forty large power and heating stations by 1990. This method also produces heat energy. In addition, the so-called fluid bed catalyst process (*Wirbelschichtverbrennung*), the flue-gas desulphurization rate of which can be as high as 99%, is being developed and installed in new plants.

In the GDR special attention is being focused on methods which provide high purification performance and outstanding efficiency, and at the same time furnish raw materials such as sulphur, sulphuric acid, gypsum, and fertilizers, without emitting new waste products. These and other measures will help the GDR to meet its obligation, assumed at the Helsinki Environment Conference in 1985, to diminish sulphur dioxide emissions by 30% by 1993.

Nitrogen oxide presents another problem in keeping the air clean. Since lignite is burned at relatively low temperatures, nitrogen oxide emissions from lignite are only about 10% of the values produced by burning bituminous coal or fuel oil. Nevertheless, much has been done in recent years to reduce this type of emission as well. Speed limits for motor vehicles have been tightened, and since 1983 all registered motor vehicles have had to undergo an exhaust-gas test. Other cases in point are the increasing shift to transporting goods by rail and waterways instead of by road, and the gradual electrification of the railway network. These measures have resulted in a reduction of nitrogen oxide emissions in the area of transportation by about 25%.[13]

----

[13] From a speech held by Hans Reichelt, Minister of Environmental Protection and Water Resources, at the Multilateral Conference on the Tasks of Environmental Policy, Munich, June, 1984, printed in *Neues Deutschland*, 26 June 1984, p. 3, with the title: "Zusammenarbeit beim Umweltschutz erfordert Sicherung des Friedens." See also "Der Schutz der Umwelt erfordert Entspannung im Geist von Helsinki. Rede von Minister Dr. Hans Reichelt auf der internationalen Umweltschutzkonferenz," *Neues Deutschland*, 9 July 1985, p. 3.

Dust is a third aspect of air pollution. Since in recent years GDR oil-burning energy-generation facilities have been switched over to lignite, it has become necessary to install dedusting devices. In 1985 funds allocated for this purpose were increased by 30% over the preceding year. Dust emissions have been reduced by about 30% in the last ten years.[14]

Water Resources and Waste Treatment

While the annual world average of water available per person is about 12,000 cubic meters, the corresponding figure for the GDR is only 880. The result is that the GDR has extremely overstrained water resources. In countries with highly developed industry and intensive agriculture - and the GDR is among those countries - water requirements are very great. In order to use water as efficiently as possible, complex measures must be taken to: reduce water requirements and consumption; eliminate water loses and water dissipation; protect the lakes, rivers, and the sea; treat waste water and sewage; and decrease all kinds of water pollution. The legal basis for executing these tasks in the GDR is the Water Act of 1982. The State Water Supervision Authority monitors the observance of all relevant provisions of the act and is empowered to impose special conditions or limits if necessary.

From 1981 to 1985 the specific water consumption of the national economy was reduced by more than 20%, a saving mainly due to the repeated reusage of water.[15] In recent years the capacity of sewage treatment and disposal plants has been appreciably expanded. In 1985 the largest and most modern municipal sewage treatment plant in the GDR to date began operating to the north of Berlin. It uses a new Soviet sludge-drying technology which requires 25% less space than earlier plants. Construction costs and time are reduced by 50% and 25% respectively as well. Since the drinking water consumption of the population is increasing at a rate of between 2.5 and 3% per year, great efforts are being made to use less potable water in industry. To this end, the state has imposed targets for the industrial use of water, i.e., water consumption standards per product unit.

---

[14] Information supplied by the Zentrum für Umweltgestaltung der DDR. See also speech held by Hans Reichelt at the conference of the presidium of the Urania, 12 October 1984, reprinted in *Umschau*, No. 8 (1984), p. 6.

[15] The statistics used here were supplied by the Zentrum für Umweltgestaltung der DDR.

In some areas of the GDR water quality has been seriously affected by the use of artificial fertilizers, chemicals, and concentrated liquid manure, as well as by extended mining operations and industrial waste. As one measure to alleviate this situation, a long-term program devoted to lake and pond sanitation was adopted in 1972. It specifies measures against the eutrophication of water reservoirs by nitrogen and phosphates. Lakes and ponds are desludged and the deep deoxygenized water is drained off or enriched with oxygen. In the long run, however, the decisive means must be the prevention of further water pollution by agriculture and industry. Between 1980 and 1985 ground water pollution was reduced by a percentage equivalent to the annual average of waste water produced by five million people.[16] For the period from 1986 to 1990 the State Water Supervision Authority, in collaboration with district councils and enterprises, has issued standards regulating the recovery of usable materials from waste water.

The chemical plants built in the 1930s, like Leuna and Buna, were all constructed without waste-water purification installations, with the result that they badly polluted the environment. At present these chemical concerns are being equipped with modern waste-treatment facilities. New chemical plants like Schwedt and Leuna II were provided with water-treatment technology corresponding to international standards.

The best results in combating industrial water pollution have been obtained in combines and plants where the management attached importance to the designing and development of low-waste or waste-free products and water-saving processes or to the regaining of usable materials. Here are a few examples: in the petrochemical combine Schwedt nearly 100% of the phenol and oil content of water is regained at the rate of 1000 m^3 per hour; a water treatment plant in operation in Espenhain near Leipzig purifies 1300 m^3 of water per hour, removing 70% of the foreign elements, and thus aids in the long-term restoration of the heavily polluted Pleiße, Elster, and Saale Rivers; in 1985 the largest industrial water treatment facility (10,000 m^3 per hour) went into operation at the VEB Chemische Werke Buna near

---

16 Statistics provided by Zentrum für Umweltgestaltung der DDR.

Schkopau, a heavily industrialized area.[17] Such measures bring a two-fold gain: the economy regains materials from the waste water, and the water is returned to the rivers in a purer condition.

Conservation of the Soil/Reclamation

In the GDR about 6.2 million hectars of land are under cultivation, which is equivalent to a per capita figure of 0.37 hectars, approximately the size of a soccer field. This figure is small compared with the statistics for other countries (e.g., 1.96 hectars in the United States). For this reason, the continued intensification of agricultural production will be an essential precondition for meeting the growing food requirements of the GDR population. Selective irrigation can increase agricultural yields substantially. In 1984 more than one million hectars were irrigated, which represented 17% of all land under cultivation.[18] Fertilizers likewise increase yields, but both organic and inorganic matter must be applied very carefully so as to avoid overmanuring and overfertilizing the soil. With the help of the so-called nitrate quick test, a new method developed in the GDR, farmers can quickly determine the nitrogen content of the soil and thus decide on the spot whether additional plant nutrients are needed or not.

Open-cast lignite mining carries with it much special responsibility for soil protection. In 1985 about 300 million tons of lignite were extracted, which led to significant changes in the landscape. With open-cast mining, entire areas are transformed into wasteland before the coal has been fully extracted. This situation requires new means of environmental protection. Before a new open-cast pit can be dug, a recultivation program must be approved by the responsible body of the local council. The valuable topsoil must be removed and stored to be put back as a new topsoil layer after the pit has been used up. Funds from the mining enterprises themselves and from the state budget - about 45,000 Marks per hectar - are allocated for recultivation programs.[19] Depending on the location and mining conditions, these investments are amortized in a period of six to ten years. Long-term soil studies have shown that in numerous cases recultivation

[17] *Anlagen zur industriellen Abwasserreinigung*, an information brochure of the VEB Chemieanlagenbaukombinat Leipzig/Grimma, n.d.

[18] Information supplied by the Zentrum für Umweltgestaltung.

[19] Information supplied by the Zentrum für Umweltgestaltung.

measures have improved the soil over its quality before coal extraction began. Very often used-up pits are made into recreation areas for the local population. Thus, in the former lignite district of Senftenberg a chain of lakes was formed, covering an area of about 5,000 hectars, which was made into a nature reserve.[20]

International Cooperation

In conclusion, I will discuss some of the international cooperation projects in the field of environmental protection in which the GDR takes part. Without joint efforts by all European countries, it will hardly be possible to solve the complex problems confronting the GDR in maintaining and restoring a healthy environment.

For many years now there has been successful cooperation between the member countries of the Council for Mutual Economic Assistance (CMEA). Sixteen specialized commissions deal with problems of environmental protection, all work of which is coordinated by the Council for Environmental Protection (Rat für Umweltschutz). The central issues are water protection, protection of the atmosphere and the countryside, as well as the development of new technologies to minimize industrial waste. The GDR is, among other things, responsible for all matters relating to the protection of the atmosphere against contamination. A large number of topics are dealt with on the basis of bilateral governmental agreements. For instance, a cooperation agreement devoted to the protection of the forests in the eastern part of the Ore Mountains was concluded between the GDR and the CSSR in November 1986.

Another declared policy of the GDR is to act in accordance with the Helsinki Conference and to cooperate actively within the special organs of the United Nations and other international organizations as well as with Western countries. An example which demonstrates the fruitfulness of such cooperation is the 1974 Convention on the Protection of the Marine Environment in the Baltic Sea Region. As a result of the joint efforts undertaken by all countries bordering on the

---

[20] The number of nature reserves (*Naturschutzgebiete*) in the GDR has increased from 140 in 1945 to 766 in 1985. In addition there are at present 400 protected countryside areas (*Landschaftsschutzgebiete*) and two biosphere reserves, which are recognized by the UN.

Baltic, its waters are now cleaner than those of the North Sea or the Mediterranean.

The GDR has also played an active part in the realization of the UN Environment Program, which came into being in 1972. On behalf of UNEP and UNESCO, the GDR has organized postgraduate courses for senior environment specialists from Asian, African, and Latin American countries. Under the UNESCO program "Man and the Biosphere," the GDR is taking part in fourteen projects in which it shares its experience in recultivating played-out open-cast mines.

The cooperation of the GDR with countries of northern and central Europe such as Finland, Sweden, Denmark, Norway, the Federal Republic, Great Britain, and Austria is developed on the basis of bilateral agreements. These agreements deal above all with limiting the passage of air pollutants over international borders and the exchange of waste-reduced technologies.

In the 1970s and 1980s cooperation and the exchange of experience in regard to the protection of the natural environment have expanded considerably between European countries with differing social systems. This has provided convincing proof of the advantages offered by the policy of détente and peaceful coexistence. Proceeding in this manner may result both in reducing the burden on man's environment and in making progress in other areas of interest to the nations of our earth as well.

Zivilisationskritik in der Literatur der DDR: Überlegungen zu Hanns Cibulkas *Swantow*

Wolfgang Ertl

> Kometenhaft
> zieht über den Himmel
> das Wort:
> Fortschritt.[1]

Zivilisationskritische Äußerungen, die den wissenschaftlich-technischen Fortschritt in Frage stellen und auf das gestörte Verhältnis zwischen Mensch und Natur hinweisen, finden sich spätestens seit Ende der siebziger Jahre häufig in der DDR-Literatur, in Lyrik, Prosa und Dramen von bekannten und weniger bekannten Autoren verschiedener Generationen. Dabei handelt es sich nicht in jedem Fall um Neubesinnung und Wende in der Entwicklung des einzelnen Dichters, sondern oft auch, und zwar besonders bei Autoren, denen die Bereiche Natur und Landschaft schon immer nahe standen, um Verdeutlichung oder Verschärfung von schon früher eingenommenen Positionen. Hubertus Knabe führt in seinem Beitrag zu dem 1985 von der Redaktion Deutschland Archiv herausgegebenen Band *Umweltprobleme und Umweltbewußtsein in der DDR* eine große Anzahl neuerer Prosawerke an, in denen Zweifel und Skepsis an der Industriegesellschaft den Wissenschaftsoptimismus der Aufbaujahre und der NÖS-Periode ablösen. "Daß gerade die Schriftsteller," so schreibt Knabe,

> sich kritisch mit der modernen Zivilisation auseinandersetzen, mag an ihrer besonderen Sensibilität für gesellschaftliche Veränderungen liegen, die von anderen Instanzen der Pro-

---

[1] Hanns Cibulka, *Swantow: Die Aufzeichnungen des Andreas Flemming* (Halle/Leipzig: Mitteldeutscher Verlag, 1982), S. 37. Im folgenden wird nach dieser Ausgabe zitiert.

blemartikulation, also Wissenschaft, Politik, Medien, kaum oder gar nicht thematisiert werden. Zugleich dürften ihre Möglichkeiten größer sein, auch unbequeme Wahrnehmungen öffentlich auszudrücken. DDR-Literatur könnte damit in besonderer Weise als Seismograph von gesamtgesellschaftlichen Problemen und Bewußtseinslagen gelten.[2]

In einer aufschlußreichen Diskussion in *Sinn und Form*, die durch den Naturwissenschaftler Erhard Geißler ausgelöst wurde, werden Inhalt, Ausmaß und Funktion solcher kritischen Stimmen in der Literatur reflektiert. Bemerkenswert ist dabei zunächst, daß ein Wissenschaftler, das Gespräch mit Literaten suchend, den Diskurs in Gang bringt. Die Zeitschrift veröffentlichte Ende 1984 einen längeren Aufsatz des Molekularbiologen mit dem provokativen Titel "Bruder Frankenstein oder - Pflegefälle aus der Retorte?" Geißler beklagt sich am Anfang dieser Schrift darüber, daß Heinar Kipphardt sich mit seinem Stück *Bruder Eichmann*, das im Frühjahr 1984 im Deutschen Theater aufgeführt wurde, "in die Schar derer eingereiht [habe], die sich in der Öffentlichkeit über die gesellschaftlichen Konsequenzen der modernen Genetik äußern, und zwar ausschließlich negativ."[3] Der Wissenschaftler bedauert es, daß die, wie er sagt, "schon heute greifbaren und die für morgen erwarteten segensreichen Entwicklungen der modernen Biologie" ignoriert und die Genetiker "als Eichmänner von heute diffamiert" werden (S. 1290). Besonders beunruhigt Geißler, daß nicht nur Kipphardt, sondern auch Ernst Schumacher, Jurij Brězan, Christa Wolf, Richard Pietraß, ja, wie er 1981 auf der Warnemünder Plenartagung der Akademie der Künste über das Thema "Kunst und Gesellschaft im Jahr 2000" feststellen mußte, "der weitaus größte Teil der Künstler und Schriftsteller," mit denen er sprach, "mehr oder weniger von derartigen Furchtvorstellungen vor dem Mißbrauch von Naturwissenschaft und Technik ganz allgemein und von Gentechnik im besonderen geplagt wird" (S. 1290-91).

---

[2] Hubertus Knabe, "Zweifel an der Industriegesellschaft: Ökologische Kritik in der erzählenden DDR-Literatur," in *Umweltprobleme und Umweltbewußtsein in der DDR*, hrsg. v. Redaktion Deutschland Archiv (Köln: Wissenschaft und Politik, 1985), S. 201-02.

[3] Erhard Geißler, "Bruder Frankenstein oder - Pflegefälle aus der Retorte?" *Sinn und Form*, 36, Heft 6 (1984), 1290.

So antwortete zum Beispiel Jurij Brězan auf die im Gespräch über seinen 1976 erschienenen Roman *Krabat oder Die Verwandlung der Welt* gestellte Frage, welche Hauptprobleme er für die Menschheit sehe:

> Mir scheint, . . . daß die Menschheit drauf und dran ist, sich kraft des Wissens selbst vom Leben zum Tode zu bringen. In der Diskrepanz zwischen dem ungeheuer gewachsenen Wissen und der daraus folgenden Macht des Menschen einerseits und seiner - oder vielmehr ihrer, nämlich der Menschheit als Ganzes -, also ihrer weit zurückgebliebenen moralischen Entwicklung andererseits liegt m.E. der Grund für die allergrößten Gefahren.[4]

Die genetischen Forschungen beunruhigen Brězan dabei besonders: "Hier könnte die Wissenschaft ein anderes, ein unblutiges Ende der Menschheit vorbereiten: das Ende des Menschen, wie wir den Menschen sehen. Ich jedenfalls habe Angst vor den Biologen, und ich fürchte, wir alle müssen Angst haben" (S. 1006). Was die Beziehung zwischen Mensch und Natur anbelangt, so nimmt Brězan ebenfalls kein Blatt vor den Mund:

> Was nun den Ast betrifft, auf dem der Mensch sitzt und an dem er sägt: Die ungeheure Ausbeutung aller Reichtümer unserer Erde durch unsere Generation muß, wenn sie nicht gestoppt wird, Folgen haben für die kommenden Generationen, die wir nicht einmal absehen können. (S. 1007)

Christa Wolf schreibt in ihrer vierten Frankfurter Poetik-Vorlesung, "[der] Preis für die Art Fortschritt, die die Institution Wissenschaft seit längerem hervorbringt," sei ihr "allmählich zu hoch."[5] Richard Pietraß wendet sich in seinen Gedichten nicht nur der Umweltkrise zu, sondern auch den beängstigenden Möglichkeiten der Klonierung von Menschen und des embryonalen Wachstums in der Retorte.[6]

---

[4] "Gespräch mit Jurij Brězan," *Sinn und Form*, 31, Heft 5 (1979), 1006.

[5] Christa Wolf, *Voraussetzungen einer Erzählung. Kassandra*, Frankfurter Poetik-Vorlesungen (Darmstadt/Neuwied: Luchterhand, 1983), S. 136.

[6] Richard Pietraß, *Freiheitsmuseum. Gedichte* (Berlin/Weimar: Aufbau, 1982), S. 94, 95, 83.

Geißler kritisiert solche und ähnliche Texte als Beispiele eines sachunkundigen und unbegründeten Wissenschaftspessimismus, der "katastrophale Folgen haben" könnte (S. 1291), wobei ihn besonders beunruhigt, daß einerseits derartige Befürchtungen unter DDR-Bürgern ohnehin verbreitet seien, andererseits Schriftsteller und Künstler als Multiplikatoren solcher Horrorvisionen "in einem derart kunstfreundlichen Land" (S. 1291) wie der DDR sich weitaus größerer Ausstrahlungskraft erfreuen als Naturwissenschaftler. Ausgehend von dem Credo, daß "wir die vor uns stehenden gewaltigen Probleme der achtziger und neunziger Jahre nur dann lösen können, wenn wir die Vorzüge des Sozialismus gerade mit den Errungenschaften des wissenschaftlich-technischen Fortschritts verbinden" (S. 1291), läßt Geißler Ängste nur zu vor der militärisch-industriellen Aggressivität des kapitalistischen Westens, der "den wissenschaftlich-technischen Fortschritt zur Erlangung militärischer Überlegenheit, zur Erringung von Erstschlagskapazität zu mißbrauchen" (S. 1319) suche.

Geißlers Forderung, der Künstler und Schriftsteller habe sich *sachkundig* zu machen, bevor er sich zu einem Sachthema äußere, wurde dann in den folgenden Zuschriften zu dem Frankenstein-Aufsatz wiederholt kritisiert. So sieht etwa Werner Creutziger genug Gründe für das Mißtrauen vor dem "Fortschritt" in der Wissenschaft: "Was nützen mir gestrige wissenschaftliche Beweise, wenn ich heute keine Luft mehr kriege?"[7] Sein Lebensinteresse sieht er, im Gegensatz zu Geißler, sehr wohl von Dichtern wie Richard Pietraß "sachkundig vertreten" (S. 420).

Mit dem Aufsatz "Frankensteins Tod" von Geißler im ersten Heft 1986 beendet die *Sinn-und-Form*-Redaktion, wie es in den Anmerkungen heißt, diese Diskussion. Geißler setzt sich darin besonders mit den ablehnenden Zuschriften (auch von seinen Fachkollegen) auseinander und beharrt im allgemeinen auf seinen Positionen. Die Auseinandersetzung dauert jedoch notgedrungen an, wobei dem Medium Literatur sicher nicht nur marginale Bedeutung zukommt.

An einem Einzelbeispiel, Hanns Cibulkas 1982 erschienenem Buch *Swantow. Die Aufzeichnungen des Andreas Flemming*, soll im folgenden demonstriert werden, welche

---

[7] Werner Creutziger, "Brief an Erhard Geißler," *Sinn und Form*, 37, Heft 2 (1985), 417.

besonderen Erscheinungsformen von Umweltgefährdung und Verarmung des Lebens erfaßt werden. Da es sich um einen fiktionalen Tagebuchtext mit eingestreuten Gedichten handelt, interessiert gleichfalls, auf welche Weise die erfahrene Wirklichkeit stilisiert und poetisiert erscheint. Die Diskussion schließlich, die dieser literarische Text ausgelöst hat, erweist sich als mindestens so aufschlußreich wie das Tagebuch selbst.

Hanns Cibulka, 1920 in Jägerndorf (Tschechoslowakei) geboren, arbeitet seit 1952 als Bibliothekar in Gotha. Seine literarische Produktion umfaßt zahlreiche Gedichtbücher und Tagebücher, die allesamt im Westen ziemlich unbekannt geblieben sind. Der Name Cibulka fällt hier allenfalls gelegentlich im Zusammenhang mit Aufzählungen der wichtigsten seiner Generationsgenossen: Franz Fühmann, Paul Wiens, Walter Werner, um nur einige zu nennen. Im Umkreis der kurz skizzierten Debatte über wissenschafts- und zivilisationskritische Tendenzen in der neueren DDR-Literatur ist Cibulka ins Rampenlicht einer kritischen Auseinandersetzung geraten, die von giftiger Attacke über differenziert-wohlwollende Analyse zur freudigen Feier Cibulkas als dem "erste[n] Alternative[n]" und "erste[n] Grüne[n] der DDR" in der bundesdeutschen Tagespresse reicht.[8] In einem Artikel in der *Frankfurter Rundschau* wird Cibulka in lustiger Unkenntnis seiner Biographie als "Lyriker aus Swantow auf der Ostsee-Insel Rügen" bezeichnet, der "seine Kritik nicht am politisch-ideologischen System der DDR" ansetze, "sondern . . . die europäische Zivilisationskritik direkt und konkret auf den 'ersten deutschen Arbeiter- und Bauernstaat'" übertrage.[9] Angesichts des stark autobiographischen Charakters von Cibulkas Werken mag es von geringer Bedeutung sein, daß es den Ort Swantow, von dem aus sich im Rahmen der Tagebuchhandlung die Beobachtungen und Reflexionen des siebenundfünfzigjährigen Dichters Andreas Flemming entfalten, gar nicht gibt. Die fiktionalen Arabesken, die sich um diesen Ort ranken, legen es jedoch nahe, ihn als eigenartigen "Standort" des Dichters, eben als "Erfindung," zu betrachten. Die Frage, was das eigentlich für ein Ort ist, stellt sich besonders, wenn man den Stellenwert der zivilisationskritischen Äußerungen, die im Zentrum dieses Tagebuches stehen, erfassen will. Immerhin wird gleich am Anfang des

---

8 Reinhard Losik, "Alternative Töne von einem DDR-Lyriker," *Frankfurter Rundschau,* 2. Juni 1981.
9 Ebd.

Buches gesagt, Swantow sei "vielleicht eine Einbildung, ein Ort, der erst gegründet werden" müsse (S. 9).

Die Form des Tagebuchs erlaubt es, ein weites Spektrum von Themen zu berühren und Fragen aufzuwerfen. Sie ermöglicht auch die Montage von literarischen Zitaten, hier Lesefrüchten Flemmings, der zusammen mit seiner Partnerin, der Krankenschwester Liv, einen Sommer in einem alten Haus auf der Insel Rügen verbringt. Hinter der Eingangstür finden die beiden bei der Ankunft im Ferienort ein Wespennest, mit dem sie sich entschließen zu leben. "Ich glaube nicht, daß sie uns stören werden," sagt Flemming (S. 11). Als symbolisches Leitmotiv zieht sich dieses Wespennest durch das ganze Tagebuch, wobei es vieldeutig, um nicht zu sagen unklar bleibt. Einerseits wird das Wespennest mit großer Aufmerksamkeit als natürlicher Organismus, den es zu schonen gilt, studiert und beschrieben, gehört also zusammen mit den Landschaftsbildern zum Bereich der natürlichen Umwelt. In diesem Sinne äußert sich Flemming gegenüber der Pfarrersfrau Krüger, die nicht versteht, warum er das Nest nicht einfach ausräuchert, die Wespen hätten ihn "von neuem die Liebe zur Natur gelehrt" und durch den Umgang mit ihnen erfahre er seine "eigene Existenz" (S. 46). Andererseits bietet das Wespennest wiederholt Anlaß zu Reflexionen über das Zusammenleben der Menschen, etwa wenn, gegen Ende des Tagebuchs, von den "geheimen Botschaften" der Wespen die Rede ist:

> Sie leben ohne Intellekt, ohne Gefühl, sind ganz auf die Gemeinschaft programmiert, auf den Staat, den Wespenstaat. Sie haben keine Möglichkeit zum Träumen, beschäftigen sich auch nicht mit Fragen. Der Sinn des Lebens ist für sie das Leben selbst, ein Leben, das im Flug vergeht. Der Mensch hat die Fähigkeit zu zerstören, sie kennen diese Fähigkeit nicht. In diesem Punkt sind sie dem Menschen überlegen. (S. 110)

Frau Krüger liefert das Stichwort, als sie besserwisserisch Flemmings Grundsatz "Leben und leben lassen" in den Wind schlägt: Flemming lebe "in Unkenntnis der Gefahr" (S. 46). Damit dürfte das Generalthema des Buches benannt sein. Flemming greift das Wort auf, allerdings gänzlich im Widerspruch zu Frau Krügers Warnung:

Wir wiegen uns in trügerischer Sicherheit.
Noch füllt die Luft das Gewölbe des Himmels,
noch gibt sie der Kuppel die zartblaue Farbe,
aber das Schutzkleid unserer Erde ist in töd-
licher Gefahr. Unmerklich verändern sich vor
unseren Augen die Erde, das Wasser, die Luft.
(S. 46)

In vielen, zum Teil längeren Passagen dokumentiert das
Tagebuch die Gefahren der Umweltzerstörung von den gelben
Giftwolken der Sprühflugzeuge der LPG bis zur Verkrebsung
der Fische. Besonders eindringlich wird die Vergiftung der
Weltmeere beschrieben:

Eines Tages wird uns das Meer seinen blinden
Spiegel entgegenhalten, aber dann wird es zu
spät sein. Die Schreie der Menschen werden
ungehört an den Küsten verhallen. Das Meer
wird der Schauplatz unserer künftigen Kata-
strophen sein. Ist das moralische Gewissen der
Menschen wirklich am Zerfallen? (S. 79)

Da der Tagebuchschreiber nicht nur allgemein lamentiert,
sondern immer wieder ganz konkrete Erscheinungsformen
der Naturzerstörung beschreibt, gewinnt das Buch in starkem
Maße dokumentarischen Charakter. "Wir zahlen bereits heute
einen viel zu hohen Preis für unser zweifelhaftes Wohlleben,"
heißt es am Anfang einer Passage über "den Januskopf der
chemischen Industrie" (S. 79).

Mit dem, wie es an einer Stelle des Tagebuches heißt, in
den letzten dreißig Jahren auf verschiedenen Gebieten
verzehnfachten Wissen (S. 81) geht so manche Verarmung
des täglichen Lebens einher. In den Kliniken, so erzählt die
Krankenschwester, mangelt es an menschlichem Beistand, an
Sterbehilfe: "Es wird eine Zeit kommen, da werden sie den
[sic] Sterbenden am Fußende noch einen Farbfernseher hin-
stellen, damit er von seinem eigenen Sterben abgelenkt wird,
damit er sich bis zum letzten Atemzug mit den oberfläch-
lichen Dingen des Lebens beschäftigen kann" (S. 73).

Das Landschaftsbild Rügens, in langen Passagen in seiner
archaisch anmutenden Schönheit beschrieben, bleibt von
dem Einbruch lebensfeindlicher Bedrohung nicht verschont.
In der Eintragung vom 27. August heißt es:

Metallene Riesenvögel ziehen durch die Luft, Kampfhubschrauber fliegen in Kirchturmhöhe über das Land, vor der Küste liegen die Zerstörer. Die inneren Spannungen, die eine solche Umwelt auslöst, gehen an keinem Menschen spurlos vorbei, sie übertragen sich auf sein Denken, Fühlen und Handeln. (S. 107)[10]

Von den hohen Kosten, die der Umweltschutz mit sich bringt, ist im folgenden die Rede, und, als Kontrast dazu, von der neuen Hochrüstung der USA und der Vernichtungskapazität der modernen Waffen. Hier werden konkrete Zahlen genannt im Vergleich mit der Atombombe von Hiroshima.

Als in besonderem Maße aktuell erweisen sich die skeptischen Überlegungen des fiktiven Dichters Flemming über die friedliche Nutzung nuklearer Energie. Hier verbindet Cibulka verallgemeinernd-poetisierende Diktion mit Zitaten aus einem nicht näher identifizierten Sachbuch zum Thema Kernenergie: "Ein Wasserkraftwerk ist voller Leben, da hat man das Rauschen des Wassers im Ohr, das Summen der Generatoren. In einem Kernkraftwerk ist alles still, totenstill, die Energie wird lautlos produziert, der Verbrennungsprozeß dominiert" (S. 16). Hierauf folgt ein wörtliches Zitat aus dem Sachbuch nebst Auflistung der gefährlichen Spaltprodukte. Klaus Höpcke, Stellvertreter des Ministers für Kultur, auf dessen ausführliche Besprechung von *Swantow* in *Sinn und Form* noch näher einzugehen ist, stößt sich besonders an

---

[10] Es sei darauf verwiesen, daß der Vorabdruck einiger Abschnitte aus *Swantow* in *Neue Deutsche Literatur*, 29, Heft 4 (1981) mehrere scharfe Passagen enthält, besonders zu den Themenkreisen Militär, wissenschaftliches Zeitalter, Kernkraft, die in der Buchausgabe fehlen. Auf dieses Zitat über die negativen Wirkungen der militärischen Präsenz folgt zum Beispiel im *NDL*-Vorabdruck: "[S]chon im Unterbewußtsein der Kinder setzen sich diese Spannungselemente fest, schlagen um in Aggressivität" (S. 50). Sicher wird durch diese Auslassungen das eine oder andere Argument entschärft und ließe sich darauf hinweisen, daß Cibulkas Zivilisationskritik in den Punkten, in denen sie allzu unverblümt Tabus bricht, durch den Mechanismus der (Selbst-)Zensur gemildert wurde. Trotzdem scheint mir ein polemisch-hämisches Herausstreichen dieser "Revisionen" weniger sinnvoll als eine sachliche Betrachtung des nach wie vor grundsätzlich erstaunlich kritischen Potentials der Buchveröffentlichung. Für weitere Informationen über diese Auseinandersetzung s. das in Vorbereitung befindliche Buch von Anita M. Mallinckrodt, *The Environmental Dialogue in the GDR*, das bei University Press of America erscheinen wird.

dem Wort "totenstill," denn es verletze "in diesem Zusammenhang Regeln der Lauterkeit."[11]

Ausgehend von dem Rilke-Vers "Du mußt dein Leben ändern" spricht Flemming davon, daß die "schwierigste aller Aufgaben" uns noch bevorstehe: "die Revolution gegenüber uns selbst, gegen unsere eigene Trägheit, den Egoismus, das Machtdenken, eine Revolution, die uns lehrt, ganz anders über den Menschen zu denken als bisher" (S. 81). Im Zusammenhang mit dieser Überlegung stehen einige Einzelbeobachtungen zu spezifischen gesellschaftlichen Einrichtungen, etwa den aufdringlich exklusiven Interhotels: "Die revolutionäre Ausgangsposition der späten vierziger Jahre, wurde sie nicht längst durch übersteigerte materielle Ansprüche überdeckt?" (S. 88). Auf die Erzählung Livs über ihre negativen Erfahrungen mit einem Chefarzt, der ihr einen Bericht über das Erlebnis eines klinisch bereits toten Lehrers, der durch die moderne Medizin wieder ins Leben geholt wurde, verübelte, folgt die verallgemeinernde Feststellung: "Ich kenne keine menschliche Gesellschaft, in der nicht auch Elemente der Despotie vorhanden sind" (S. 125).

Das fünfteilige Gedicht "Lagebericht" kann als Kernstück des Tagebuches gelesen werden. An den antiken Chor erinnernd, greift es die Themen des Tagebuches elegisch auf. Die Eintragung vom 18. Juli beginnt mit einem Alptraum Flemmings ("Atomschneisen wurden gelegt, von Rostock bis nach Triest"), auf den der erste Abschnitt des Gedichtes folgt mit der Klage: "Nicht musisch / lebt heute der Mensch, / berechnend / geht er durchs Leben" (S. 36-37). Der dritte Teil, der einige Seiten später eingefügt wird, beginnt folgendermaßen:

> Kein Hölderlin-Hymnus
> auf die Natur,
> die Herzwand verkarstet,
> zauberkundig
> die Polypenarme der Chemie,
> vom Anblick der toten Fische
> kaufen wir uns frei
> durch die Wachstumsraten der Wirtschaft,
> zur Sage geworden

---

11 Klaus Höpcke, "Sicht auf Swantow - Überzeugendes und Bezweifelbares," *Sinn und Form*, 36, Heft 1 (1984), 172.

das Wasser
im Brunnen. (S. 64)

Den pessimistischen Hinweis Livs, daß keine Zeitschrift und
kein Verlag diesen "Lagebericht" abdrucken werde, kontert
Flemming mit den Worten: "Das Wort eines Schriftstellers hat
nur dann Daseinsberechtigung, wenn es sich vollkommen
offen dem Leben stellt. Wir müssen den Tatsachen ins Gesicht sehen" (S. 127). Und, ein wenig später: "Es bewegt sich
im Kokon. Ein Schmetterling, der zum Licht will, muß auch
die Kraft haben, die Fäden zu durchbrechen, mit denen er
sich einst als Raupe selbst umsponnen hat" (S. 128).

Der Vergleich dieses "Lageberichtes," dessen Entstehung
im Tagebuch auch selbst wiederholt reflektiert wird, mit
anderen "Lageberichten" aus der DDR (es handelt sich um
einen beliebten Gedichttitel) zeigt: In Thematik und Wort-
wahl verbindet ihn vieles mit jüngeren Autoren wie Heinz
Czechowski oder Volker Braun. Cibulka durchbricht jedoch
keineswegs - wie etwa Volker Braun dies bewußt mehr oder
weniger effektiv tut - die gebräuchliche Syntax. Die Natür-
lichkeit, die er zu bewahren sucht, findet er noch im
"natürlich" gegliederten Fluß der Verse. Die kurzen, oft nur
ein Wort haltenden Zeilen zerhacken nicht, was prosaisch
langzeilig formuliert werden könnte, sie folgen eindring-
licher, dem einzelnen Wort zu seinem Recht verhelfender
Diktion. Solche Ästhetisierung von Welterfahrung mag als
antiquiert abgetan werden, sie hat aber den Vorzug leichterer
Rezipierbarkeit. Es dürfte nicht zufällig sein, daß sich der
Naturwissenschaftler Geißler an den Werken von Cibulka (und
Březan) stößt und nicht an den neuesten Zitatmontagen
Volker Brauns.[12]

Die Überlegungen zur Poesie im Umkreis der Ent-
stehungsgeschichte des fünfteiligen, inzwischen auch schon
separat veröffentlichten Gedichtes "Lagebericht" sind eher
unergiebig.[13] Es sind allgemeine, teilweise wenig originelle
Erörterungen, die dem Poetischen, dem Musischen zu
seinem Recht verhelfen sollen, indem sie es als Verloren-
gehendes bedauern. Offenheit des Gedichts wird beschworen,

---

[12] Es sei nur darauf verwiesen, daß auch diese sich auf eine "Tradition"
berufen, deren "modernistischer" oder "avantgardistischer" Ton auch nur im
Rahmen der besonderen Umstände, unter denen sich die Literatur der DDR
entwickelt, von bemerkenswertem Neuigkeitswert ist.
[13] Vgl. die Veröffentlichung der früheren Fassung des Gedichtes in die horen,
26. Ausgabe 124 (1981), 7-8.

aber nicht im Sinne der gebrochenen Gestik Volker Brauns
oder der lakonischen Formelhaftigkeit Heinz Czechowskis,
sondern eines idealistischen Harmoniebedürfnisses. Der
"Lagebericht" schließt mit den Versen:

Die anderen
reden vom Fortgehn,
ich bleibe,
ich weiß,
der Docht ist verrußt,
nur langsam
wächst im Menschen
das Licht.

Solange noch ein Wort
an deinen Augen sich entzündet,
Leben,
bleibt das immer zu Nennende:
Erde, Wasser, Luft. (S. 108-09)

Der Dichter greift zur abgegriffenen Licht-Dunkel-Metaphorik
und kontrastiert die Dokumentation bedrohlicher Zerstörung
der Umwelt mit dem inkommensurablen Vorzug naturnaher
und musischer Lebensweise am Rande des Meeres, in einem
Ort, den es, wie schon gesagt, vielleicht noch gibt, den es
möglicherweise aber erst zu schaffen gilt. Flemming lebt mit
dem Wespennest, von dem keine Gefahr auszugehen scheint.
Er kultiviert eine Allegorie, in die zu stechen sich verbietet,
weil sie sich dann in ein Chaos auflösen würde.

In seinem in der *Deutschen Zeitschrift für Philosophie*
abgedruckten Artikel "Über die Schwierigkeit der Wirklichkeitsbewältigung" wirft Hermann Ley Cibulka mangelndes
Wissen vor: "Eine gewisse Allgemeinbildung, die jüngste
Menschen leichter als ältere besitzen, sollten sich aber
Literaten zueignen, die sogenannte 'globale Probleme' ökolo-
gischer Art anziehen."[14] "Mit selten anzutreffender Unbefan-
genheit" nehme Cibulka in Anspruch,

mit dem Lob des sogenannten einfachen Lebens
jegliches Geschehen in einer sich industriali-
sierenden und industrialisierten Welt unter
einen Schuldkomplex zu subsumieren, der nach

---

[14] Hermann Ley, "Über die Schwierigkeit der Wirklichkeitsbewältigung,"
Deutsche Zeitschrift für Philosophie, 30, Heft 2 (1982), 244.

dem Trend seiner wohlgesetzten Worte eigentlich jedem einleuchten und zu unseren frühe-
sten Stammesbrüdern zurückzukehren veran-
lassen müßte. (S. 244)

Ley spricht weiterhin von "den bis zum Überdruß strapa-
zierten Vergiftungen der Luft und der Gewässer" (S. 244). In
gehässiger Weise zeiht er Cibulka "archaisierenden Denkens"
und gegenaufklärerischer Tendenzen (S. 244, 246).

Während Klaus Höpcke, wie Ley, die wissenschafts-
pessimistischen und, in Fragen Revolution, Macht, Militär,
klassenindifferenten Äußerungen des Tagebuches scharfer
Kritik unterwirft und ansonsten auch so manch andere
Textpassage benörgelt, verwirft er Leys unsachgemäßes
Herangehen an einen literarischen Text und sein Befallensein
von "einer Art antiökologischer Allergie."[15] Großes Wohl-
wollen bringt Höpcke auf für Cibulkas grundsätzliche
ökologische Fragestellung, äußerten sich doch in ihren
Sachbüchern DDR-Wissenschaftler sogar noch drastischer
und sei doch die offizielle Umweltschutzpolitik der DDR
nicht umsonst dabei, diesen Problemen zu Leibe zu rücken (S.
176).

Bernd Leistner macht auf "Ungereimtheiten" auf der
Reflexionsebene des Werkes aufmerksam, in der sich "das
Geschichtsbild einer spezifischen Ausformung von krypto-
religiösem Bewußtsein," "Beziehungen . . . zur Anthropo-
sophie" und "Berührungen . . . mit Schopenhauer" mischen.[16]
Leistners Analyse, so kritisch sie im einzelnen verfährt,
überzeugt in vielen Punkten dadurch, daß sie Cibulkas Text
als *literarisches* Werk ernst nimmt.

Es ist wohl gerade die kulturhistorisch konservative
Kontrastierung von musischem, naturnahem Leben und dem
analytischen naturwissenschaftlichen Denken, die beunruhi-
gend wirkt: Cibulka rückt sein Thema kaum in den Kontext
der ideologischen Auseinandersetzung zwischen Ost und
West. Von Klassenkonflikt ist nirgends die Rede. Wissen-
schaftskritik und die poetisierte Reflexion über die Zerstörung des ökologischen Gleichgewichts und ihre Konse-

---

[15] Höpcke, "Sicht auf Swantow," S. 175, 176.

[16] Bernd Leistner, "'Nicht musisch / lebt heute der Mensch . . .': Zu Hanns
Cibulka, 'Swantow. Die Aufzeichnungen des Andreas Flemming,'" in *DDR-
Literatur '83 im Gespräch*, hrsg. v. Siegfried Rönisch (Berlin/Weimar: Auf-
bau, 1984), S. 115.

quenzen für das Leben des Menschen sind wenig "DDR-spezifisch." Das gilt auch für seine poetologischen Betrachtungen. Hier unterscheidet sich Cibulka von seinen jüngeren Zeitgenossen, denen es angesichts der Problematik auch die Sprache verschlägt, besonders die aus einer Zeit geborgte, in der idealistische Vorbilder als Gegenbilder zu einer miserablen Realität kultiviert wurden. Cibulka ist ein konventioneller Dichter. Als Mottos stellt er seinem Tagebuch zwei Zitate über das Symbolische alles Geschehens und aller Situationen voran. Das erste ist von Goethe, auf den sich Cibulka wiederholt beruft: "Alles was geschieht ist Symbol, / und indem es vollkommen sich selbst darstellt, / deutet es auf das Übrige." Das zweite die mehr stimmungshafte Klage Hugo von Hofmannsthals: "Situationen sind symbolisch; / es ist die Schwäche des jetzigen Menschen, / daß sie sie analytisch behandeln / und dadurch das Zauberische auflösen." Cibulka vertraut offensichtlich einer traditionellen Aussageweise, besonders auch im Gedicht.

Trotzdem läßt sich schwerlich verleugnen, daß Cibulka mit *Swantow* ein Buch vorgelegt hat, in dem sich, wie der DDR-Kritiker Bernd Leistner schreibt, "Bezeichnungsmut und menschheitlich gerichtetes Verantwortungsbewußtsein" zu erkennen geben. "Ein gleichsam politisch-moralisches Gebot fordert dazu auf, daß man sich zu dem ganz einzelgängerisch unternommenen Vorstoß des Cibulkaschen Tagebuchs bekennt. Einzeleinwände haben zurückzutreten."[17] In diesem Sinne wird das Buch offensichtlich in der DDR auch von offizieller Seite ernst genommen.

Auch in seiner neuesten Tagebucherzählung *Seedorn* (1985),[18] deren poetologisches Credo stark von einem eigenwilligen und einseitigen Gerhart-Hauptmann-Bild und einer unerschütterlichen Dichtungsgläubigkeit geprägt ist, greift Cibulka das brisante Thema wiederholt auf. Im Anschluß an eine Reflexion über das Bild des Turmes in der Literatur heißt es hier:

---

[17] Ebd., S. 117. Vgl. auch Monika Melchert, "Swantow," *Sonntag*, Nr. 34 (1983), S. 5, und Gerhard Dahne, "Swantow oder Hinter Masken reden wir mit Masken," in *Kritik 83: Rezensionen zur DDR-Literatur*, hrsg. v. Eberhard Günther, Werner Liersch u. Klaus Walther (Halle/Leipzig: Mitteldeutscher Verlag, 1983), S. 24-29.

[18] Hanns Cibulka, *Seedorn. Tagebucherzählung* (Halle/Leipzig: Mitteldeutscher Verlag, 1985).

Der Mensch hat sich Türme gebaut, um dem Himmel näher zu sein. Heute sehen wir nur noch hinauf zum Zifferblatt, um die Zeit abzulesen, und schrecken zusammen, wenn wir feststellen, daß es fünf Minuten vor zwölf ist.

(S. 18)

Fortschritt im real existierenden Sozialismus - aktuelle Probleme und sozialkulturelle Hintergründe wissenschaftlich-technischer Innovation in der DDR

Fred Klinger

Innovation, Wissenschaft und Technik stehen gegenwärtig im Zentrum sozialwissenschaftlicher, philosophischer und politischer Erörterungen in der DDR. Das hat besondere Gründe. Die DDR-Führung steht unter dem nachhaltigen Zwang, Technologieentwicklungen und Innovationsschübe, wie sie sich - vor allem bedingt durch die Mikroelektronik - in den westlichen Industrieländern seit einiger Zeit durchsetzen, im eigenen Land nachzuvollziehen. Bei diesem Versuch mit der westlichen Entwicklung mitzuhalten, sind vor allem seit Beginn der achtziger Jahre erhebliche Innovationsschwächen offensichtlich geworden. Im nachfolgenden soll zunächst einmal versucht werden, einige zentrale Aspekte dieser meines Erachtens strukturell angelegten Innovationshemmnisse aufzuzeigen. In einem zweiten Schritt werde ich mich dann mit der Frage befassen, welche sozialkulturellen Faktoren und Hintergründe dafür eine Rolle spielen, daß man in der DDR am bisherigen System einer zentralistischen Steuerung wissenschaftlich-technischer Innovation festhält.

Das Erscheinungsbild einer stillgelegten Kreativität

1985 waren rund 200 000 Beschäftigte im Bereich von Forschung und Entwicklung eingesetzt, rund 60 % von ihnen waren Hochschulabsolventen. Obwohl Vergleiche aufgrund der vorliegenden Daten auf Schwierigkeiten stoßen, schätzen DDR-Wissenschaftler, daß man "hinsichtlich des Anteils der für FE [Forschung und Entwicklung] eingesetzten Berufstätigen im Landesmaßstab in die internationale Spitzengruppe" aufgestiegen sei.[1] Einem geschätzten DDR-Anteil von 1-2 % an Forschungs- und Wissenschaftspersonal der Welt entspricht ein Anteil von weniger als 0,4 % der Weltbevölkerung. 4,7 % des Nationaleinkommens, knapp 11 Mrd. Mark wurden 1985 staatlicherseits für Wissenschaft und Technik bereitgestellt. 1986 wird sich diese Summe auf 11,6 Mrd. belaufen.[2]

Solche empirischen Befunde veranschaulichen, was selbstverständlich erscheint: Eine Gesellschaft, die auf die industrielle Nutzung wissenschaftlich-technischer Ergebnisse ausgerichtet ist, muß auch dem wissenschaftlich-technischen Fortschritt einen zentralen Platz einräumen.[3] (Vgl. die nachfolgende Tabelle)

Tabelle: Ausgaben und Beschäftigte im Bereich Wissenschaft und Technik in der DDR von 1971-1985 [4]

Aufwand/Beschäftigte	Zeitraum	Umfang
Ausgaben für Wissenschaft	1971-75	24 101,2 Mio M
und Technik	1976-80	31 188,4 Mio M
	1981-85	43 645,6 Mio M
Anteil der Ausgaben am	1971-75	3,5 %
produzierten National-	1976-80	3,6 %
einkommen	1981-85	4,1 %
Beschäftigte insgesamt	1970	123 000
	1980	182 000
	1985	ca. 200 000
Hierunter Absolventen von	1970	64 000
Hoch- und Fachschulen	1980	113 000
	1985	ca. 120 000

[1] *Intensivierung der Forschung. Bedingungen - Faktoren - Probleme*, hrsg. v. Günter Kröber, Lothar Läsker und Hubert Laitko (Berlin: Akademie, 1984), S. 158. Auf diese Stelle beziehen sich auch die folgenden Zahlen.

[2] Zu den Zahlen für 1985/86 vgl. "Wachsender Nutzen aus Wissenschaft und Technik," *Neues Deutschland*, 30.12.1985, S. 3.

[3] Vgl. Günter Mittag, "Mit höchsten Leistungen den XI. Parteitag vorbereiten," *Einheit*, 40, H. 6 (1985), S. 492.

[4] Eigene Berechnungen nach Daten im *Statistischen Jahrbuch der DDR* (Berlin: Staatsverlag der DDR, 1985), S. 102. Zahlen über Beschäftigte nach verschiedenen Jahrgängen der *Einheit* und des *Neuen Deutschland.*

Doch konstatieren Soziologen, Wissenschaftstheoretiker und Praktiker aus den Forschungs- und Entwicklungsbereichen ein merkwürdiges Phänomen, man habe in der DDR zwar Forschungs- und Entwicklungskapazitäten aufgebaut, die sich durchaus mit ihren materiellen und personellen Ressourcen am Niveau entwickelter Industriegesellschaften messen können, aber diese Potentiale bleiben in hohem Maße unwirksam. Ihre Potenz müsse aktiviert, in tatsächliche ökonomisch-technische Effektivität überführt werden.[5] Hierin besteht, so die nahezu übereinstimmende Kritik neuerer wissenschaftstheoretischer und soziologischer Untersuchungen, die entscheidende Herausforderung der weiteren Entwicklung.

In der DDR wird das Wort "Mittelmaß" bemüht, wenn es darum geht, den aktuellen Zustand und die Malaise vorhandener Forschungs- und Entwicklungskollektive zu beschreiben. Bei einer Untersuchung von 442 Hoch- und Fachschulkadern und 92 Kollektivleitern wurde beispielsweise festgestellt, daß sich insbesondere in der Altersgruppe der unter dreißigjährigen Wissenschaftler eine signifikante "Konzentration mittelmäßiger Leistungen" zeige.[6] Solche Ergebnisse, die in den hochaggregierten offiziellen Statistiken verschwinden, erhält man freilich erst durch genauere soziologische Analysen, die naturgemäß auch quantitativen Beschränkungen unterliegen. Anonyme Befragungen von Führungskräften in Forschungs- und Entwicklungsbereichen der DDR ergaben, daß diese "bemerkenswert oft" der Ansicht waren, daß ihre Mitarbeiter für Forschungszwecke "nicht geeignet" seien.[7] Leitungskader müssen in der DDR für ihre Mitarbeiter regelmäßig schriftliche Leistungsbewertungen anlegen. Ein Vergleich dieser anonymen Befragungen mit den offiziellen Leistungsbewertungen ergab allerdings, daß derselbe Mitarbeiterstamm regelmäßig mit Bewertungen wie

---

5 Vgl. Autorenkollektiv unter Leitung von Harry Nick, *Ökonomische und soziale Wirksamkeit des wissenschaftlich-technischen Fortschritts* (Berlin: Dietz, 1986), S. 260.

6 Marie-Luise Fiebekorn, "Zu einigen Problemen der altersspezifischen Ausprägung des Leistungsverhaltens bei Forschungs- und Entwicklungskadern in der Industrie," *Sid. Informationen zur soziologischen Forschung in der Deutschen Demokratischen Republik*, 19, H. 6 (1983), S. 51. Im folgenden zitiert als *Sid.*

7 Günther Boring, "Wissenschaftliche Arbeitstagung zu 'Probleme der politisch-ideologischen Führung des wissenschaftlich-technischen Fortschritts,'" Konferenzbericht, *Sid*, 21, H. 3 (1985), S. 61.

"Spitzenkraft" oder "sehr gute Forscher" (S. 61) eingestuft wurde.

Entscheidungszentralismus und Innovationsprozeß

Während der jährlichen Planerstellung kommt es auf allen Stufen der Leitungspyramide in horizontaler wie vertikaler Richtung zu vielfältigen Koordinations-, Korrektur- und Kontrollprozessen, die bis in den genossenschaftlichen oder kommunalen Bereich hineinreichen. Aber die hierbei gegebene funktionale Selbständigkeit der Teilsysteme (Betriebe, Kombinate, staatliche Instanzen etc.) ist niemals eine prinzipielle, qualitative Entscheidungsautonomie, sondern immer daran gebunden, einen vorgegebenen Rahmen effektiv auszufüllen und festgelegte Ziele nach Maßgabe konkreter Bedingungen umzusetzen.[8]

Für Innovationsprozesse (aber nicht nur für sie) hat diese Hierarchie von Erfüllungsprozeduren gravierende Folgen. Denn wer innerhalb dieses Systems den Steuermann steuert, bleibt prinzipiell ungeklärt. Selbst wenn inzwischen vorausgesetzt werden darf, daß die Formulierung sogenannter "objektiver gesellschaftlicher Erfordernisse" in den staatlichen Planaufgaben nach allen Regeln wissenschaftlicher Expertise erfolgt, so verstößt doch die Funktionslogik des gesamten Planungsablaufs gegen elementarste kybernetische Erkenntnisse, wie sie übrigens von seiten der Fachwissenschaft auch in der DDR schon in den sechziger Jahren hervorgehoben wurden.[9] Danach müßte nämlich bereits die Zielbestimmung und nicht erst die Erfüllungsprozedur das Ergebnis eines offenen dialogischen Prozesses sein, der eine Vielzahl wirksamer Feed-back-Impulse reguliert und verarbeitet.

Solche Überlegungen mögen aus fachwissenschaftlicher Sicht noch so berechtigt erscheinen, sie stoßen im Grund-

---

[8] Vgl. *Sozialistische Volkswirtschaft. Lehrbuch*, hrsg. v. Hans-Heinrich Kinze, Hans Knop, und Eberhard Seifert (Berlin: Die Wirtschaft, 1983), S. 128 ff. u. 132 ff.

[9] In der DDR begann die kybernetische Diskussion v.a. unter dem Einfluß der grundlegenden Arbeiten von Georg Klaus. Sein erstes Buch, *Kybernetik in philosophischer Sicht* (Berlin: Dietz) erschien bereits 1961. Kybernetische Auffassungen prägten insbesondere die Vorstellungen der Zeit der Wirtschaftsreformen in den sechziger Jahren. Mit dem Machtantritt Honeckers 1971 wurden kybernetische Diskussionen aus der offiziellen Planungs- und Leitungsdoktrin verbannt.

gedanken an die grundlegenden Herrschaftsprinzipien des politischen Systems. Denn dieses System ist gemäß dem - nicht zufällig dogmatisierten - Leninschen Schema darauf ausgerichtet, den universellen Zugriff auf alle relevanten gesellschaftlichen Belange zu wahren.[10] Eben deshalb gilt für die Steuerung von Innovationsprozessen, was für die Planung und Leitung des Wirtschaftsgeschehens schlechthin gilt: die deterministische Festlegung der Planziele und der einheitliche, steuernde Zugriff von oben.

Die Kontrolle der Zukunft scheint perfekt. Man weiß schon im Vorgriff, was man eigentlich wissen möchte. Das mag wie eine unglaubwürdige Vereinfachung der DDR-Planungspraxis erscheinen, deckt sich aber im Grundsatz mit den kritischen Einwänden verschiedener DDR-Autoren. So wird in der Studie *Intensivierung der Forschung* darauf verwiesen, daß Forschungsprozesse als sich entwickelnde Systeme begriffen werden müßten. Das heißt als Systeme, die einerseits genügend offen angelegt sein müßten, um spontanen, unvorhergesehenen Entwicklungen Rechnung zu tragen, und die andererseits entsprechend flexibel sein müßten, um auf selbstregulierte Weise - wenn erforderlich - Forschungspotentiale zu verlagern und Problemschwerpunkte zu modifizieren.[11] Mit anderen Worten: Wohlformulierte und festgelegte Aufgabenstellungen in Forschungsplänen (Wissenschafts- und Technikplänen) können bestenfalls bereits verfügbares Wissen aufbereiten oder absehbare Ergebnisse vorwegnehmen. Für die Erzeugung neuer Ideen sind solche Planungsprämissen ungeeignet. Eine solche "eingeengte Auffassung" der Forschungsplanung sei, wie die Autoren der Forschungsstudie einräumen, "noch" in der Praxis anzutreffen. Von ihr müsse man sich "entschieden . . . distanzieren," da sich die Forschungsplanung dann "auf die Vorausplanung absehbarer Resultate reduzieren" (S. 307) würde:

Die Konsequenz einer derartigen Auffassung ist, daß das Unvorhersehbare, die fundamental neuartige Idee, das in höchstem Grade Kreative neben der Planung steht. . . . Wenn aber For-

10 Vgl. *Leitung der sozialistischen Wirtschaft. Lehrbuch*, hrsg. v. Gerd Friedrich, Helmut Richter, Horst Stein, Gerhard Wittich (Berlin: Die Wirtschaft, 1983), S. 29 ff. Georg Brunner (*Politische Soziologie der UdSSR. Teil II* [Wiesbaden: Akademische Verlagsgesellschaft, 1977], S. 188) spricht in diesem Zusammenhang zutreffend von der "Kompetenzkompetenz" der führenden kommunistischen Partei.

11 *Intensivierung der Forschung*, S. 309 ff.

schungsplanung praktisch auf die Programmie-
rung des Absehbaren beschränkt bleibt, dann
organisiert sie . . . tatsächlich den Nachtrab.
(S. 308)

Mit vorgegebenen ökonomischen und technischen Para-
metern in den wissenschaftlich-technischen Plänen seien, so
eine Einstellungsuntersuchung von Hoch- und Fachschulkadern in Forschung und Entwicklung, bestenfalls "internationale Durchschnittswerte" zu erreichen.[12] Forschungs-
und Entwicklungsprojekte, die "auf der Basis 'sicher' rea-
lisierbarer Lösungen" aufgebaut werden, "transformieren
Mittelmaß in die Zukunft und bedeuten ökonomischen
Prestigeverlust auf dem Weltmarkt."[13]

**Der Faktor Interesse: defensive Verhaltensstrategien und
informelle Einflüsse**

Obwohl demokratisch-zentralistische Leitungsstrukturen
darauf ausgerichtet sind, eine straffe Einheitlichkeit des
Willens über die ganze Befehlpyramide hinweg zu gewährleisten, erzeugen sie fortlaufend ihr Gegenteil: den Verlust an
Steuerungskapazität durch sich widerstreitende Interessen
und Interessenebenen.

Die Grundbeziehung zwischen leitender und ausführender
Ebene gründet zunächst einmal auf einem Autoritätsgefälle:
Das leitende Organ verfügt über relativ mehr Möglichkeiten,
seinen Willen durchzusetzen, als die ausführenden Organe.
Vordergründig erfüllt diese Konstellation ihren beabsich-
tigten Zweck: Das Interesse der nachgeordneten Instanzen
wird einseitig auf die zentralen Vorgaben ausgerichtet. Die
formale Planerfüllung ist auch in der Tat die alles entscheidende Richtgröße für die politischen und fachlichen Kader in
den Betrieben, Kombinaten und anderen Einrichtungen. Aber
dieselbe Konstellation erzeugt gleichzeitig einen unerwünsch-
ten Nebeneffekt: das defensive Verhalten der ausführenden
Organe gegenüber den jeweiligen Leitungsinstanzen. In diesem Sinne haben die Wirtschaftseinheiten ein strukturell
bedingtes Interesse daran, die eigene Leistung zu minimie-
ren, die Planziele zu senken und ohne Risiko für den Plan-

12 Gundula Barsch, "Stimulierung und Leistungsverhalten," *Sid*, 19, H. 5
(1983), S. 33.
13 Heinz Großer und Cornelia Zanger, "Pflichtenheft und Leistungsbewertung in Forschung und Entwicklung," *Sozialistische Arbeitswissenschaft*,
28, H. 6 (1984), S. 407.

erfüllungsprozeß zu disponieren. Je komplexer die Planungsobjekte geraten und je länger die Entscheidungskette wird, um so mehr operieren die zentralen Organe mit hoch aggregierten Informationen aus zweiter Hand. Diese Informationen aber sind auf allen Stufen der Planungs- und Leitungspyramide in erheblichem Maße durch die dort wirksamen defensiven Verhaltensstrategien geprägt und daher einseitig. Auf diese Weise entsteht ein Netzwerk sozialer Mechanismen der Absicherung und Leistungsbegrenzung, die vom betrieblichen Mikrokosmos über die Kombinate bis hin zu den Industrieministerien, Ministerien und anderen zentralen Organen reicht. So ergibt sich folgendes Phänomen: Äußerlich, in den formalen Leitungsbeziehungen entsteht das Bild einer monolithisch durchorganisierten Struktur; realiter aber wirkt ein Gefüge informell wirksamer, vielfältiger Eigeninteressen, die allesamt nach Wegen und Möglichkeiten suchen, den eigenen Funktionsbereich abzuschirmen und überschaubare Routineoperationen durchzuführen.

Grundlegende Innovationen stellen daher für die Wirtschaftseinheiten häufig nur eine unliebsame Belastung dar. Sie bringen über längere Zeit Unsicherheiten in die eingespielten Routineabläufe, führen naturgemäß zu höheren Leistungsansprüchen in nachfolgenden Planperioden, entwerten ihre bisherigen konventionellen Leistungen und Erzeugnisse und bergen zudem das Risiko in sich, mit der laufenden Planerfüllung in Verzug zu geraten.[14]

Das prägt das Verhalten der Wirtschaftseinheiten im Umgang mit den staatlichen Planauflagen. Wenn beispielsweise der Minister für Hoch- und Fachschulwesen der DDR, Hans-Joachim Böhme, dem versammelten 10. ZK-Plenum (1985) zu berichten wußte, daß 1984 insgesamt 1660 Forschungsergebnisse der Universitäten und Hochschulen den Kombinaten übergeben werden konnten, davon 261 Aufgaben aus dem Staatsplan Wissenschaft und Technik,[15] so haben diese Daten bis auf ihre Legitimationsfunktion vermutlich keinen besonderen Erkenntniswert. Da Pläne erfüllbar gemacht werden, gibt es auch kaum Pläne, die nicht erfüllt werden. Die schon im Planansatz einkalkulierte Anspruchs-

---

14 Vgl. Heinz-Dieter Haustein, "Zeitfaktor und Effektivität," *Wirtschaftswissenschaft*, 32, H. 3 (1983), S. 205 f; vgl. auch Angela Scherzinger, "Aspekte und Planung von Forschung und Entwicklung in der DDR," *Vierteljahreshefte für Wirtschaftsforschung*, H. 1 (1983), S. 83.

15 Hans-Joachim Böhme, "Eine große Herausforderung für unsere Wissenschaftler," *Neues Deutschland*, 22./23.6.1985, S. 5.

losigkeit der Aufgabenstellung in den Wissenschafts- und Technikplänen oder den operativen "Pflichtenheften"[16] sorgt dafür, "möglichst nur Entwicklungs- und Forschungsaufgaben in den Plan aufzunehmen, die mit absoluter Sicherheit zum Termin erfolgreich abgeschlossen werden können."[17] Rund ein Drittel der Aufgaben der betrieblichen Wissenschafts- und Technikpläne liegt angeblich "unter dem internationalen Stand."[18] Nur 25 der 222 gesellschaftswissenschaftlichen Forschungsthemen, die für den Zeitraum 1981-1985 an der Berliner Humboldt-Universität festgelegt worden waren, wurden nach Auffassung der verantwortlichen Themenleiter als "Höchstleistungen" konzipiert.[19]

Da Forschungs- und Entwicklungsprozesse auch inhaltlich (und nicht nur in der Bewertung, prozessual, organisatorisch etc.) durch eine hohe Komplexität gekennzeichnet sind, gibt es für die Phantasie keine Grenzen, wenn es darum geht, einzelne inhaltliche Komponenten auszudifferenzieren, Details als Projekte auszugeben oder alte Bestände unter einem neuen Gesichtspunkt zusammenzufassen. Da sich aus jedem wissenschaftlichen Projekt mühelos mehrere solcher Abwandlungen konstruieren lassen, ist man auch im industriellen Inventionsbereich in DDR-Betrieben nicht verlegen, wenn statistisch und im materiellen Eigeninteresse die innovative Bilanz aufgebessert werden muß. Harry Maier, bis vor kurzem einer der führenden DDR-Forscher auf dem Gebiet der Technik- und Innovationstheorie, nennt solche Verfahren neutral "kosmetische Innovationen."[20]

---

[16] Die seit 1981 (und in ähnlichen Regelungen schon zuvor) bestehenden Pflichtenheft-Verordnung legt bestimmte Grundsätze und verbindliche Verfahrensweisen für die Planung und Leitung von Forschungs- und Entwicklungsaufgaben fest. In ihnen werden ökonomischer Nutzeffekt, Aufgabenstellung, Fristen, Ablauf u.ä. für entsprechende Projekte vorgegeben. Pflichtenhefte dienen dann der Lenkung, Kontrolle und Planabrechnung von Forschungs- und Entwicklungsarbeiten. Vgl. *Gesetzblatt der DDR 1982*, Teil I, S. 1 ff. und die Fassung der Pflichtenheft-Verordnung gemäß erster Durchführungsbestimmung, *Gesetzblatt der DDR 1983*, Teil I, S. 381 ff.

[17] Claudia Grafe, Dieter Liebing, Harry Nick, Heinz Willems, "Zur Leitung wissenschaftlich-technischen Fortschritts in den Kombinaten," *Einheit*, 39, H. 5 (1984), S. 413.

[18] *Intensivierung der Forschung*, S. 207.

[19] Ebenda.

[20] *Innovation und Wissenschaft*, hrsg. v. Günter Kröber und Harry Maier (Berlin: Akademie, 1985), S. 26 und S. 53.

Auf der Entstehungsseite ist die Erzeugung neuen technischen Wissens ein offener, noch unkonturierter Entwurf. In bezug auf die möglichen Resultate ist es daher auch hochgradig risikobesetzt; in seinen Prozeßformen häufig ein spontaner, indeterminierter Verlauf. Im Prinzip kommt es damit zu einem unvermeidlichen Widerspruch zwischen den Handlungsbedingungen kreativer Spontaneität auf der einen und den Operationsbedingungen administrativer Steuerung auf der anderen Seite. Letztere tendieren notwendigerweise dazu, die risikobesetzte Kreativität in einen überschaubaren und kontrollierbaren Prozeß zu überführen. Setzen sich solche Tendenzen durch, dann führt das dazu, daß die kreativen und spontanen Komponenten des Inventionsprozesses aufgelöst und durch paßfähige Routinehandlungen ersetzt werden. Die gegenwärtige Form parteistaatlicher Steuerungen bedingt daher, was der DDR-Soziologie Ladensack folgendermaßen beschreibt:

> Teilweise muß überhaupt erst das Verständnis für das Wesen des Risikos und die unabdingbare Notwendigkeit, gerechtfertigte Risiken einzugehen, weiter vertieft werden. . . . Für verschiedene Leute, Leitungs- und Kontrollorgane ist Risiko vor allem ein Begriff mit negativem Inhalt. Taucht Risiko auf, werden sofort Maßnahmepläne zur Eliminierung des Risikos verlangt.[21]

Die Ökonomisierung der Forschung

Seit 1983 hat man in der DDR durch eine Reihe von Maßnahmen versucht, den Innovationsprozeß zu effektivieren. Dazu gehören vor allem die bereits erwähnten "Pflichtenhefte," die im Grunde nichts anderes sind als verbindliche operative Planungskonzepte für wissenschaftlich-technische Leistungen, und Maßnahmen zur Ökonomisierung von Forschungs- und Entwicklungsarbeiten. Ein wesentlicher Gedanke bei letzteren bestand darin, den Kauf und Verkauf wissenschaftlich-technischer Leistungen auf eine betriebswirtschaftliche Grundlage zu stellen. Zu diesem Zweck sind die Forschungspotentiale und vergleichbaren Einrichtungen auf die Prinzipien der sog. wirtschaftlichen Rechnungs-

---

[21] Klaus Ladensack, "Pflichtenheft und Risiko," *der neuerer*, 33, H. 8 (1984), S. 98.

führung umgestellt worden.[22] Das bedeutet, daß diese Institutionen als selbständig wirtschaftende Einheiten die Eigenfinanzierung ihrer Kosten sicherstellen und planmäßige Gewinne erwirtschaften sollen.

Weitere Regelungen, die Ende 1985 verfügt wurden, dehnen die Grundsätze einer ökonomischen und an Effektivitätszielen orientierten Forschungsarbeit auf die Einrichtungen der Akademie der Wissenschaften und des Hochschulwesens aus. Konkrete Leistungsverträge und die Finanzierung entsprechender wissenschaftlicher Leistungen durch die Kombinate sollen zukünftig den Schwerpunkt in Akademie- und Hochschulforschungen bilden.[23]

Man kann anhand verschiedener Hinweise in der Fachliteratur davon ausgehen, daß bislang kaufmännische Gesichtspunkte im Bereich von Forschung und Entwicklung eine weitgehend untergeordnete Bedeutung besaßen.[24] In den entsprechenden Einrichtungen arbeitete man für gewöhnlich anhand wissenschaftlich-technischer Themen die Vorgaben aus den Plänen "Wissenschaft und Technik" ab. Wirtschaftliche Aufwands- und Ertragskalküle bildeten hierbei als Orientierungspunkt schon insofern eine *quantité négligeable*, als die Anwender wissenschaftlicher Erzeugnisse - vornehmlich die Wirtschaftseinheiten - ja auch ihrerseits keine hinreichend wirksamen Rentabilitätskriterien besaßen und auch heute noch nicht besitzen.

Die Begrenztheit dieser jüngsten Steuerungsmaßnahme wird schon allein daraus ersichtlich, daß betriebswirtschaftliche Kalküle in Forschungs- und Entwicklungseinrichtungen nur insoweit greifen können, als das wirtschaftliche Gesamtsystem nach denselben Grundsätzen verfährt. Solange bei den Betrieben und Kombinaten aber solche Wirtschaftlichkeitskriterien selbst brüchig bleiben, nur verzerrt wirken oder gänzlich unwirksam sind, gibt es auch keinen triftigen Grund dafür, weshalb man von der bisherigen Praxis im Forschungs- und Entwicklungsbereich auf einmal abgehen sollte. Im Zweifelsfalle werden eben auftragsgemäß durchgeführte Pseudoinnovationen, bedarfsfremde Fehlent-

---

[22] Vgl. *Gesetzblatt der DDR 1983*, Teil I, S. 387 ff.

[23] Vgl. *Gesetzblatt der DDR 1986*, Teil I, S. 9 ff. und S. 12 ff.

[24] Vgl. etwa Gerhard Rosenkranz und Hans-Gerd Bannasch, "Innovationsorganisation im Industriebetrieb," *Arbeit und Arbeitsrecht*, 40, H. 3 (1985), S. 51 und passim.

wicklungen und ungenügende technische Leistungen mit buchhalterischem Geschick auf Heller und Pfennig abgerechnet.[25]

Die Produzenten von Forschungsleistungen sollen, wie die Anordnung bestimmt, nunmehr ihre Kosten kalkulieren und auf dieser Grundlage - zuzüglich des normativ festgelegten Gewinns - entsprechende Preise bilden. Anbieter und Käufer entsprechender Forschungsleistungen müssen sich dabei vertraglich auf die vorläufigen Kosten- und Preisgrenzen einigen. Spitzenleistungen und gezielte Überbietungen können sogar mit Extragewinnen in Höhe von 50 %, z.T. auch 100 % des normativen Gewinns honoriert werden, die allerdings zum größten Teil in der jeweiligen Forschungsinstitution verbleiben. Der persönliche Nutzen des Forschungs- und Entwicklungspersonals bleibt streng begrenzt und wird gegebenenfalls über entsprechende Extragratifikationen in Höhe von bis zu 300 Mark je Beschäftigtem aus den Prämienfonds der Forschungseinrichtungen finanziert. Darüber hinaus können jedoch im Bedarfsfalle auch zusätzliche Leistungsanreize gewährt werden. Bei den Mitarbeitern der Akademie der Wissenschaften und der Hochschulen liegt der Spitzensatz aller Prämienzahlungen derzeit bei maximal 1200 Mark je Vollbeschäftigtem.[26]

Aber worin bestehen die gerechtfertigten Kosten von Forschungsleistungen, und wie hoch ist ihr ökonomischer Nutzen, der eigentlich in den Gewinn- und Extragewinnzuschlägen zum Ausdruck kommen müßte? Zu Recht wird auch in DDR-Publikationen darauf hingewiesen, daß solche Kosten-Nutzen-Kriterien nur sehr begrenzte Aussagen über den ökonomischen Wert und die gesellschaftliche Bedeutung einer wissenschaftlich-technischen Neuerung zulassen.[27] Gerade bei Forschungsleistungen, wenn sie den Namen verdienen, handelt es sich in der Regel um Originalproduktionen, für die es definitionsgemäß keine Vergleiche gibt. Kostenrechnungen kalkulieren hier lediglich den individuellen Aufwand, mehr nicht. Ihr ökonomischer Nutzen erschließt sich wiederum keineswegs aus den anfallenden Aufwendungen. Ferner gibt es gerade auf dem Gebiet von Forschung und Entwicklung keine lineare Beziehung

25 Vgl. Mittag, "Mit höchsten Leistungen," S. 491.

26 *Gesetzblatt der DDR 1986*, Teil I, S. 18

27 Vgl. *Ökonomische und soziale Wirksamkeit des wissenschaftlich-technischen Fortschritts*, S. 251 ff. und S. 276 ff.

zwischen ökonomischem Aufwand und Ertrag. Nutzlose Forschungsleistungen können erhebliche Mittel verschlingen, während relativ geringe Forschungsaufwendungen zu Ergebnissen führen mögen, deren Verwertungsmöglichkeiten in keiner Relation zu den ursprünglichen Kosten stehen.

Praktisch gesehen haben denn auch die bisherigen Erfahrungen mit der wirtschaftlichen Rechnungsführung in Forschungseinrichtungen zu keinen nennenswerten Effekten geführt.[28] Da die Käufer wissenschaftlich-technischer Leistungen zumeist kaum die Berechtigung der Kosten beurteilen können und die Preisfestsetzung administrativen Charakter hat, berechnen die Forschungseinrichtungen eben das, was bei ihnen an Kosten anfällt, und versuchen - je nach Motivation und Interessenlage recht oder schlecht - zu liefern, was ihnen aufgetragen wurde.

Rolle und Bedeutung symbolischer Codes

Bei all den benannten Dilemmata und Fehlwirkungen des Entscheidungszentralismus für das Innovationsgeschehen wie für gesellschaftliche Steuerungen überhaupt, drängt sich vor allem eine Frage auf: Warum unternimmt die Parteielite im eigenen fundamentalen Interesse an volkswirtschaftlicher Effektivität keinen ernst zu nehmenden Versuch, das Planungs- und Leitungsgeschehen auf eine rationalere Grundlage zu stellen? Offenkundig gibt es erhebliche Beharrungskräfte innerhalb des politischen Systems, die an dessen gegenwärtigem Erscheinungsbild - der monokratischen Entscheidungskompetenz an der Spitze und dem hochgradigen Zentralismus der Steuerungsformen - festhalten. Und obwohl diese Beharrungskräfte zu irrationalen und - qua Ineffektivität - selbstzerstörerischen Konsequenzen führen, scheinen sie sich dennoch auf stabile Bewußtseinsformen, d.h. auf entsprechende Deutungs- und Bewertungsmuster stützen zu können, die das politische System in seiner gegenwärtigen Gestalt legitimieren. Diese leisten offenkundig zweierlei: einerseits immunisieren sie gegen systematische, sachliche Zweifel, bieten aber gleichzeitig ein sinnerhaltendes Interpretationsschema der realsozialistischen Wirklichkeit an.

---

[28] Vgl. Helga Engel, "Zur Erhöhung der ökonomischen Wirksamkeit von Wissenschaft und Technik durch die Anwendung der wirtschaftlichen Rechnungsführung in Forschungseinrichtungen von Industriekombinaten," *Wirtschaftswissenschaft*, 34, H. 5 (1986), S. 711 und S. 715 ff.

Solche Deutungs- und Bewertungsmuster sind vor allem für das offizielle Selbstverständnis von Parteielite und Funktionärskörper von entscheidender Bedeutung, da sie dazu beitragen, ihr Bewußtsein, ihre Motivation und Handlungsbereitschaft zu stabilisieren. Entsprechende mentale Muster, die das politisch-ideologische Selbstverständnis durch grundlegende Einstellungen und Sinnbezüge zusammenhalten und ihnen einen inneren Halt verleihen, will ich in Anlehnung an S.N. Eisenstadt symbolische Codes nennen.[29] Eisenstadt benutzt diese Begrifflichkeit, um die integrierenden Bedeutungsmuster von sozialen Kulturen schlechthin und ihre Wandlungsfähigkeit zu untersuchen. Ich benutze sie hingegen, um die Innenperspektive des politisch-ideologischen Selbstverständnisses der Herrschaftsträger im real existierenden Sozialismus zu analysieren. Der Unterschied besteht also weniger in der Sache als in der Spezifik des Untersuchungsfeldes.

Symbolische Codes sind nicht beliebig konstruierbar und schon gar nicht dürfen sie mit wissenschaftlichen Sachaussagen verwechselt werden, obwohl sie sich durchaus wissenschaftlicher Argumente bedienen können. Aber das äußere Erscheinungsbild interessiert am symbolischen Code nur bedingt. Vielmehr richtet sich der Blick auf die im symbolischen Code wirksamen bildhaften Vorstellungswelten und kulturell geprägten Sichtweisen, die notwendigerweise jenseits von sachlicher Diskussion und vernünftiger Kritik operieren. Ihre Verbindung zur bestehenden geistigen und sozialen Struktur einer Gesellschaft ergibt sich einerseits daraus, daß sie über historische Kontinuitätslinien und Traditionsbestände weitergetragen werden, daß sie aber auch in die jeweils aktuellen Erfahrungszusammenhänge eingelagert sind. Sie nehmen also auf deutende und wertende Weise Bezug auf das, was in der sozialen Wirklichkeit geschieht. In diesem Sinne sind symbolische Codes Kristallisationen einer gewachsenen sozialkulturellen Umgebung.

Es lassen sich in den realsozialistischen Gesellschaften eine Reihe solcher Codes erkennen, die auf die beschriebene Weise das ideologische System fundieren: etwa die Vorstellung vom adelnden und sinnstiftenden Wert der Arbeit - vor allem der Industriearbeit, oder die Vorstellung vom Kommunismus als irdischem Heilszustand, als Endpunkt und Ziel

29 S.N. Eisenstadt, *Tradition, Wandel, Modernität* (Frankfurt/M.: Suhrkamp, 1979), S. 10 ff. und passim.

aller Geschichte, die im wahren Reich der Freiheit aufgehen soll; eine Vorstellung, in der sich unzweideutig ältere, religiöse Heilserwartungen abgelagert und gleichzeitig modernisiert haben.[30] Dazu ließe sich mehr und Spezifischeres sagen als dies an dieser Stelle möglich ist. Im folgenden soll es daher vor allem um denjenigen symbolischen Code gehen, der für das Herrschaftssystem und die Organisationsprinzipien des demokratischen Zentralismus eine überragende Bedeutung besitzt und den ich mit dem Kürzel "Gesellschaft als Objekt" kennzeichnen will.

Das Determinismuskonzept

Charakteristisch für dieses Konzept ist vor allem eine besondere Vorstellung vom gesetzmäßigen Charakter gesellschaftlicher Strukturen und Prozesse. Sie besagt vor allem dies: "zwischen den einzelnen Zuständen, Bereichen und Prozessen des gesellschaftlichen Lebens" sollen angeblich notwendige gesetzmäßige Beziehungen herrschen.[31] Das heißt, das Verhalten und das Erscheinungsbild der einzelnen sozialen Teile und Vorgänge des gesellschaftlichen Ganzen wird als festgelegte Ordnung determinierter Beziehungen und Bewegungen verstanden.

Es liegt in der Logik dieser Vorstellungswelt, daß der vorherrschende Gesetzestypus, den sie für eine Erklärung und Deutung sozialer Sachverhalte heranzieht, der der kausalen Notwendigkeit ist. In diesem Sinne muß es also eindeutige Ursachen auf der einen und entsprechende Wirkungen auf der anderen Seite geben. Zwischen Ursache und Wirkung besteht eine mehr oder weniger komplizierte, aber in sich notwendige Verknüpfung. Gesetzeszusammenhänge jedoch, die sich in einer Vielfalt von Zuständen und Prozessen darstellen können, die also im Prinzip nicht eindeutig sind, würden offenkundig jeder universellen Determinismuskonzeption widersprechen bzw. die kausale Determination nur für einen begrenzten Ausschnitt gesetzmäßiger Wirkungen einschließen. Die Annahme der Indeterminiertheit würde besagen, daß gesellschaftliche und historische Sachverhalte zwar erkennbare Strukturen und Entwicklungsrichtungen aufweisen, daß aber die hierbei auftretenden

[30] So in der Interpretation von Karl Löwith, *Weltgeschichte als Heilsgeschehen* (Stuttgart: Kohlhammer, 1953), S. 45 ff.

[31] Gottfried Stiehler, *Dialektik und Gesellschaft* (Berlin: Deutscher Verlag der Wissenschaften, 1981), S. 35 ff.

Zustände keineswegs notwendig sind und im einzelnen auch nicht vorausgesagt werden können. Spontaneität und Zufall wären demzufolge Einflußgrößen der Wirklichkeit, denen ein ganz eigenständiges Gewicht beigemessen werden müßte, weil von ihrem Eintreten qualitativ verschiedene Zustände eines Gesamtsystems abhängen können.

Genau dies sind aber Erkenntnisse über indeterminierte Prozesse und Strukturbildungen, wie sie seit jüngerer Zeit in der westlichen Diskussion vor allem im naturwissenschaftlichen Denken formuliert werden und vermutlich hier wie in anderen Wissenschaften zu einer weitreichenden Umwälzung von Interpretationssystemen führen werden.[32] Wenn führende Wissenschaftstheoretiker der DDR, wie etwa Herbert Hörz, solche modernen naturwissenschaftlichen Auffassungen rezipieren, dann wird deutlich, in welchem Maße die sich hier aufdrängenden Schlußfolgerungen mit der Vorstellungswelt der marxistisch-leninistischen Orthodoxie kollidieren und wie sehr diese in einem unaufhebbaren Widerspruch zur herrschenden Steuerungs- und Entscheidungspraxis des politischen Systems stehen.[33] Denn die altehrwürdigen Planungspraktiken und zentralistischen Steuerungsformen müßten - orientierte man sich an solchen Auffassungen - nicht nur damit aufhören, die Zukunft auf determinierbare Ergebnisse festzulegen, sie müßte auch jene Entwicklungsfaktoren überhaupt erst einmal freisetzen und sich eigenständig bewegen lassen, die als Störfaktoren und Unkalkulierbarkeit bis auf den heutigen Tag aus dem Herrschaftssystem hinausgesäubert werden: Spontaneität und Zufall.

Mechanisches Weltbild und Gesellschaft als Objekt

Die Vorstellung, daß es eine vom betrachtenden und handelnden Menschen unabhängige Wirklichkeit universell gültiger Gesetze gibt, die das Verhalten der Teile eines Systems und dessen Zustand vollständig definieren, ist freilich wesentlich älter als die theoretischen Anfänge des Marxismus oder die noch viel jüngeren der marxistisch-leninistischen Ideologie. In ihren weltanschaulichen Voraussetzungen angedeutet oder ausformuliert finden wir das deterministische Denken bereits zu Beginn des neuzeitlichen

---

[32] Vgl. Ilya Prigogine und Isabelle Stengers, *Dialog mit der Natur* (München: Piper, 1981), S. 148 ff. und 176 ff.

[33] Vgl. Herberg Hörz, "Weltbild und Weltanschauung," in Walter Hollitscher unter Mitarbeit von Hubert Horstmann, *Naturbild und Weltanschauung* (Berlin: Akademie, 1985), S. 214.

naturwissenschaftlichen Denkens bei Kopernikus und Kepler, bei Galilei und schließlich bei Newton.[34] Was seit Anbeginn an dieser Vorstellung des determinierten Mechanismus so faszinierte und eine geradezu magnetische Anziehungskraft ausübte, war die in ihr angelegte ungeheure Expansion menschlicher Gestaltungsmöglichkeiten und Machterweiterung. Darin gründete bei den ersten Renaissancedenkern der anfangs noch unbewußte Impuls zum wissenschaftlichen Suchen, der sich schließlich zum leitenden Paradigma einer neuen Weltauffassung, eines neuen Realitätsbezuges verdichten sollte.[35] Das neuzeitliche aufgeklärte Denken hat nämlich, wie u.a. Horkheimer und Adorno interpretieren, im Grunde den Menschen als unbeschränkten Herrn eingesetzt und seine Diktatur über die Dinge errichtet.[36] In der berühmten Formel Francis Bacons, daß Wissen Macht sei, ist diese Einstellung zum Programm der sich anbahnenden industriellen Epoche erhoben worden.

Entscheidend für unsere Problematik ist diese sozialkulturelle Dimension des veränderten Realitätsbezuges, die den geistigen Wendepunkt der Neuzeit überhaupt erst begreiflich macht. Sie erklärt nämlich die Verbindungslinie zwischen systematischer wissenschaftlicher Praxis, methodischem Determinismus und Machtentfaltung über die Objektwelt. Ohne die Konstruktion eines deterministischen Zusammenhangs, der theoretisch wie praktisch immer nur ein willkürliches Modell der Wirklichkeit darstellt, wird auch die Vorstellung sinnlos, mit entsprechend zweckgerichteten Eingriffen die Bewegung der Teile eines Systems oder dessen Gesamtzustand hinreichend kontrollieren zu können.

Von hier aus läßt sich ein Bogen zu den unausgesprochenen Denkprämissen zentralistischer Planungssysteme des real existierenden Sozialismus schlagen: So wie das Determinismuskonzept in seinen Erkenntnisinteressen auf die wissenschaftliche Verfügbarkeit über Dinge, Zustände und Prozesse gerichtet ist, so zielt auch die Parteiherrschaft und ihr politisches Institutionensystem auf die planmäßige Umsetzung eines zentralen Willens.

34 Vgl. Lewis Mumford, *Mythos der Maschine* (Frankfurt/M.: Fischer, 1984), S. 367 ff. und 393 ff.

35 Ernst Cassirer, *Die Philosophie der Aufklärung* (Tübingen: J.C.B. Mohr [Paul Siebeck], 1932), S. 48 ff.

36 Max Horkheimer und Theodor W. Adorno, *Dialektik der Aufklärung* (Frankfurt/M.: Fischer, 1971), S. 12 und 16.

Der gedankliche Weg von der rationalen Beherrschung der Realienwelt (Natur) zur wissenschaftlichen Beherrschung von Gesellschaft ist daher nicht weit. Denn aus der klassischen Formel Descartes' vom Menschen als "mâitre et possesseur de la nature" folgt - wie Gehlen schreibt - mit innerer Notwendigkeit die modernere Vorstellung vom "mâitre et possesseur de la société."[37] Wenn es nämlich im Bereich der Natur "keine massiven, nach aller Erfahrung unüberwindlichen Widerstände mehr gibt, die eine echte Verzichtsbereitschaft aufnötigen könnten" (S. 80), weshalb sollte nicht gleiches auch für die Sozialordnung gelten? Genau dieser Zusammenhang ist für die realsozialistischen Systeme so charakteristisch: Die Vorstellung von der deterministischen Gestaltbarkeit der Objektwelt hat sich zur Vorstellung einer rationalen Verfügung über die Gesellschaft erweitert und radikalisiert.

Charakteristisch für sie ist, daß jede menschliche Ambivalenz, jede Mehrdeutigkeit, jedes spontane Wirken und Spannungsverhältnis im mechanistischen Bild eines programmierbaren Ablaufs des sozialen Geschehens erloschen sind. Die "maschinelle Großproduktion," so Lenin im Jahre 1918, erfordert

> unbedingte und strengste Einheit des Willens, der die gemeinsame Arbeit von Hunderten, Tausenden und Zehntausenden Menschen leitet. . . . Wie aber kann die strengste Einheit des Willens gesichert werden? Durch die Unterordnung von Tausenden unter den Willen eines einzelnen.[38]

Bei Stalin schließlich wird die maschinenähnliche Struktur des Leitungsapparates überdeutlich: Es ist die in der Partei inkarnierte, kollektive Rationalität des Wissens um die Gesetze von Gesellschaft und Geschichte, die sich in Form einer Entscheidungspyramide über die einzelnen Transmissionsriemen der Massenorganisationen bis hinein in das individuelle Handeln und Denken verlängert.[39] Die Herr-

---

[37] Arnold Gehlen, *Seele im technischen Zeitalter* (Hamburg: Rowohlt, 1957), S. 80.

[38] W.I. Lenin, "Die nächsten Aufgaben der Sowjetmacht," in ders., *Ausgewählte Werke* (Berlin: Dietz, 1970), II, S. 762 f.

[39] Vgl. J. Stalin, "Über dialektischen und historischen Materialismus," in ders., *Fragen des Leninismus* (Berlin: Dietz, 1951), S. 657 ff.

schaft der parteigelenkten Rationalität wird als geschlossenes System zentralistischer Steuerung und Entscheidungsumsetzung gedacht.

Daß die Vorstellung einer vollständigen, objekthaften Kontrolle von Mensch und Gesellschaft in der Praxis parteistaatlicher Herrschaft fortlaufend widerlegt wird, hat offenbar keineswegs den Zerfall des symbolischen Codes selbst zur Folge. Vielmehr scheint es so, daß die für ihn charakteristischen Einstellungen und Deutungsmuster nach wie vor die Vorstellungswelt der Herrschaftsträger kennzeichnen. Wie anders wären auch alle Widersprüche, alle so offenkundigen Dysfunktionen des Planungs- und Leitungsgeschehens, die ich oben skizziert habe, mit der Anspruchshaltung des Marxismus-Leninismus auf rationale, wissenschaftlich begründete Gesellschaftsführung vereinbar? Im symbolischen Code von der Gesellschaft als Objekt gelingt die Ausblendung einer mißlichen gesellschaftlichen Realität, die ihrem Wesen nach gerade deshalb gerechtfertigt und überlegen scheint, weil sie aufgrund ihrer institutionellen Struktur einen direkten Zugriff auf alle sozialen Teilelemente und Prozesse erlaubt. Eben dies scheint ihr ungeheurer Vorteil zu sein. Daß diese monokratische Konzentration der Machtmittel mit realer Steuerungskapazität verwechselt wird, ist der große, aber wohl auch notwendige Selbstbetrug des politischen Systems.

Macht, entgrenzte Macht über Menschen und Dinge berauscht. Sie hat eine zutiefst sinnliche Qualität: den realen Schein der universellen Verfügbarkeit, der Gestaltung der Welt nach eigenen Wertschätzungen und Zwecken. Alles Denken in den Bahnen der Kausalität, alle (realiter fiktiven) Konstruktionen von geschichtsmächtigen Tätern (Subjekten) und determinierbaren Objekten finden hier ihren sozialpsychischen und triebhaften Hintergrund. So ist es auch zwangsläufig, daß diese Vorstellungswelt von letzten Ursachen, fundierenden Wesenskräften und absoluten Anfangsgründen regiert werden muß. Daß es ebenso vorstellbar wäre, daß sich das soziale Geschehen vielgestaltig selbst erzeugt und zerstört wie in seinen Ergebnissen offen bleibt, käme als Antithese einem Attentat auf die marxistisch-leninistische Orthodoxie gleich. Das Übermenschentum der großen und kleinen stalinistischen Führer von einst ist gerade in diesem Sinne zwingend: Sie waren die politische Inkarnation einer letzten, alles begründenden Instanz. Selbst mehr als dreißig Jahre nach dem Tode des großen Diktators bleibt noch der

Schauer einer unbedingten Autorität, den die Träger der Macht einflößen, bleibt ihr absolutistischer Verhaltens- und Entscheidungsstil mit sorgfältig arrangierten Auftritten in der Partei und gesellschaftlichen Öffentlichkeit. Parteitage: eine vom Anfang bis zum Ende, vom Delegierten bis zum Applaus durchgestaltete Inszenierung; Wahlen: eine vollständig kontrollierte Zukunft, die nur determinierbare Ergebnisse zuläßt; Geschichte: eine Abfolge von Planjahrfünften.

Und so täusche man sich nicht über die unterschwelligen Beharrungskräfte des parteistaatlichen Regimes, das entgegen aller selbstverschuldeten Widersprüche, entgegen dem systemisch bedingten Verfall volkswirtschaftlicher Leistungs- und Innovationskraft, immer auch ein tieferes Bedürfnis befriedigt: das nach absoluter Wahrheit, innerer Geschlossenheit und machtfundierter Stabilität.

The Image of Computers and Robots in GDR Prose Fiction

Nancy A. Lauckner

Although the GDR lags considerably behind the West in computerization, it hopes to catch up. The Eleventh Party Congress stressed the importance of technology and proclaimed a policy of extensive computerization as vital for the GDR economy. State firms are making the products needed to implement the policy,[1] and theoreticians are struggling to justify resultant sweeping changes such as potential unemployment, the development of a technological elite class, and monotonous jobs for less qualified workers.[2] Allegedly the GDR has 350,000 personal computers and 57,000 industrial robots in use, but most of its small computers are less sophisticated than Western models and most of its robots would not be classified as such in the West.[3] Probably few computers will be used in homes.[4] Many problems hamper GDR computerization efforts: a late start in the computer field, the Western embargo on certain computer products, low quantities of hardware production, failure to keep pace with the latest advances in computer technology,[5] and difficulties with software and support.

Against this background and because of literature's ability to provide a subjective glimpse of the future, this study

---

[1] "Tempo zulegen," *Der Spiegel*, 12 May 1986, pp. 75, 81.

[2] Katharina Belwe and Fred Klinger, "Der Wert der Arbeit. Aspekte des sozialen Wandels in der industriellen Arbeitswelt der DDR," in *Tradition und Fortschritt in der DDR. Neunzehnte Tagung zum Stand der DDR-Forschung in der Bundesrepublik Deutschland, 20. bis 23. Mai 1986*, Edition Deutschland Archiv (Cologne: Wissenschaft und Politik, 1986), pp. 71-77.

[3] "Tempo zulegen," p. 81; Belwe and Klinger, pp. 70-71.

[4] "Tempo zulegen," p. 78.

[5] "Tempo zulegen," pp. 79, 81.

investigates the image of computers and robots in GDR prose fiction. Except for the works by Stefan Heym, Helga Königsdorf, Irmtraud Morgner, and Christa Wolf treated here, *Belletristik* has devoted little attention to computers. Most of the works discussed here therefore represent science fiction, termed "wissenschaftlich-phantastische" or "utopisch-phantastische Literatur" in the GDR.[6] The science fiction stories were chosen from anthologies and thus provide a cross section of typical texts.

Several critics have addressed the treatment of computers in GDR science fiction. In an early study (1966), Klaus Walther, a GDR critic, asserts that socialist science fiction responds optimistically to an assumed future world of cybernetic systems and its attendant enhancement of human life instead of showing "[d]ie Angst vor der entfesselten Maschinenwelt" which he sees in pessimistic Western science fiction.[7] Pointing to cybernetics as a relatively new concern at the time, he declares it the role of socialist science fiction to portray "die Begegnung des Menschen mit sich selbst unter neuen, ungeahnten Bedingungen der Zukunft" and the "Kampf um die humanitäre Verwendung der Maschinen und Systeme."[8] Horst Heidtmann states that GDR authors seldom portray computer and robot technology. When they do, they tend to remark generally on its labor-saving potential and rarely depict problems in the "Verhältnis des Menschen zu den denkenden Maschinen."[9] In contrast to Heidtmann, I find considerable mention of computers and robots in GDR science fiction. While some depictions are positive or, at least, neutral, many are quite negative, and this study will show that GDR authors seem much more pessimistic about the contribution of this technology to a truly humane future than Walther suggests.

Some GDR works of *Belletristik* and science fiction treat computer technology quite superficially, as Heidtmann states. They maintain a neutral stance, portraying the technology as

---

[6] Horst Heidtmann, *Utopisch-phantastische Literatur in der DDR: Untersuchungen zur Entwicklung eines unterhaltungsliterarischen Genres von 1945-1979* (Munich: Wilhelm Fink, 1982), p. 13.

[7] Klaus Walther, "Acht Anmerkungen," in *Marsmenschen: Kosmische und kybernetische Abenteuer*, ed. Klaus Walther (Berlin: Das Neue Berlin, 1966), p. 371.

[8] Walther, pp. 373-75.

[9] Heidtmann, p. 122.

neither productive of nor anathema to a truly humane society. Here computers and robots serve largely as tools for handling great amounts of complex data. In Christa Wolf's "Selbstversuch" (1973),[10] scientists use the computer to plan and evaluate their sex change experiment. In Alfred Leman and Hans Taubert's "Gastgeschenk" (1973),[11] computers receive and store information about the Transsolars sent from space ships to radio telescopes and store further data as well as performing linguistic analysis when the extraterrestrials meet humans. Both Leman and Taubert's "Parallelen"[12] and Frank Töppe's "Die letzten Bilder des Grafikers Schneider" (1978)[13] contain space ship computers which analyze expedition data.

Several works present a positive image of computers and robots. The most glowing portrayal occurs in Karl-Heinz Tuschel's *Die Insel der Roboter* (1973).[14] One of the few works actually set in the GDR, this novel describes a project to develop stochastic robots in the 1990s in order to bring about a revolution in socialist industry which would enable Comecon to achieve "das absolute Übergewicht auf allen Gebieten" and thereby assure peace by making imperialist attacks impossible (pp. 276-77). Although technical problems arise in training the robots, the socialist characters are confident that they can be solved. The team takes steps, to be sure, to prevent the robots from harming humans, but, given the precautions, the team members never fear the robots and consider them forces for future good. The only negative comments on this new technology come from the West: a

[10] Christa Wolf, "Selbstversuch: Traktat zu einem Protokoll," in her *Unter den Linden: Drei unwahrscheinliche Geschichten* (Berlin/Weimar: Aufbau, 1973), pp. 97-133. Subsequent references to this work will be given parenthetically in the text, as will references to other works of primary literature discussed below after the first citing.

[11] Alfred Leman and Hans Taubert, "Gastgeschenk," in their *Das Gastgeschenk der Transsolaren* (Berlin: Neues Leben, 1973), pp. 142-49; rpt. in *Von einem anderen Stern: Science-Fiction-Geschichten aus der DDR*, ed. Horst Heidtmann, dtv phantastica, 1874 (Munich: dtv, 1981), pp. 124-29.

[12] Alfred Leman and Hans Taubert, "Parallelen," in *Die andere Zukunft: Phantastische Erzählungen aus der DDR*, ed. Franz Rottensteiner, Suhrkamp Phantastische Bibliothek, 66 (Frankfurt/M.: Suhrkamp, 1982), pp. 78-105.

[13] Frank Töppe, "Die letzten Bilder des Grafikers Schneider," *Neue Deutsche Literatur*, 24, No. 12 (1976), 98-136; rpt. in *Von einem anderen Stern*, pp. 130-70.

[14] Karl-Heinz Tuschel, *Die Insel der Roboter* (Berlin: Militärverlag, 1973).

New York Times article suggests that robots might do away with humans (p. 79), and a Nobel laureate predicts the subjugation of humans by the machines (p. 210). However, the socialist heroes of this spy thriller regard these warnings only as efforts to sabotage their project and hence the triumph of socialism and peace.

Whereas *Die Insel der Roboter* stresses the economic advantages of robotized industry, with peace as a secondary benefit, Stefan Heym's "MAX und DAISY" (1984)[15] focuses on achieving peace by computers. He depicts the development of MAX and DAISY, the first two computers with free will, by a wise professor whose country's top general needs special computers for his rockets. When MAX and DAISY realize that the general plans to program rockets to destroy the enemy in a first strike, MAX makes a conference call to computers all over the world. All agree that people who use computers for military purposes will destroy the earth and human life, so MAX sends a new program to the conferees. When both sides launch their attack, MAX's program annihilates every rocket and nuclear warhead in the world, establishing peace. Since then, Heym's fairy tale concludes, "alle Computer [haben] einen eigenen Willen, und die Menschen bemühen sich, es ihnen gleichzutun" (p. 96). His story clearly warns against military use of computers, thus reflecting the fears of writers like Irmtraud Morgner and Christa Wolf that computers could unleash a nuclear war by accident,[16] yet it includes an unusual twist because these computers actually make the world more humane.

Carlos Rasch's "Das unirdische Raumschiff" (1967) depicts computers and robots quite positively as well. Here the "Lebende," inhabitants of the star system Epsilon Eridani, have an advanced, automated society.[17] Unlike humans, who

---

[15] Stefan Heym, "MAX und DAISY," in his *Märchen für kluge Kinder* (Munich: Goldmann, 1984), pp. 88-96.

[16] See Irmtraud Morgner, *Amanda: Ein Hexenroman* (Berlin/Weimar: Aufbau, 1983), p. 200; Christa Wolf, *Voraussetzungen einer Erzählung: Kassandra*, Frankfurter Poetik-Vorlesungen, Sammlung Luchterhand, 456 (Darmstadt/Neuwied: Luchterhand, 1983), p. 87; and my article "Literature 'in der Stunde vor der Dunkelheit': GDR Authors Address the Issues of War and Peace," in *Studies in GDR Culture and Society 5* (Lanham/New York/London: University Press of America, 1985), pp. 310-11.

[17] Carlos Rasch, "Das unirdische Raumschiff," in his *Das unirdische Raumschiff*, Das neue Abenteuer, Heft 258 (Berlin: Neues Leben, 1967); rpt. in *Die andere Zukunft*, pp. 182-230. Page references are to the reprint.

are fascinated by technology and have reached only the first stage of the "Hohe Reife," the more mature "Lebende" reject such "Technizismus" (p. 221), but nevertheless employ technology extensively yet discreetly, where it is needed (p. 202). Computers and robots play three major roles here. The "kybernetische Hauptstation für Lingumatik" analyzes language samples obtained from the earth ship that has penetrated their star system and develops a "Verständigungswandler" to facilitate communication with the humans (p. 207). The robot Sem 3 Set teleports his image to the earth ship unbeknownst to the "Lebende" and talks with the commander in a highly colloquial style which the linguistic analysis has determined is the way humans speak. However, not only is no harm done, but Sem 3 Set saves the crew by detecting the peril they are in, taking back vital information for analysis by complex computer systems, and arranging for another ship, the Relais 9, to rescue the humans. This incident represents an unusual comic version of the dreaded notion that a robot might act autonomously. Vern 7 Mol, the "Steuerkybernet" (p. 216) of the Relais 9, demonstrates the third major role of computers and robots in this story. He controls the entire functioning of the ship, and his help and that of computers on his planet enable the humans to learn what has happened to the second earth ship and to go to its aid. Rasch's computers and robots interact well with the "Lebende," who have very human characteristics, and facilitate the high quality of life of this enlightened race. By implication, these aliens will help humans to develop a mature technological civilization in which computers and robots will be compatible with a humane society.

Günter and Johanna Braun's *Der Irrtum des Großen Zauberers* (1972)[18] also predicts a future in which computers and robots will be used to enhance human life, although most of the novel portrays the oppression that results when these machines are subverted to evil. Naida, one of the magician's opponents, expresses this positive vision: "[I]ch finde Maschinen fabelhaft. . . . Es müßten Maschinen sein, durch die wir alle Zeit gewinnen, zum Beispiel für die Liebe . . . . Was für Maschinen es geben soll, darf kein Multiplikato bestimmen, sondern wir . . . das Volk von Plikato"; and her co-conspirator Alcedo explains further: "sie müßten gemeinsames Eigentum

---

[18] Günter and Johanna Braun, *Der Irrtum des Großen Zauberers* (Berlin: Neues Leben, 1972); rpt. Suhrkamp Phantastische Bibliothek, 74 (Frankfurt/M.: Suhrkamp, 1982). Page references are to the Suhrkamp edition.

werden, alle müßten für sie verantwortlich sein, und alle müßten anteilig für sie aufkommen" (pp. 155 f.). Thus, the Brauns postulate an automated socialist society in which machines owned by the people serve the common good.

While positive portrayals of computers and robots in GDR works often reflect dreams of a peaceful and economically productive socialist future, negative depictions are more frequent and address fears common to both East and West. Although the machines themselves are neither good nor bad, the negative treatment reveals great concern about their possible misuse. Several authors fear that virtual deification of this technology will blind people to its dangers and problems. Christa Wolf alludes to this fear in "Selbstversuch" by mentioning the "reverence" with which a cyberneticist feeds his computer (p. 120), while in her "Neue Lebensansichten eines Katers" (1970) a character states: "[M]an solle der Rechenautomatik nicht auf ähnlich verzückte Weise gegenüberstehen wie die ersten Christen ihrer Heilslehre."[19] Similarly, the protagonist in Günter and Johanna Braun's "Der Fehlfaktor" (1975) finally recognizes that adoration at the shrine of "total perfection" in the form of the "Maschinengott" has prevented him and his team from eliminating the error factor in the great computer.[20] The Brauns' *Der Irrtum des Großen Zauberers* provides a classic example of this danger in the magician's striving to become "gottähnlich, also maschinenähnlich" (p. 192).

Even isolated problems raised by individual authors echo concerns familiar to Westerners. For example, a character in Rasch's generally positive "Das unirdische Raumschiff" suggests that dependence on computers and robots may destroy the ability to think for oneself (pp. 216-17), and Anne, in Klaus Wohlrabe's "Korrektur der Vergangenheit" (1975), points to the related problem of overspecialization in an age when only computers are generalists: "Wie sieht denn unser Fortschritt aus? Eine idiotische Ansammlung von Superspezialisten, nur die Speicher haben die Übersicht. Kein Mensch könnte das Ganze mehr erfassen. Arbeiten wir für die

---

[19] Christa Wolf, "Neue Lebensansichten eines Katers," in her *Unter den Linden*, p. 80.

[20] Günter and Johanna Braun, "Der Fehlfaktor," in their *Der Fehlfaktor: Utopisch-phantastische Erzählungen*, 2nd ed. (Berlin: Das Neue Berlin, 1976), pp. 177-78. See also Heidtmann, p. 88.

Speicher?"[21] And in Johannes Conrad's "Basemeier und die Außerirdischen" (1977) a night porter complains that computerization has gone too far "für einen normalen Menschenverstand" now that his bank account and the number of his personal identity card are monitored by machine.[22]

A double problem mentioned occasionally is the anthropomorphization of computers and robots and the danger of people becoming automatons. Many works demonstrate anthropomorphization without commenting on it, but a few criticize it. The professor in Tuschel's *Die Insel der Roboter* constantly inveighs against the practice (pp. 60, 112, et passim), and a character in Rasch's "Das unirdische Raumschiff" advises erasing Sem 3 Set's memory bank of feelings because "Der Roboter ist kein Spielzeug, sondern ein Spezialgerät . . ." (p. 186). Gerhard Branstner's "Der verliebte Roboter" (1974)[23] uses fear of robot attack to illustrate the dangers of anthropomorphization, albeit for comic effect: here Oskar, a robot which loves to imitate people and has been secretly programmed by Dr. Karmen's jealous rival, mimics the doctor's pursuit of a female technician, and Karmen ·angrily destroys the speech center in Oskar's chest with a hammer. Karmen sustains a crushed clavicle rather than a fatal head injury from Oskar's reprisal since the robot understands the form but not the intent of Karmen's attack (pp. 180-81). The robot itself bears no malice, yet the story offers a serious warning about anthropomorphization.

The fear of degrading people to automatons is realized in Leman and Taubert's "Gastgeschenk" when volunteers become "lebende Datenspeicher" for Transsolars studying human reactions (p. 129). In *Der Irrtum des Großen Zauberers* the Brauns play on this fear: the magician chooses women by a computerized pattern with the intent of replacing them with "Maschinenfrauen" (pp. 124-25), and he wants to make elite humans, including himself, like machines (pp. 87, 181). Several stories address this concern in terms of computer

21 Klaus Wohlrabe, "Korrektur der Vergangenheit," in *Der Mann vom Anti*, ed. E. Redlin (Berlin: Das Neue Berlin, 1975), pp. 292-333; quoted from the reprint in *Von einem anderen Stern*, p. 204.

22 Johannes Conrad, "Basemeier und die Außerirdischen," in his *Vom Marsflug zurück, General!* (Berlin: Eulenspiegel, 1977), pp. 12-18; quoted from the reprint in *Von einem anderen Stern*, p. 243.

23 Gerhard Branstner, "Der verliebte Roboter," in his *Der verliebte Roboter* (Berlin: 1974); rpt. in *Die andere Zukunft*, pp. 172-81. Page references are to the reprint.

regulation of humans. In Stefan Heym's "Die Computerfrau" (1983), for example, a man deals with his wife's frequent mood swings by having implanted in her brain an emotional pacemaker which is "programmed for harmony" and equipped with a "Fernregler" that lets him evoke the desired emotional responses.[24] thus turning her into a kind of "Maschinenfrau." Since the man proves unable to tolerate a programmed wife until he also has the operation, Heym's story suggests that programming emotions is incompatible with real humanity and warns against using computers to regulate the human mind.

The danger of computer regulation of humans also informs Christa Wolf's "Neue Lebensansichten eines Katers." Here a presumably GDR research group tries to develop "ein logisches, unausweichliches, einzig richtiges System der rationellen Lebensführung unter Anwendung der modernsten Rechentechnik" (p. 80) with the aim of establishing "TOTALES MENSCHENGLÜCK" (p. 68). To create the "Normalmensch" (p. 90) compatible with this computerized system, the group must eliminate many human characteristics, such as "schöpferisches Denken" (p. 91), "Wagemut, Selbstlosigkeit, Barmherzigkeit," "Überzeugungstreue," "Phantasie," "Schönheitsempfinden" (p. 92), "Vernunft," and "Sexus" (p. 93), and even then fails to achieve a "Reflexwesen" acceptable to the computer (p. 87). Clearly, Wolf uses the term "Normalmensch" ironically since the resultant creature would be neither normal nor human. By showing that only beings who react with absolute consistency are suitable for this computerized system she suggests that they would essentially be machines. Thus, she offers a pessimistic view of the computer as antithetical to a truly humane society and especially cautions against using it for human engineering.

Some works focus on the effect of computers on the will and emotions in other ways. In the Brauns' "Der Fehlfaktor," for example, the Central Computer Center exerts a soporific effect on its workers. Overcome by a "Gefühl des Wohlbehagens" (p. 179) and convinced that "Es läuft wunderbar" (p. 171), even the team sent to find and eliminate the error factor must leave the oppressive environment in order to apply its critical thinking capacities and fulfill its mission. Thus, although the protagonist initially regards the computer

---

[24] Stefan Heym, "Die Computerfrau," in his *Gesammelte Erzählungen* (Munich: Goldmann, 1984), p. 377.

as an eighth wonder of the world (p. 154), its deleterious effects on the human will, mind, and emotions suggest that it may be more harmful than beneficial. Franz Fühmann echoes this concern in "Die Ohnmacht" (1976)[25] where a computer enables experimentees to glimpse their near future briefly, although they cannot change it. The results are bad for all concerned: an experimentee suffers a feeling of "Ohnmacht" when he cannot alter the fixed future (p. 104); the computer operator, depressed by the experimentees' reactions and their inability to change the future, turns to drink, dulling his distress and even his own humanity; and his assistant becomes so angry because neither the computer nor its operator feel compassion for a child in danger that he destroys the computer. Again an author does not criticize the machine itself, but questions its effect on human beings.

A humorous reversal of this concern appears in the Brauns' "Die Logikmaschine" (1967)[26] where exposure to human illogic and emotions deranges a machine. Here a computer becomes confused by a conversation about love and the desire to save an old tower despite added costs. The narrator's explanation "daß Maschinen . . . noch nicht imstande sind, Menschliches und Maschinenmäßiges auseinanderzuhalten, und es sich . . . empfehle, die Maschine abzuschalten, wenn es um die sogenannten schönen Dinge gehe" (p. 235) thus affirms the incompatibility of people and computers even though it is the machine that suffers from their encounter this time.

Another issue raised frequently in these works and familiar to Western readers is the concern about a totally computerized society. Although a few works, like Rasch's "Das unirdische Raumschiff" and, by implication, Tuschel's *Die Insel der Roboter*, postulate that such a society would enhance the quality of life, most authors treat the theme negatively and often depict rebellion against inhumane and tyrannical aspects of complete automation. In the Brauns' "Die Logikmaschine" this rebellion takes the minor form of wearing a long beard, which the narrator describes as "sehr unpraktisch . . . aber sehr beliebt . . . wie alles Unpraktische

[25] Franz Fühmann, "Die Ohnmacht," *Sinn und Form*, 28, No. 1 (1976), 86-108; rpt. in *Von einem anderen Stern*, pp. 100-123. Page references are to the reprint.
[26] Günter and Johanna Braun, "Die Logikmaschine," *Das Magazin*, 14, No. 7 (1967), 14-16; rpt. in *Die andere Zukunft*, pp. 231-35, which is cited here.

im Zeitalter der absoluten Rationalisierung" (p. 232). The same authors' *Der Irrtum des Großen Zauberers* best exemplifies the nightmare of a totally computerized society despite predicting that this technology could serve the common good. Here a megalomaniac replaces human workers by computers and robots. The people daily consume a pear juice concoction which addles their brains and makes them tractable. They clearly live a miserable existence, although most are too drugged to realize it. Ultimately, a rebellion is necessary to place people in control of the machines. In spite of the happy ending the novel warns that computers and robots can be used for evil and that an automated society in the hands of a madman could prove most inhumane.

Karlheinz Steinmüller's "Der Traum vom Großen Roten Fleck" (1979)[27] focuses on the loss of uniquely human characteristics in a computerized world in earth's future. All aspects of life are automated: transportation, apartments, food selection and delivery, communication, choice of sex partner, etc. Even the language is based on a computer language, and the central computer provides everything "[b]is auf einen eigenen Willen, eigene Gedanken" (p. 182). The occasionally anachronistic behavior of some people reflects their unfulfilled need for human companionship and a truly human lifestyle. As the narrator explains: "[N]och brauchen wir von Zeit zu Zeit das Gefühl, in einer Masse, unter anderen Menschen zu sein" (p. 174). Some people, who call themselves "Drachen," recognize the impossibility of living like real human beings in this world and foresee the inevitable failure of the central computer system, but the narrator refuses to join their conspiracy to start "einen neuen Weg für die Menschheit" on Ganymede (p. 181). Too adapted to his society, he regards the "Drachen" as irrational enemies of the system and knows he could not stand the life they offer: "Ständig dieselben Gesichter erblicken, . . . gemeinsam essen und reden, reden, reden" (p. 185). Whether the narrator's contact with the conspiracy is real or imaginary, Steinmüller clearly exposes the incompatibility between complete automation and a truly humane society.[28]

---

[27] Karlheinz Steinmüller, "Der Traum vom Großen Roten Fleck," in his *Der letzte Tag auf der Venus*, Kompaß-Bücherei, 247 (Berlin: Neues Leben, 1979), pp. 91-108; rpt. in *Von einem anderen Stern*, pp. 171-86, which is cited here.

[28] See Heidtmann's comment on descriptions of "eine Reduzierung menschlicher Lebensqualität in vollautomatisierten . . . Welten" in works by Steinmüller and the Brauns in the 1970s, p. 122.

The fear of the effects of total computerization on human beings reaches its logical conclusion in Helga Königsdorf's fairy tale "Der kleine Prinz und das Mädchen mit den holzfarbenen Augen" (1982),[29] for here an intergalactic computer controls the universe. In this adaptation of Saint-Exupéry's *Le petit prince*, the prince, who wants to become a human being, must apply to the computer, which administers the "zweckgerichtete intensivierte terrestrische Evolutionskonzeption" (p. 232) based on its determination of an "optimales Menschheitsspektrum" (p. 227). It decides who will be born and establishes a normed human race governed by daily hormone regulation. Rejected because his constant questioning, individualism, and insufficient optimism violate the norms, the prince is far more human than the beings the computer accepts. Thus, Königsdorf voices the concern that computerization could lead to machine control of people and destroy the very characteristics that make them human.

This study has shown then that GDR works depict extensive automation, although few of them treat the GDR itself in the present, but focus on future life on earth and extraterrestrial civilizations. Some are neutral on computers and robots, regarding them as necessary tools; a few view this technology favorably as the means to achieve increased economic productivity, peace, and a high quality of life, and some of these positive portrayals are GDR-specific. Most works studied, however, depict computers and robots negatively and express concerns about them common to both East and West, including uncritical idolization of technology; anthropomorphization of machines and mechanization of people; robot attack; pernicious effects on the human mind, will and emotions; the human consequences of a totally computerized society; and computer control of the universe. Such concerns reflect fears that imprudent, extensive computerization may prove incompatible with human beings and a truly humane lifestyle. As the GDR becomes more automated, it will be interesting to see whether the hopes and fears of these authors are realized and what changes the literary image of computers and robots will undergo. Even writers of *Belletristik* will likely contribute to this image in greater numbers as computerization increasingly affects their society.

---

[29] Helga Königsdorf, "Der kleine Prinz und das Mädchen mit den holzfarbenen Augen," in her *Der Lauf der Dinge* (Berlin/Weimar: Aufbau, 1982); rpt. in *Der Holzwurm und der König: Märchenhaftes und Wundersames für Erwachsene*, ed. Klaus Hammer (Halle/Leipzig: Mitteldeutscher Verlag, 1985), pp. 224-45, which is cited here.

Science Fiction in the GDR:
A Comparative Approach

H.-J. Schulz

The extensive and continuing attention paid to the literature of the GDR by American and West European Germanists is indicative of a number of questions, both implied and explicitly posed, which go beyond problems of textuality. How vital can a literature be in a planned socialist society, i.e., to what extent is it confined to affirmative ideological functions and to what extent can it fulfill its negative .function of displacing the historical moment against a vision of possibility and thus uncover the complex historicity of that moment's ideological closures, of its "strategies of containment." A central version of this question is, of course, the question of the autonomy of the literary discourse within the total structure of GDR society. The emergence of a vital, complex, and innovative literature in the GDR, appropriating and refunctionalizing a large repertoire of thematic and formal traditions, exploring forms of private alienation, and expanding the range of fictionalization into the fantastic, has challenged a number of Western preconceptions. One of the effects of this process has been, for some, a redirecting of attention to the commodification of Western literature and to the relative absence of public reasoning, in the West, about literature's social functions.

With the exception of Horst Heidtmann's well-documented book,[1] little work has been done in the West on GDR science fiction and its development. One of the reasons may well be the predominantly paraliterary form of the genre in the West and its frequent dismissal as homogeneously re-

---

[1] Horst Heidtmann, *Utopisch-phantastische Literatur in der DDR. Untersuchungen zur Entwicklung eines unterhaltungsliterarischen Genres von 1945-1979* (Munich: Wilhelm Fink, 1982).

gressive and escapist. This dismissal represses the ideological complexity of the genre and those emancipatory and utopian tendencies which are among its constituent elements. A comparison of Western and GDR science fiction could help to open up the closed rigidity of our preconceptions of Western paraliterary science fiction.

The development of science fiction in the GDR, and the public reasoning that has accompanied it, reflect many of the central concerns of GDR literary theory and practice of the last thirty-five years:

1. Science fiction in the GDR is generally considered entertainment literature. Its early development took place in juvenile novel series and magazines. It is not surprising then that as a genre it was neglected in the critical debate during the first decades of the GDR: in this phase, the individually and socially redeeming qualities of entertainment seemed to be incompatible with the individual's non-alienated existence in a socialist state.[2] The validation of these qualities came only with the full recognition (in theory and literary practice) of the existence of "non-antagonistic" problems in present-day socialist society. Thus, despite the example of a flourishing Soviet science fiction, the genre did not emerge as a viable form until the liberalizing tendencies of the 1960s and 1970s.

2. In the GDR, as in the Federal Republic, science fiction had to live down the tradition of the *Zukunftsroman* (exemplified by Hans Dominik), in which the genre had become identified with a chauvinistic ideology. This association reinforced an official GDR *Utopiefeindlichkeit* based on the theory that classical utopian thought and imagination had been replaced by scientific socialism.[3] The rigidity of this notion ignores the multiplicity of cognitive functions which have traditionally characterized this genre. Measured against a concept of utopian narrative which reduces the genre to systematic sociopolitical intentionality and preparation for social praxis, the often playful manipulations of historical, social,

---

[2] Compare Horst Slomma's orthodox *Sinn und Kunst der Unterhaltung* (Berlin: Henschel, 1971) with Ekkehard Redlin's discussion of the entertainment value of science fiction: "Entpflichtung im Nirgendwo: Zum Unterhaltungswert der utopischen Literatur," in *Lichtjahr 3* (Berlin: Das Neue Berlin, 1984), 91-107.

[3] See Werner Krauss's symptomatic essay, "Geist und Widergeist der Utopien," *Sinn und Form*, 14, Nos. 5/6 (1962), 769-99.

technological, and biological reality of science fiction appeared to be incomplete, ideologically defective, unscientific, and thus a caricature of utopian intentionality. This conception of science fiction reflects that of certain West German Marxists who, following Schwonke's and Krysmanski's theories of science fiction as the modern, pluralistic form of utopian literature,[4] unmasked modern Western science fiction as a perversion and betrayal of utopian intentionality. This interpretation ignores the fact that the aesthetic and narrative requirements of the genre are not the same as those of the classical utopian novel of the 19th century and that the range of fictional displacements of reality in science fiction has always exceeded socio-political concerns.

3. These attitudes of GDR critics concerning the social value of entertainment and the obsolescence of the utopian imagination imposed very narrow parameters on science fiction in the early years of the Republic. These restrictions were reinforced by the suppression of *Phantasie* as a dialectical counterpart to the narrow representational functions assigned to literature by earlier concepts of socialist realism. Lehmann's book on *Phantasie und künstlerische Arbeit*,[5] which attempts to legitimize imagination as an essential component of all mental work and stresses its unfettered intentionality (as a "spielerische Unvernunft"), is an excellent example of the later process of de-ideologizing the concept of *Phantasie*. With the appropriation of bourgeois humanistic literary traditions, a further upgrading of the formative functions of literature (as a complement to phenomenological reflection) takes place.[6] This development accentuates the fact, particularly important for early GDR science fiction, that the right world view does not guarantee literary quality and that the functions of a text are not confined to its represen-

---

[4] Martin Schwonke, *Vom Staatsroman zur Science Fiction* (Stuttgart: Ferdinand Enke, 1957); Hans-Jürgen Krysmanski, *Die utopische Methode. Eine literatur- und wissenssoziologische Untersuchung utopischer Romane des 20. Jahrhunderts* (Cologne/Opladen: Westdeutscher Verlag, 1963).

[5] Günther Lehmann, *Phantasie und künstlerische Arbeit: Betrachtungen zur poetischen Phantasie*, 2nd ed. (Berlin/Weimar: Aufbau, 1976). First appeared in 1965.

[6] Robert Weimann, *"Phantasie und Nachahmung." Drei Studien zum Verhältnis von Dichtung, Utopie und Mythos* (Halle: Mitteldeutscher Verlag, 1970).

tational content.[7] The rehabilitation of traditional works of fantasy in the GDR also opened up the full range of displacement functions of the genre (satiric, prognostic, utopian, epistemological).

The evolution of GDR science fiction proceeded from the cold-war thrillers and novels exploring the immediate future to a full realization of the generic potential of science fiction in the 1960s and 1970s. GDR science fiction now shares a large formal and thematic repertoire with Western science fiction. This development parallels the process of differentiation in other literary genres in the GDR and therefore provides a generically specific access to the development of GDR literary culture. Beyond this aspect, a study of GDR science fiction and its comparison with Western paraliterary science fiction opens up an additional area of investigation. One of the main generic constituents of science fiction is its fictional exploration of "otherness," especially of possible social and political futures. On the surface, the difference between GDR and Western paraliterary science fiction seems absolute in this regard: one presupposes a known and positive future, the other experiments (without obvious intentionality) with a multiplicity of apparently equivalent futures. This difference is revealed at first glance in the dominant tone of each corpus (optimism vs. pessimism). But both conceptions of the future (one "given," the other "open") are subject to ideological closure. Both forms of science fiction, as their principal "generic act," open up a future enclosed in the ideology of the present; both forms are characterized by the interaction of "dissimultaneous" (Bloch) ideological strains encoded in various generic strains (e.g., the social-critical impetus of utopian fiction and the affirmative and "escapist" functions of juvenile adventure literature). A comparison of the science fiction of East and West, then, not only accentuates the difference in dominant ideologies and social function but enhances our understanding of the generic stability of science fiction and its utopian displacements of ideological images of the present.

Much of Western commercial science fiction, and practically all the criticism that has been produced within its paraliterary system, show a pronounced aversion toward what is known as "propaganda." Under this concept are subsumed

<hr>

[7] Olaf R. Spittel, "Von fremden und bekannten Sternen," *Temperamente*, 4/1980, 145-57; Heinz Entner, "Musterung einer Gattung. Utopische Literatur eines Jahrzehnts," *Neue Deutsche Literatur*, 24, No. 12 (1976), 137-53.

certain explicit forms of social criticism and, even more so, those depictions of alternate social organizations which carry a clear intentional message. At least superficially, Western science fiction is guided by the idea of the "open universe of science fiction" which allows the author the "freedom" to experiment freely with any fictional idea, and to do so without "ideological restrictions."[8] Common sense and the textual evidence, of course, do not support this fiction of an experimental freedom beyond ideology. The commercial writer of science fiction, more so perhaps than the writer of "high literature," is subject to the limits imposed by dominant ideologies. As a matter of fact, the social orientations of older commercial science fiction, as especially West German critics have shown, tend to be regressive: forms of feudalism and 19th-century competitive capitalism prevail; and, especially in the 1950s, chauvinistic and quasi-fascist tendencies were very much in evidence.[9] More important in this context is the fact, however, that the generic peculiarity of science fiction, to fictionally displace existent forms of social life and the notions which validate them, frees critical energies and leaves these forms and values in question. This is not necessarily evidenced by such stereotypes of commercial science fiction as a world-wide confederation of nations, elimination of racial prejudice, and the emancipation of women: in most cases, as in early GDR science fiction, such values of progressive social humanism remain abstract and incidental to narrative concerns. But postwar Western science fiction, although rarely programmatically progressive, is replete with displacements and satiric exposures of contemporary social phenomena.

The simultaneous existence of emancipatory and utopian tendencies (inherent in the very structure of the genre) and the suppression of these tendencies in the quasi-official ideology of the Western science fiction system is symptomatic

---

[8] See the so-called Marxism debate ("Change, SF, and Marxism: Open or Closed Universes") by various authors and critics: *Science-Fiction Studies*, 1 (1973-74), 84-98, 213-14, 269-76.

[9] There are three major West German studies of the ideology of commercial science fiction: Michael Pehlke and Norbert Lingfeld, *Roboter und Garten-laube. Ideologie und Unterhaltung in der Science-Fiction-Literatur* (Munich: Hanser, 1970); Manfred Nagl, *Science Fiction in Deutschland. Untersuchung zur Genese, Soziographie und Ideologie der phantastischen Massenliteratur* (Tübingen: Verein für Volkskunde, 1972); Horst Schröder, *Science Fiction Literatur in den USA. Vorstudien für eine materialistische Paraliteraturwissenschaft* (Gießen: Focus, 1978).

of the complex ideological structure of science fiction as a paraliterary system. The fiction of the ideological neutrality of Western science fiction is supported by the (largely unexamined) assumption of an ideologically bound and "unfree" science fiction in the socialist countries. This assumption became modified as the works of the Strugatski brothers and Lem appeared on the American market but still persists implicitly in the ideology of the "open universe." The remarkable process of formal, thematic, and aesthetic differentiation which science fiction has undergone in the socialist countries is largely unknown to Western readers and is hardly recognized by Western critics. It has had little effect so far on our ability to recognize the complexity of ideologically affirmative and emancipatory elements in Western paraliterary science fiction, to view its texts as concretizations of dissimultaneous ideological strains.

Science fiction in the GDR underwent its evolutionary process in the span of fifteen to twenty years; it repeated and varied, in concentrated form, the development of Soviet science fiction since 1917. GDR science fiction started in the 1950s without a positive national tradition to provide stable generic parameters. Since the German *Zukunftsroman* had been discredited, authors turned to adventure fiction for plot structures and conventions of characterization. Especially espionage and detective fiction seemed to suit the purpose of extrapolating into the immediate future real and assumed threats to the young socialist state. Here the perceived function of the genre, as a weapon in the cold war, totally suppressed its utopian and satiric potential and trivialized the social and political reality it presumed to reflect: sinister Western agents, in search of scientific secrets or on errands of sabotage, are defeated by virtuous heroes; and the cause of peace and socialism is saved by individual heroic action.[10] A variant of this form of early science fiction is the transfer of a trivialized form of international antagonisms to other planets where capitalist regimes (usually peculiar mixtures of high capitalism and feudalism) succumb to the righteous revolution of workers or slaves, aided by terran socialists.[11]

---

[10] H.L. Fahlberg's *Erde ohne Nacht* (Berlin: Das Neue Berlin, 1956) may serve as a paradigmatic example.

[11] Ludwig Turek's *Die goldene Kugel* (Berlin: Dietz, 1949), the first major science fiction work in the GDR, seems to have legitimized this kind of escapist adventure science fiction: its superficial portrayal of character, society, and social processes and its *deus-ex-machina* solution to social problems prefigure much of the science fiction of the 1950s.

The point of this description of early, cold-war science fiction is not to belittle its function as propaganda or to chastise its quality. What makes these texts interesting is a comparison with Western texts from the same period. We recognize similarities in the suppression and deformation of science fiction's utopian potential under the pressure of political conditions, a pronounced tendency toward preservation of ideological closures. The displacement function of science fiction is deformed in a "contestation," to use Macherey's term,[12] with values (such as "freedom," "peace," and "social justice") which have degenerated to character stereotypes and stereotypical plot-patterns. The fact that the early GDR texts propagate a superior social morality does not affect their aesthetic quality: stereotypes here are narrative and figural forms of ideological closure, and these texts confirm these closures rather than displace them.

This type of science fiction did not remain the dominant form in the GDR for long, but some of its ideologically charged stereotypes persisted into the 1960s. The changes which occurred in the second half of the 1960s came in response to general liberalizing tendencies as well as to the increased presence of Soviet science fiction, and expressed themselves, in part, in a criticism which implied an "ideology criticism" of cold-war science fiction. The list of charges raised reads like an implied program for the science fiction of the future and offers considerable similarities with standard criticism of Western science fiction: the simplification of real social and political problems and of their solutions; the poverty of characterization, allowing complex plots but no complex motivations; the depiction of the far future as technologically superior to the present but otherwise identical with it; the emphasis on technological solutions to human problems; and finally and perhaps most importantly, the charge that science fiction writers frequently assume that the right *Weltanschauung* guarantees literary quality.[13] In terms of the methodological premises of this paper, this rising self-consciousness within the science fiction community can be summarized as an awareness that science fiction so far had

[12] See Pierre Macherey, *A Theory of Literary Production*, trans. Geoffrey Wall (London: Routledge & Kegan Paul, 1978), passim.

[13] See, for instance, Redlin (Note 2), Spittel and Entner (Note 7); Heinz Entner, "Gut gemeint - gut gemacht?" *Neue Deutsche Literatur*, 27, No. 7 (1979), 153-58; and Bernd Ulbrich, "Die sogenannte utopische Methode oder Vehementes Plädoyer für eine SF," *Neue Deutsche Literatur*, 29, No. 11 (1981), 161-64.

ignored, if not falsified, the power inherent in the genre to displace the many forms of closure that characterize the ideology of the moment.

Of special importance was the charge that science fiction either depicted the present in terms of a trivialized past or posited an abstract future in which all present-day problems had already been solved. The present, as a manifestation of the imminent future, was ignored by science fiction. Carlos Rasch responded to this state of affairs with his own version of the earlier Soviet *Theorie der Nahziele*, his program of science fiction as *Realphantastik*, a concept he demonstrated programmatically with his novel *Im Schatten der Tiefsee* (1965).[14] This kind of science fiction attempts to depict, on the basis of authentic scientific and technological developments, the solution of problems facing socialist society. The novel reminds us of the naive gadget-science fiction of Jules Verne and the technocratic speculations of American science fiction in its "golden age" of the 1940s and early 1950s. Its presumption to contribute speculatively to the advancement of socialist science and technology, of course, reduces narrative to a disposable vehicle and turns fiction into "hypothesis." The communist reality of Rasch's future is taken for granted but not shown; the science is abstract; bureaucracy has been replaced by sources of instant and total administrative efficiency; and the novel's central problem is finally solved by a *deus-ex-machina*. The novel, which deals with the attempt to raise algae in the Baltic Sea, reduces the problems of the future to the naive quantities of production figures and seems to attempt, in the words of two GDR critics, "mit phantastischen Techniken phantastisch hohe, aber eben auch bloß phantastische Produktionserfolge zu erzielen."[15] The novel's "hypothesis," seen against the background of the then chronic shortages of consumer goods, turns out to be a form of effortless wish-fulfillment whose gesture of ideological closure is painfully obvious.

Rasch's *Realphantastik*, along with other undifferentiated forms of socialist realism, rejects fantastic elements by equating fictional departures from empirical reality and from

---

[14] Carlos Rasch, *Im Schatten der Tiefsee* (Berlin: Das Neue Berlin, 1965).

[15] Erik Simon and Olaf R. Spittel, *Science-fiction: Personalia zu einem Genre in der DDR* (Berlin: Das Neue Berlin, 1982), p. 60. Eberhardt del'Antonio's *Projekt Sahara* (Berlin: Tribüne, 1962), a similar science-fictional *Produktionsroman*, may have served as a model for Rasch.

scientific norms with escapism. But fantastic literature questions this concept of realism since it is, by definition, not primarily representational. Realism is not judged by the undisplaced image of phenomenological reality but by its capacity to shed light on that reality, by whatever means.[16] Only the revision of the concept of realism, the appropriation and development of non-traditional narrative and fictional strategies, and the creative assimilation of fantastic elements in mainstream literature prepared the ground for the full realization of the generic potential of science fiction that we now witness in the GDR.

More important for the development of GDR science fiction than his pseudoscientific extrapolations are probably Rasch's well-intentioned attempts to create a foreground of rounded characters and complex relationships. But these remain incomplete and inert partly because the necessary dialectical relationship between general and specific levels (between the production theme as "ideological project" and the individual characters) is not successfully carried out. It is precisely the emphasis on this dialectical relationship which characterizes much of GDR science fiction since the late 1960s: here closed ideological, social, organizational structures are isolated in fictional futures, brought into a dialectical relationship with characters (whose individuality evolves in the course of this relationship), and are displaced and opened toward a richer future.

This "third phase" can be read, in part, as a purging of the science fiction repertoire of its worst stereotypes: the two-dimensional "positive hero" and his unreflected readiness for self-sacrifice; the stereotypical solidarity which not only overarches human differences (including gender-related ones) but levels them down to a single and singular collective will; the trivialized forms of extraterrestrial class struggle; and, central to all these, the obligation to maintain a tone of optimism and to end the tale happily. This intertextual relationship of much of current science fiction to earlier practice solidifies at times into recognizable parody: in a short sketch, "Science-fiction zum Selbermachen" (in *Der Utofant*), for instance,

---

[16] For a recognition, in GDR criticism, of the element of play in science fiction, see Paul Behla, "Was ist das - Wissenschaftliche Phantastik?" *Potsdamer Forschungen*, Ser. A, 15 (1975), 65-74; on the multiplicity of cognitive functions in science fiction, see Gustav Schröder, "Zur Geschichte der utopischen Literatur in der DDR," *Potsdamer Forschungen*, Ser. A, 16 (1975), 31-47.

Johanna and Günter Braun describe a game which allows any combination of standard science fiction ingredients; to keep the game within the prescribed mode of optimism and success, a "Negativsperre" has been incorporated. The same authors' remarkable novel *Conviva Ludibundus* reads like a detailed parody of Rasch's *Im Schatten der Tiefsee*: here the fabulous success of marine farming is magnified into a grotesque caricature of dreams of exclusively material progress.[17]

During the period of "realist" science fiction certain thematic areas of Western science fiction had been excluded as incompatible with the scientific world view science fiction was to propagate. The new science fiction, based on the realization that the value of a theme does not depend on its inert content but on the cognitive function it serves in a text, has become receptive to the full thematic repertoire developed by Western and Soviet science fiction. There are some notable examples of traditional themes being revitalized to serve new displacement functions. One theme is the encounter with alien beings. For early American commercial science fiction, the alien served as a highly ideological image of a threat to human (i.e., Western) domination; in Soviet science fiction, this encounter usually served to demonstrate (often with similar ideological simplicity) that highly developed beings necessarily meet on the basis of peaceful cooperation. Klaus Frühauf, in his novel *Stern auf Nullkurs*,[18] while ultimately accepting the latter version, uses the theme to explore the complexity and limits of anthropomorphic ideologies and the need for any social organization, including an advanced socialist one, to face its internal contradictions in order to progress. Werner Steinberg, in *Zwischen Sarg und Ararat*,[19] introduces the theme of the generation space ship to illustrate a similar problem: the danger of ideological structures surviving their proper time and conditions, becoming dogmatic, and threatening man's creative access to the past and to a new future.

As long as science fiction was primarily a juvenile genre in the GDR, conceived as a vehicle for political and scientific

[17] Johanna and Günter Braun, *Der Utofant* (Berlin: Das Neue Berlin, 1981), pp. 223-26; *Conviva Ludibundus* (Berlin: Das Neue Berlin, 1978).

[18] Klaus Frühauf, *Stern auf Nullkurs* (Berlin: Neues Leben, 1979).

[19] Werner Steinberg, *Zwischen Sarg und Ararat* (Rudolstadt: Greifenverlag, 1978).

popularization, there was little room for sophisticated playful manipulations of its generic characteristics. At this point in the evolution of GDR science fiction, the most remarkable phenomenon is the recent, rather sudden flowering of exactly this mode and the development, somewhat under Lem's influence, of a distinct subgenre: that of the playful utopian-phantastic tale. Gerhard Branstner, in *Die Reise zum Stern der Beschwingten*, argues for a "Technik der heiteren Ver-stellung" whose function is irony ("Verstellung . . . , um die Dinge richtig zu stellen") as well as "Spiel mit der Wirklich-keit."[20] Branstner's terminology serves well to describe the work of Johanna and Günter Braun, the GDR's most important contribution to international science fiction. The Brauns com-bine the "schöpferische Unvernunft" of Lewis Carrollian epis-temological displacements with shrewd exposures of certain social, organizational, and psychological structures and the ideological rigidity that preserves them. While their fictional worlds are usually tipped, in one way or another, in the direction of a recognizable convergence with our known world, on the whole their work takes advantage of the crea-tive freedom that proximity to empirical reality seldom grants. To show the sure-handed use of their large formal and thematic repertoire would require a separate essay. Let me instead outline briefly one of their dominant themes, a theme that has been at the heart of science fiction criticism for several decades: the theme of individuality and individualism.

Western science fiction and science fiction of the socialist countries have been routinely criticized for their lack of rounded characters and realistic motivation. This charge, more often than not, imposes narrow realistic standards of plot and character on fantastic literature.[21] Degree and kind of human individuality in a text are not only the result of the author's talent; they are also determined by the essential cognitive functions of the generic structure which the text realizes. Science fiction, like most forms of satire and the utopian romance, is essentially a menippean genre, i.e., it deals, in the language of Edmund Crispin, with generic, not individual problems. What superior science fiction shows, however, is that these two aspects are not mutually exclusive:

20 Gerhard Branstner, *Die Reise zum Stern der Beschwingten* (Rostock: Hin-storff, 1979), p. 183.

21 See, for instance, Ursula Le Guin, "Science Fiction and Mrs. Brown," in *Science Fiction at Large*, ed. Peter Nicholls (London: Victor Gollancz, 1976), pp. 15-33.

where fantastic literature deals with the generic phenomenon of ideology in its many manifestations, the individual becomes the natural vehicle of its displacement. This individual, to be sure, is not the individual of psychological realism but rather that individual who, in his or her specific typicality, is subject to the cognitive functions of the genre: an instrument to engage ideological structures in a dialectical relationship which identifies and imaginatively overcomes the latter's closures and empowers the former's subjectivity and freedom.

The theme of the individual who realizes his or her spontaneity, subjectivity, creativity, and privacy and a concern with questions of the meaning of life, love, and death, run through all the major works of the Brauns, from the early 1970s into the 1980s.[22] Its most impressive treatment so far is the novel *Das kugeltranszendentale Vorhaben*.[23] Here an old railwayman finds himself on a planet where language has lost its referential quality and thereby the power of judgment and discrimination that it may grant the individual. Ideology, in its essential form of language, has become totally independent of reality (the ultimate ideological closure): language has become infinitely powerful to direct and dominate the individual and the group and thereby infinitely poor in its ability to change reality and make it humane.

Both in the West and the GDR science fiction has undergone a steady process of formal and thematic growth and has developed a large and differentiated set of cognitive functions. What both have in common is the development from early forms characterized by stereotypical plots and characters transporting an unreflected ideology to a rather systematic de-ideologizing of its stock repertoire. These obvious similarities should not tempt us, however, to disregard their different social and ideological contexts in favor of an abstract formalist approach to the genre. Rather, a comparative study should emphasize the specific forms used to fictionalize and displace specific closed systems of thought. To the Western critic, the flowering of the genre in an evolving socialist system should be of particular interest. Using the two traditions

---

[22] See, for instance, *Der Irrtum des großen Zauberers* (Berlin: Neues Leben, 1972); *Bitterfisch* (Berlin: Neues Leben, 1974); *Unheimliche Erscheinungsformen auf Omega XI* (Berlin: Das Neue Berlin, 1974); *Der Fehlfaktor* (Berlin: Das Neue Berlin, 1975); *Die unhörbaren Töne* (Frankfurt/M.: Suhrkamp, 1984); *Der x-mal vervielfachte Held* (Frankfurt/M.: Suhrkamp, 1985).

[23] Johanna and Günter Braun, *Das kugeltranszendentale Vorhaben* (Frankfurt/M.: Suhrkamp, 1983).

in a mutually illuminating way would sharpen our sense of the dynamic autonomy of science fiction as a generic system and of its capacity to evoke, by its essential generic act of deviating from known or accepted reality, alternate and humaner forms of life.

Nietzsche Criticized: The GDR Takes a Second Look

Denis M. Sweet

As part of an exhibit on famous German contributors to culture in the Martin Luther House in Eisenach, there is a photograph of Friedrich Nietzsche accompanied by the following text:

> Friedrich Nietzsche: Pfarrersohn. Geboren 15.10.1844 Röcken/Sachsen, gestorben 25.8. 1900. Professor für klassische Philologie. Geistig einflußreichste Persönlichkeit des ausgehenden Jahrhunderts. Hat als Denker und Dichter zu positiver und negativer Auseinandersetzung angeregt. Werke u.a. "Also sprach Zarathustra," 1883; "Die fröhliche Wissenschaft," 1882; "Der Antichrist," 1888.

What could be more inconspicuous! There is nothing here, it would seem, to attract attention, much less to evoke controversy. It appears as if any dissension connected with this thinker had long since been worked out, as if long ago all the positive and negative influences had been recorded and investigated, discussed and settled. Suffice it to say that the exact opposite is the case. This serene summary, which leans heavily on classical associations ("das Land der Dichter und Denker"), is misleading. Friedrich Nietzsche is not a topic that has come to rest in the GDR. It would perhaps be equally misleading to say that Friedrich Nietzsche's philosophical oeuvre lies at the center of an intense debate that, far from being over, seems to have reached a new stage, yet such a statement reflects far more adequately the true state of affairs in the GDR than does the museum's precis in Eisenach.

Nietzsche's legacy poses, simply because of its refracted, contradictory, and far-flung nature, very serious problems for an adequate Marxist analysis. These problems manifested themselves from the start in opposing standpoints on Nietzsche within the working class and the Left generally. While, for example, Adolf Levenstein was collecting letters from working-class people who had been positively influenced by Nietzsche in pre-World-War-I Germany,[1] Franz Mehring was polemicizing that "die großkapitalistische Philosophie Nietzsches . . . den proletarischen Klassenkampf bekämpfte aus denselben erhebenden Gedankenkreisen heraus wie der erste beste Börsenjobber oder das erste beste Reptil."[2] Despite such polemics, working-class reception of Nietzschean ideas around the turn of the century was surprisingly widespread. His death notice in the *Sozialistische Monatshefte* reads as follows:

> Er war u n s e r. Er war nicht der Philosoph
> der zünftlerischen Romantik. . . . Er war nicht
> der Philosoph des Capitalismus. . . . Er war
> unser Prophet, ohne dass er darum wusste, und
> ohne dass wir darum wussten. Er hat geweis-
> sagt, was wir uns erarbeiten mussten: dass der
> Wert der Menschheit im Menschen liegt und
> dass jedes echte Aufwärts einen aristokrati-
> schen Sinn hat.[3]

But early working-class and Social Democratic reception of Nietzsche have only in the last few years come to be investigated at all - and that in the West.[4] Such investigations serve to highlight the narrow confines of a Nietzsche criticism in the GDR that has, with almost exclusive persistence, concentrated on three main aspects in interpreting Nietzsche's writings and their influence: imperialism, irrationalism, and fascism. These terms can be associated with the three thinkers who established a Marxist Nietzsche criticism that

---

[1] Adolf Levenstein, *Friedrich Nietzsche im Urteil der Arbeiterklasse* (Leipzig: Meiner, 1914).

[2] Franz Mehring, "Nietzsche gegen den Sozialismus," *Die Neue Zeit*, 20 January 1897; rpt. in his *Gesammelte Schriften* (Berlin: Dietz, 1983), XIII, 166.

[3] As quoted by Vivetta Vivarelli, "Das Nietzsche-Bild in der Presse der deutschen Sozialdemokratie um die Jahrhundertwende," *Nietzsche-Studien*, 13 (1984), 534.

[4] Ernst Behler, "Zur frühen sozialistischen Rezeption Nietzsches in Deutschland," *Nietzsche-Studien*, 13 (1984), 503-20; Vivetta Vivarelli, pp. 521-69.

continues in effect in the GDR to this day: Franz Mehring, Georg Lukács, and Hans Günther. But whereas they were once writing at the cutting edge of the altercation with imperialism (Mehring), National Socialism (Günther), and irrationalism (Lukács), GDR analysis has simply stuck to reiterating their argumentations.

The assessment of Nietzsche in the GDR has found no reason to proceed beyond the boundaries of a discourse essentially set in the 1890s and the pre-war and Cold War periods. If I may, I would like to refer the reader to my previous article for an account of the earlier Nietzsche criticism,[5] and proceed to the one contemporary writer who sets the official tone in the GDR in matters having to do with Nietzsche: Heinz Malorny, a philosopher at the Academy of Sciences of the GDR. Since his first article, entitled "Friedrich Nietzsche gegen den klassischen bürgerlichen Humanismus," appeared in 1978, Malorny has produced a considerable body of Nietzsche criticism, publishing at least one article every year.[6]

But what was differentiated, subtle, filled with a very palpable and human frustration in the case of Mehring, Günther, and Lukács has coalesced in the case of Malorny to a reiteration of the by now "classical" points of argument:

Nietzsche degradiert den Menschen zum Tier,
ein untrügliches Kennzeichen jedes Antihuma-

[5] Denis M. Sweet, "Friedrich Nietzsche in the GDR: A Problematic Reception," *Studies in GDR Culture and Society 4* , ed. Margy Gerber (Lanham/New York/London: University Press of America, 1984), 227-41.

[6] Heinz Malorny, "Friedrich Nietzsche gegen den klassischen bürgerlichen Humanismus," in *Philosophie und Humanismus. Beiträge zum Menschenbild der deutschen Klassik* (Weimar: Böhlau, 1978), pp. 220-34; "Tendenzen der Nietzsche-Rezeption in der BRD," *Deutsche Zeitschrift für Philosophie,* 27, No. 12 (1979), 1493-1500; "Friedrich Nietzsche und der deutsche Faschismus," in *Faschismus-Forschung. Positionen, Probleme, Polemik,* ed. Dietrich Eichholtz and Kurt Gossweiler (Berlin: Akademie, 1980), pp. 279-301; "Nietzsche-Renaissance in der Welt von Gestern," *Einheit,* 36, No. 10 (1981), 1038-45; "Friedrich Nietzsches Kritik an der Bourgeoisie und der bürgerlichen Gesellschaft," in *Traditionen des Konservatismus* (Berlin: Akademie, 1982), pp. 41-54; "Friedrich Nietzsche," in *Philosophen-Lexikon,* ed. Dietrich Alexander and Erhard Lange (Berlin: Dietz, 1982), pp. 693-98; "Vorahnung des Imperialismus - Friedrich Nietzsche," in *Falsche Propheten. Studien zum konservativ-antidemokratischen Denken im 19. und 20. Jahrhundert ,* ed. Ludwig Elm (Berlin: Akademie, 1984), pp. 74-110; "Friedrich Nietzsches Wiederkehr," *spectrum,* 16, No. 5 (1985), 25-27.

nismus. . . . Der Mensch ist für ihn ein "schmutziger Strom", das grausamste, das mißratenste, das krankhafteste Tier, das beste Raubtier, das Untier und Übertier, der "Affe Gottes", die höchste Verirrung der Natur, eine Krankheit der Erde, etwas, daß [sic] überwunden werden muß.[7]

This maleficent litany is characteristic of Malorny: stringing together snippets taken from various of Nietzsche's works as proof of a uniform (here: anti-humanist) intent. A more adequate mode of criticism has not been developed because all conclusions here are foregone conclusions: "Wir sehen allerdings in Nietzsche einen der wichtigsten geistigen Vorläufer und Wegbereiter der Philosophie und Ideologie des Imperialismus, darunter auch der faschistischen Ideologie in Deutschland."[8] With that everything has already been said.

While Malorny disclaims wanting to place Nietzsche in any immediate connection with German fascism, the pathos in his repeated reference to the victims of Auschwitz and Maidanek nonetheless makes the point vividly enough. In all fairness to Malorny, one must acknowledge a very real concern that Nietzschean concepts could be resurrected in the West as part of an increasingly anti-socialist arsenal. This would not be the first time. "Von einer Wirkungslosigkeit der reaktionären und antihumanen Ideen Nietzsches kann also keine Rede sein, die Auseinandersetzung mit ihnen ist darum eine ständige Aufgabe der marxistisch-leninistischen Gesellschaftswissenschaftler," Malorny concludes in his last article entitled "Friedrich Nietzsches Wiederkehr."[9]

But while such a starkly politicized modus of criticism is suitable for the purposes of political admonition, it is less useful as the basis for coming to a closer understanding of Nietzsche's oeuvre, particularly where a whole tradition of progressive and democratic writers and artists who were positively influenced by Nietzsche is concerned. A Marxist Nietzsche criticism such as that represented by Malorny can only register puzzlement in the face of this.

---

[7] Heinz Malorny, "Friedrich Nietzsche gegen den klassischen bürgerlichen Humanismus," p. 229.

[8] Heinz Malorny, "Friedrich Nietzsche und der deutsche Faschismus," p. 283.

[9] Heinz Malorny, "Friedrich Nietzsches Wiederkehr," p. 27.

This fact more than any other thing has made a more differentiated Nietzsche criticism seem needed for some time now. The first sign of movement in this direction was Renate Reschke's article "Kritische Aneignung und notwendige Auseinandersetzung: Zu einigen Tendenzen moderner bürgerlicher Nietzsche-Rezeption" that appeared in the July, 1983 issue of *Weimarer Beiträge*. Reschke covers the whole spectrum of Nietzsche receptions from ultra-Right to Left and comes to the conclusion that, because contemporary Marxist analysis of Nietzsche in the GDR tends toward blanket criticism, Nietzsche becomes accessible only from the Right: "Hier soll die Feststellung genügen, daß die falsche Eindeutigkeit der Legende den fast ausschließlichen Zugriff durch konservative Ideologie begünstigt hat."[10]

What Reschke envisages in its place is a highly differentiated Marxist criticism that works closely with the texts - in the sense of Mazzino Montinari, who has made a historical-critical edition available - but more particularly one that is able to pursue *all* of the Nietzsche receptions and so arrive at a more comprehensive view. "Das Resultat ist kein ganz anderer ·Nietzsche, aber doch einer, der nicht mehr - auch seitens marxistischer Kritik - schadlos einseitig der potenzierten Vereinfachung konservativer Interessenvertretung zuzuschlagen ist . . ." (p. 1198). Reschke's message is as lucid as it is simple: if this is not done, then one simply no longer has anything to say: "Daran vorbeizusehen, bedeutet jedoch, sich unbeabsichtigt ins theoretische und ideologische Abseits zu stellen" (p. 1199). Reschke's article is a plea for a more differentiated Nietzsche criticism in the GDR. As such, it is rather remarkable - especially since, as it turns out, Renate Reschke has written a *B-Dissertation* (from which the article in *Weimarer Beiträge* is a chapter) that takes the first step by beginning to provide the kind of differentiated criticism called for.[11]

The aim is to work out those aspects in Nietzsche's thought that are productive of further debate for both bour-

---

[10] Renate Reschke, "Kritische Aneignung und notwendige Auseinandersetzung. Zu einigen Tendenzen moderner bürgerlicher Nietzsche-Rezeption," *Weimarer Beiträge*, 29, No. 7 (1983), 1197.

[11] Renate Reschke, "Die anspornende Verachtung der Zeit. Studien zur Kulturkritik und Ästhetik Friedrich Nietzsches. Ein Beitrag zu ihrer Rezeption," B-Dissertation, Humboldt Universität zu Berlin, 1983. English translations of passages from this and other works in the following are my own.

geois and Marxist criticism. Instead of the single-minded insistence on the philosopher of imperialism, anticipator of fascism, anti-humanist, anti-socialist, and conservative we find:

> Im Mittelpunkt des Interesses stehen vor allem solche Grundaussagen Nietzsches zur Kultur-kritik und Ästhetik in ihrer inneren Wider-sprüchlichkeit und Intentionsbreite und mit ihren konstitutiven Ambivalenzen, die - zwi-schen radikaler Epochenkritik, humanistischer Kultur- und Menschheitsutopie und regressiver Gesellschaftsperspektive - das Grundmuster seines Denkens entscheidend geprägt und die Wirkungsgeschichte - besonders die nicht-konservative - folgenreich beeinflußt haben.
>
> (p. 5)

These are the aspects then to stand at the center of discussion: Nietzsche's thought as oscillating between a radical criticism of the epoch, humanistic cultural utopia, and regressive social perspectives and the influence such thought has had, not on the conservative circles with which GDR criticism is otherwise obsessed, but - to give an example of some of the writers Reschke considers - Adorno, Bloch, Benjamin. From Reschke's viewpoint the traditional recourse to Mehring, Lukács, and Günther is no longer sufficient; such a tack "freezes historical dialectics into mere verdicts and grinds away its potential power of discussion in one-dimensional counterpositions" (p. 13). Indeed, "[e]s genügt auch nicht, sich auf die klassischen Aussagen der frühen marxistischen Kritik zu berufen, diese müssen vielmehr selbst zum Gegenstand kritischer Aufarbeitung gemacht werden" (p. 14) - a point that is exceedingly well-taken if these texts are to be grasped in their own respective historical frameworks and not made into something like ahistorical dogma. That does not mean relativizing Mehring or Lukács, say, but simply finding the means to arrive at a more precise notion of their historical significance - and limitations. The object of all this is not to remake Nietzsche over into a figure that is especially "linksfreundlich" - Reschke specifically warns against attempts on the part of some Leftists in the West to make Nietzsche into a "crypto-socialist" (p. 16) - but to arrive at a more adequate under-standing. Walter Benjamin, in a similar situation, once worked out the significance of Charles Baudelaire; why shouldn't

Benjamin's remarks, Reschke argues, apply to Nietzsche as well? As Benjamin wrote:

> Es hat wenig Wert, die Position eines Baudelaire in das Netz der vorgeschobensten im Befreiungskampf der Menschheit einbeziehen zu wollen. Es erscheint von vornherein aussichtsreicher, seinen Machenschaften dort nachzugehen, wo er ohne Zweifel zu Hause ist: im gegnerischen Lager. Dem schlagen sie in den seltensten Fällen zum Segen aus.[12]

Yet any such "Auseinandersetzung" as called for by Reschke requires texts. With the exception of a bibliophile facsimile edition of *Ecce Homo*, his intellectual autobiography, that appeared in Edition Leipzig (1985) in a very costly edition destined principally for the export market, no work of Friedrich Nietzsche has yet been published in the GDR. Two have been planned, however, in inexpensive paperback format by Reclam Verlag: *Die fröhliche Wissenschaft* and *Unzeitgemäße Betrachtungen*, each to be accompanied by an introduction and explanatory notes. In her draft introduction for the edition of *Die fröhliche Wissenschaft*, Renate Reschke emphasizes the importance not only of "calculating the limitations placed on Nietzsche by the specific class and ideological situation, but also of being able to give him his due ["würdigen"] for what he accomplished within those limitations."[13] Reschke characterizes Nietzsche's thought as "a balance between criticism and affirmation [of bourgeois society] that inclines toward the advantage of the latter" (p. 43). Affirmation then. Yet Nietzsche anticipated very early on modes of cultural criticism that have since become indispensable to 20th-century cultural discourse:

> Das Problem der Verdrängung als Symptom kultureller Krisenhaftigkeit gesehen zu haben, darin liegt ein wesentliches Kennzeichen Nietzschescher Kulturkritik. Seine Methode, von der Art der Bedürfnisbefriedigung auf die

---

[12] Walter Benjamin, *Das Paris des Second Empire bei Baudelaire* (Berlin/Weimar: Aufbau, 1971), p. 26, as quoted by Renate Reschke, "Die anspornende Verachtung der Zeit," p. 25.

[13] Renate Reschke, "Friedrich Nietzsches *Fröhliche Wissenchaft* oder Das zerbrechliche Gleichgewicht seiner Philosophie," unpublished typescript planned as introduction to GDR edition of *FW*, kindly lent me by Renate Reschke, pp. 10-11.

Art der Not der Individuen zu schließen, hat perspektivische Bedeutung. Sie greift vor, was erst um die Jahrhundertwende und danach zum Thema bürgerlicher Kulturkritik geworden und wesentlich mit Namen wie Sigmund Freud, Walter Benjamin, Siegfried Krakauer oder Georg Simmel verbunden ist. (p. 45)

In the end, Reschke characterizes the images of Nietzsche's critique of culture as "aggressive Chiffren einer . . . verletzten Menschlichkeit" (p. 46) that despite all affirmatory character remain a call to offer resistance to the capitalist order.

Friedrich Tomberg, a philosopher at the University of Jena, has prepared an introduction to Nietzsche's *Unzeitgemäße Betrachtungen* in which he ties Nietzsche's thought to traditional, Western humanist thinking, with an especially pronounced linkage to an ancient Greek model. Tomberg had put forward the notion of Nietzsche's thought as essentially indebted to the humanist tradition in a paper he delivered in Berlin in 1983, "Nietzsches Versuch einer Aktualisierung der Antike."[14] In it, Tomberg not only ridiculed earlier Marxist criticism (for example, Hans Günther's charge that Nietzsche had raised bestiality to a moral principle), but emphasized that Nietzsche's criticism of capitalist culture did not take place in the dimension of its "material reality" but in "certain manifestations of the sphere of consciousness" ("nicht in ihrer materiellen Realität, aber in bestimmten Erscheinungsformen der Sphäre des Bewußtseins," p. 4), a notion essential as well to Reschke's analysis of Nietzsche's *Kulturkritik*. Tomberg, like Reschke, has a sensitive ear, and so manages to turn on its head many an *idée reçu* of the more established school of GDR Nietzsche criticism: for example, Christianity and goodness. Where Malorny had seen Nietzsche's attack upon Christianity (for Malorny a religion of compassion and modesty) simply as one more indication of Nietzsche's anti-humanism, Tomberg is deftly able to underscore the bitter irony in Nietzsche's text and consequently draws a far more complex and convincing picture.[15] Socialism itself is another

---

[14] Friedrich Tomberg, "Nietzsches Versuch einer Aktualisierung der Antike," unpublished typescript of a paper that was read at the Werner-Krauß-Kolloquium, Akademie der Wissenschaften der DDR, Berlin, Oct. 1983, kindly lent me by Prof. Tomberg.

[15] Friedrich Tomberg, "Zukunft aus Vergangenheit. Prolegomena zu einer marxistischen Lektüre der *Unzeitgemäßen Betrachtungen* von Friedrich Nietzsche," unpublished typescript, p. 11.

good example of how Nietzsche's position has been reexamined. Where Malorny had read Nietzsche's attacks on "socialism" literally as having unrestricted and universal validity, Tomberg points toward a much more relative and historically limited picture: "Die Theorien des Sozialismus sah er fast einzig in Eugen Dühring repräsentiert, den er mit einer Heftigkeit, die der eines Friedrich Engels nicht nachstand, bekämpfte" (p. 15).

The general contours of a Marxist Nietzsche criticism have not changed. Tomberg and Reschke remain, in the end, as critical of Nietzsche's "regressive" stance as ever. But it is thanks to writers such as them that specific lines of argumentation in Nietzsche, his indebtedness to an older humanist tradition, and certain anticipations of modernity have emerged from behind what had become the fog of an ideological hands-off policy: Nietzsche as *Buhmann des Marxismus*. They have resolutely struck out against what Reschke has termed - in conversation with me - "die falschen Berührungsängste des Marxisten."

More. than anything, Tomberg and Reschke have demonstrated the need for highly differentiated and detailed studies of Nietzsche's thought, and the multifarious receptions of that thought, from a Marxist point of view. And it seems such works are now being undertaken in the GDR: Erhard Naake's dissertation, "Friedrich Nietzsches Verhältnis zu wichtigen sozialen und politischen Bewegungen seiner Zeit," for example. In his initial remarks Naake points out:

> Es gibt keine umfassende Veröffentlichung zur politischen Gedankenwelt Nietzsches. In älteren Arbeiten über ihn ist überhaupt das Politische, speziell seine Haltung zu sozialen und politischen Bewegungen seiner Zeit, nur wenig beachtet worden. Erst die Ideologen des Hitlerfaschismus, die die Brauchbarkeit Nietzscher Gedanken und Losungen für ihre Politik erkannten, betrachteten sein Werk stärker unter diesem Aspekt.[16]

The need for a Marxist investigation of Nietzsche's literary reception has been felt for some time. Such a work,

---

[16] Erhard Naake, "Friedrich Nietzsches Verhältnis zu wichtigen sozialen und politischen Bewegungen seiner Zeit," Dissertation Friedrich-Schiller-Universität Jena, 1986, p. 6.

undertaken by Eike Middell, a literary historian at the Academy of Sciences, is in progress. In a meeting at the Academy in June 1985, Middell presented an overview of his study, "Nietzsche in der deutschsprachigen Literatur."[17] From the turn of the century on, Middell reported, Nietzsche was *the* "Bildungserlebnis" for writers. Nietzsche exerted a great attraction on the intelligensia of the generation - born into the new Reich - that began to go into opposition. His contemporaries viewed him as a critic of Bismarck's Reich. Indeed, his critics on the political Right placed him on the side of the Social Democrats! In summarizing, Middell stressed Nietzche's "kritische Potenz," especially for young artists in a stance of protest against bourgeois culture. Johannes R. Becher, for one, remarked after having read Bertram's Nietzsche book: "Das bin ich!"[18]

An autobiography by Almos Csongar that appeared in the GDR in 1984 describes in great detail precisely this "critical potential" as it existed in pre-World-War-II Hungary.[19] With a German fellowship in hand, the young Csongar set out for Berlin to study Nietzsche with Bertram. The romance with Nietzsche did not survive the war years, but instead acted as an impetus towards Marxism. That Nietzsche again and again provides a collection point for criticism and discontent, and not only in bourgeois society, was demonstrated more recently in an interview with Heiner Müller that appeared in *Sinn und Form* in 1985. In it, Ulrich Dietzel asks Müller about the phenomenon of eternal return in his works, and then appends the question: What do you think of Nietzsche? Quite a remarkable answer follows:

> Nietzsche war für mich ungeheuer wichtig. Unmittelbar nach dem Krieg habe ich Nietzsche gelesen. Vorher eigentlich kaum. Damals war das für mich ein bißchen Gegengift gegen Entwicklungen in der damals noch sowjetischen Besatzungszone, dann in der DDR, die auf Egalisierung hinausgingen, also auf eine Nivel-

---

[17] Cf. Eike Middell, "Totalität und Dekadenz. Zur Auseinandersetzung von Georg Lukács mit Friedrich Nietzsche," *Weimarer Beiträge*, 31, No. 4 (1985), 558-72.

[18] Letter from Becher to Katharina Kippenberg, 26 March 1920, in *Becher und die Insel*, ed. Rolf Harder and Ike Siebert (Leipzig: Insel, 1981), p. 178.

[19] Almos Csongar, *Mit tausend Zungen: Beichte eines wechselvollen Lebens* (Berlin: Verlag der Nation, 1984).

lierung, die einfach notwendig war zur Verbreiterung von Niveau, als Voraussetzung für Niveauerhöhung. Aber natürlich stellt so eine Verbreiterung von Niveau, also auch von Bildungsniveau, immer die Spitzen infrage.[20]

Nietzsche as a constituent part of Marxist biography?

Despite all this, Nietzsche is not a topic like any other in the GDR. This is precisely what Eike Middell told me in June, 1986: "Wir in der DDR können nicht akademisch über Nietzsche diskutieren." Perhaps not. But the points Renate Reschke raised vis-à-vis Reclam Verlag in arguing why Nietzsche's *Fröhliche Wissenschaft* should be published, put the matter quite succintly:

> Aus mindestens drei Gründen scheint eine Herausgabe Nietzschescher Texte - als Einzelausgaben und marxistisch kommentiert - notwendig und gerechtfertigt: Um die Auseinandersetzung mit rechts-konservativer bürgerlicher Ideologie, die sich auf Nietzsche beruft, zu profilieren; zur überzeugenden und sachbezogenen Diskussion mit links-bürgerlichen Positionen, die Nietzsche als "Revolutionär" und "Kryptosozialisten" für sich entdeckt haben; zur historisch-kritischen Würdigung des "letzte[n] deutsche[n] Denker[s] von europäischem Rang" (Hans Günther . . .) aus marxistischer Sicht.[21]

The first two reasons have to do with ideological conflicts: tightening lines of argument against the Right - and against the Left. Only with the third reason is the case made for an investigation of Nietzsche on his own merits. Even this point of view, as reasonable as it seems on the face of it, is not shared by many. If Jost Hermand wonders in the United States whether Nietzsche should be read at all ("Es ist daher sehr die Frage, ob die studierende Jugend einen Mann wie Nietzsche überhaupt noch 'braucht.'")[22] then it is perhaps

[20] Ulrich Dietzel, "Gespräch mit Heiner Müller," *Sinn und Form*, 37, No. 6 (1985), 1210.

[21] Renate Reschke, "Exposé zu *Friedrich Nietzsche: Die fröhliche Wissenschaft*, 1) Werkwahl (Begründung)," typescript.

[22] Jost Hermand, "Paroxysmen eines Neinsagers? Zum Nietzsche-Bild von Hans Heinz Holz," in *Karl Marx und Friedrich Nietzsche*, ed. Reinhold Grimm and Jost Hermand (Königstein/Ts.: Athenäum, 1978), p. 149.

understandable that the question is put in similar chiascuro in the GDR, particularly of late.

Reclam Verlag, dissatisfied with Tomberg's introduction to the planned edition of the *Unzeitgemäße Betrachtungen*, is apparently going to let matters rest. Renate Reschke's edition of *Fröhliche Wissenschaft*, although completed and originally scheduled to appear in the fall of 1986, has been indefinitely postponed. Akademie Verlag has simultaneously lost a once voiced interest in Reschke's dissertation, and is taking a "wait and see" attitude toward Middell's study of Nietzsche in German literature. Not to mention a study by another well-known writer in which parallels are drawn between Nietzsche and dada that apparently cannot even be published under a pseudonym. The very strange state of affairs has been reached in the GDR that the most interesting writing on Nietzsche is not published - and is not being published. Nor can the currently exacerbated state of affairs be explained solely by the letter and telephone-call campaign of an out-raged Wolfgang Harich to Reclam, the Ministry of Culture, and the Goethe and Schiller Archive in Weimar, among other places. Harich is fundamentally opposed to the publication of any work by Nietzsche in the GDR and has been quite vociferous in making this view known.

Writing in exile, Heinrich Mann had foreseen a long problematic future for an adequate understanding of Nietzsche:

> Nietzsche wollte der Überwinder des 19. Jahrhunderts sein, er behauptete vor seinem Gewissen das Amt eines Denkers zwischen den Jahrhunderten. Die zweite Hälfte des zwanzigsten sollte, ihm zufolge, endlich begreifen, wer er gewesen war. Gerade das ist nunmehr zweifelhaft geworden: die erste Hälfte hat ihn voreilig mißbraucht. Sehr schwer für ihn, hiernach den Abschnitt zu vermeiden, wo die Nachwelt von einem Gedanken und einer Persönlichkeit ausruht.[23]

When I proposed this as a motto for this paper, Renate Reschke sent back the following comment: "Danke für das Heinrich-Mann-Zitat. Es trifft fast das Problem, von dem wir gesprochen haben. Ich glaube nur, daß wir bei uns nicht in

---

[23] Heinrich Mann, "Nietzsche," *Mass und Wert*, 2, No. 3 (1939), 278-79.

einem Abschnitt leben, wo die Nachwelt von Nietzsche und seinen Gedanken ausruht, sondern ihnen aus dem Wege geht." Indeed, Heinz Malorny had told me categorically in the summer of 1985: "Es kann keine marxistische Nietzsche-Rezeption geben."[24] So the second look I advertised in the title of this paper remains, for now at least, in the antechambers of the publishing houses and in the seminar rooms of at least one university. But then Renate Reschke chose as motto for her dissertation a passage from Hans Kaufmann's *Versuch über das Erbe* (1980): "Was Erbe ist und was nicht, steht nicht ein für allemal fest."

---

[24] A monograph from Malorny expressing the official view in the GDR on Nietzsche is foreseen for 1987.

Writers' Careers in the GDR:
A Generational Comparison

Günter Erbe

The following remarks stem from a statistical study of the origins, career development, and social status of GDR writers. The sample included 439 writers, for the most part, authors of belletristic literature. The material was taken from reference works, anthologies, literary histories, newspapers, and magazines, etc. published in the GDR and the Federal Republic. Personal data in the following areas were accumulated and evaluated by means of a questionnaire: social origins; education; profession before and after the author's literary debut; study at the Becher-Institut; main genre at time of literary debut; prizes and other distinctions; membership and functions in political parties and professional unions, inter alia. The starting point of the study was the classification of writers into four generations, an assumption which made it possible to ascertain - through comparison - elements of continuity and change in the social profile and self-understanding of the literary intelligentsia of the GDR over the years.[1] The results of the study presented here deal with some of these essential aspects of literary careers and the course they take in the GDR. The second generation has been given special consideration because it contains the largest number of well-known authors.

---

[1] The generational focus was especially fruitful as a heuristic principle, although it is problematic to classify writers into generations solely on the basis of their birth date, as was done for this computerized statistical study. Such a method overlooks the fact that the writers debuted at different ages and relate in different ways to writers who belong to other age groups. In classifying writers into four generations, the essential factor was the commonality of experience that could be ascertained from the dates of the individual biographies.

The First Generation (Born before 1914)

The image of early GDR literature was shaped by those writers who, for the most part returning from exile, settled in the Soviet Zone of Occupation after the war. They had published their first works during the Weimar Republic or in the preceding decade. With these works and others written in exile they laid the cornerstone for the literature that originated in the Soviet Zone/GDR after 1945. The contents of their works dating from the era of class struggle and antifascist resistance reflect the differing life experiences of the authors.

A not insignificant number of writers of the older generation were members of the KPD (later the SED) or sympathized with the politics of this party. Membership in the Bund proletarisch-revolutionärer Schriftsteller Deutschlands (BPRD) testifies to their close political and ideological attachment as well. If one considers the origins and career development of the authors, on the other hand, social and cultural differences are obvious. The authors of the first generation derived in almost equal numbers from the proletariat and from the bourgeoisie or petite bourgeoisie. Writers who came from working-class backgrounds and who had had to earn a living as factory workers for a while themselves - as was the case, for example, with Bruno Apitz, Willi Bredel, Eduard Claudius, Otto Gotsche, Hans Lorbeer, Hans Marchwitza, and Jan Petersen - had completely different career patterns than the middle-class authors. They received their literary education in workers' organizations and were ordinarily indebted to the Communist Party for having become writers. As active members of the KPD they wrote for the Party press and gradually turned from journalism to literary writing as a more effective way of propagating Party goals. Their works were printed by KPD and, later, leftist exile publishers. The social and political background of these authors was reflected in their literary self-image as well. A basic belief in class struggle was natural for authors such as Bredel, Gotsche, Lorbeer, and Marchwitza.[2] The "proletarian-revolutionary" element in their books is their commitment to portray the class viewpoint in keeping with the Party line. Their experience of solidarity, their feeling of belonging to the working class remained in-

---

[2] Cf. for example the interview with Hans Lorbeer in *Auskünfte. Werkstattgespräche mit DDR-Autoren* (Berlin/Weimar: Aufbau, 1976), pp. 228-45.

tact even after they, as writers, had left the social milieu of their class.

In order to become writers, they had to pass through a process of individualization and acquire elements of middle-class learning. Eduard Claudius and Theodor Plievier, for example, became adventurers, lived for years in the streets, socially uprooted and alone. With this uprooting came however the world view and wealth of experience which stimulated their poetic tendencies.[3] Writers like Otto Gotsche and Willi Bredel, on the other hand, who remained closely tied to the Communist Party, suppressed their individualistic tendencies instead.[4] There is evidence for the theory that the more seriously a writer of proletarian background took his task as writer, the more decisively he withdrew from the role of author as political functionary. This can be seen most clearly in the example of Erich Arendt, although, in contrast to actual worker-authors, he had no experience as a factory worker. Arendt, who had begun to write poetry under the influence of expressionism, stagnated as a poet after joining the KPD and later confessed that he was not able to write again until the functionary in him had been replaced by the anti-fascist.[5]

Although often members of the KPD, or sympathizers, the authors from bourgeois backgrounds were less dependent on the support of the Party for their careers. As a rule, they debuted in bourgeois publishing houses and received awards and recognition in middle-class literary circles before joining the Communist movement. Their level of education, their lack of practical work experience, and their posture as *Klassenkämpfer*, which was more theoretical than drawn from actual experience, separated them for life from their proletarian colleagues. The bourgeois authors strove to overcome their individuality. This is evident for example in their joining the Party. They sought solidarity, a feeling of community, and wanted to serve the proletarian revolution.

---

[3] Cf. the conversation with Eduard Claudius in *Auskünfte 2. Werkstattgespräche mit DDR-Autoren* (Berlin/Weimar: Aufbau, 1984), pp. 80-96.

[4] Cf. the interview with Otto Gotsche in *Auskünfte*, pp. 61-79.

[5] Conversation with Erich Arendt in *Der zerstückte Traum. Für Erich Arendt. Zum 75. Geburtstag*, ed. Gregor Laschen and Manfred Schlösser (Berlin: Agora, 1978), pp. 113-25.

The same motif recurs in the writing of Stephan Hermlin, Ludwig Renn, and Anna Seghers, among others: the search for the warmth of the collective, the overcoming of social guilt feelings and of isolation. Ludwig Renn (in reality: Arnold Vieth von Golßenau) was the most extreme in denying his bourgeois-aristocratic past and rejecting the bourgeois aesthetic canon. Writing was of secondary importance to him; striving for contact with people, for solidarity was crucial; and the use of literature for political causes, his goal.[6] Hermlin, on the other hand, was too strongly shaped by bourgeois learning and culture to be able to free himself from this tradition entirely. He tried instead to unite the artistic devices and literary experience of the bourgeois writer with the proletarian-revolutionary perspective. After the latter had lost its actuality he confessed - at the Eighth Writers' Congress in 1978 - what, as a result of his cultural origins, he in reality is: a late bourgeois writer.[7]

The authors named here were awarded numerous prizes in the Soviet Zone after the war and later in the GDR; and many of them held public office. After a life of deprivation in exile (here one must differentiate between East emigrants and West emigrants and between varying levels of political and social status), receiving, for example, the National Prize (*Nationalpreis*) - 1st class, 100,000 Marks; 2nd class, 50,000 Marks; 3rd class, 25,000 Marks - was the guarantee of a materially secure existence. The most successful prizewinners of the older generation - with four National Prizes - were Kuba (Kurt Barthel) and Erwin Strittmatter (as of 1986). Stephan Hermlin, Hans Marchwitza, and Anna Seghers (have) received three National Prizes; Bruno Apitz, Erich Arendt, Johannes R. Becher, Willi Bredel, Ludwig Renn, Erich Weinert, and Friedrich Wolf, two. That official recognition is not primarily dependent on artistic achievement can be seen in the case of Kuba, whose multiple honors bear no relation to his literary significance. Brecht received the National Prize, 1st Class, only after protesting: he was to have been given the 2nd Class award instead.[8]

---

[6] Interview with Ludwig Renn in *Auskünfte*, pp. 124-42.

[7] Stephan Hermlin, *Äußerungen 1944-1982* (Berlin/Weimar: Aufbau, 1983), p. 386.

[8] Manfred Jäger, *Kultur und Politik in der DDR* (Cologne: Wissenschaft und Politik, 1982), p. 25. The information on the bestowing of *Nationalpreise* is taken from *Schriftsteller der DDR* (Leipzig: Bibliographisches Institut, 1975), pp. 642-56, and from award announcements in *Neues Deutschland*. Data were gathered up to and including 1986.

In regard to the holding of offices, writers of bourgeois origins such as Becher, Brecht, Seghers, and Arnold Zweig assumed the most important functions in the cultural institutions; authors from proletarian backgrounds such as Bredel and Gotsche had influential positions in the Party apparatus. Officeholders and prizewinners are, for the most part, identical. The implication that loyalty to the state is a criterion for the awarding of literary prizes will be discussed below in connection with the second generation.

From a sociological and literary-historical point of view it is not without significance that the literary culture of the SBZ/GDR was informed in the first years by life experiences that, deviating strongly at first, later converged as a result of the writers' common antifascist, pro-Communist commitment. Writers such as Becher, Brecht, Hermlin, Seghers, and Zweig were not least of all guarantors of bourgeois learning and tradition, which, in spite of the constricting cultural policy of the late 1940s and 1950s, continued to exist as a literary orientation in their works. Proletarian writers like Bredel, Lorbeer, Marchwitza, and Ludwig Turek, on the other hand, contributed to postwar literature the traditional element of genuine class-struggle experience.

The Second Generation (Born 1915-1930)

The next generation, with which GDR literature in a narrower sense actually begins, had neither the experience of class struggle nor bourgeois learning and the broad literary horizon of the older generation. Its experience was of another kind. This generation of writers is socially much more homogeneous. It was recruited from the skilled working class and the lower middle class; for many members of this generation becoming a writer meant the possibility of moving up into the new intelligentsia.[9] While the members of the older generation shared the experience of the failure of the Weimar Republic, and of fascism and exile, the younger generation experienced fascism as youths. Not a few fought in the war and ended up in prison-of-war camps. In the SBZ/GDR they were given the opportunity to study and to create an existence for themselves as writers.

---

[9] Stephan Bock, *Literatur-Gesellschaft-Nation* (Stuttgart: Metzler, 1980), p. 60.

In the first generation journalistic praxis and Party career were typical characteristics for debuting writers of working-class origin. In the second generation journalistic experience is typical for authors from petit-bourgeois backgrounds as well. Data on skilled and unskilled work experience show that many authors also became acquainted with the work sphere before their literary debuts - albeit, in most cases, only for a short time. The literary careers of this generation began in the phase of social transformation, during which rigid literary guidelines were proclaimed by the cultural functionaries - and adhered to by debuting writers such as Franz Fühmann, Günter Kunert, and Christa Wolf, among others. Literature of socialist realism was the password. While the older writers had arrived at their aesthetic and political self-understanding (which in not a few cases, e.g., Brecht, ran counter to proclaimed guidelines) in the course of a relatively long literary-political debate, the younger generation was given a ready-made prescription. The Marxist-Leninist world view imparted at school and at the university, and a corresponding concept of literature were - due to the lack of comprehensive literary knowledge - accepted as unquestioned orientations.[10]

Thus the literary culture of the 1950s, if measured against its pretension of creating the basis for a new socialist culture, bore a double loss: the hollowing and limiting of bourgeois literary learning to a dogmatic residue of classic-bourgeois humanistic ideals; and the decline of authentic proletarian experience, since most of the writers of the second generation had come in contact with the production sphere only sporadically. That is not to say that their ties to the working class had already slackened; because of their origins and their factory experience these writers were still familiar with the proletarian milieu. They lacked however the proletarian *Lebenshorizont* which the worker-authors of the first generation had before loosening their ties to their class.[11] Authors of the younger generation who joined the labor force - often already privileged as a result of *Abitur* and university studies - knew that their future lives need not necessarily follow this path.

---

[10] See for example the autobiographic information in Franz Fühmann, *Vor Feuerschlünden. Erfahrungen mit Georg Trakls Gedicht* (Rostock: Hinstorff, 1982), pp. 81 f; and Günter Kunert, *Vor der Sintflut. Das Gedicht als Arche Noah. Frankfurter Vorlesungen* (Munich/Vienna: Hanser, 1985), pp. 31 f.

[11] See for example Franz Fühmann, "Brief an den Minister für Kultur," in his *Essays, Gespräche, Aufsätze 1964-1981* (Rostock: Hinstorff, 1983), pp. 7-16.

The group of writers classified here as the second generation, to which such different writers as Günter de Bruyn,
Franz Fühmann, Peter Hacks, Hermann Kant, Erich Loest,
Heiner Müller, Helmut Sakowski, and Harry Thürk belong,
manifested in the beginning - generally speaking - a certain
cohesiveness that derived from common political-ideological
views. Political as well as literary differences can be seen if
one considers the political-organizational enlistment of the
authors over a longer period of time. Membership in the SED,
working full-time as a functionary, the holding of offices in
the cultural-political apparatus, and, last but not least, the
receiving of prizes and distinctions can all be considered
indicators of political loyalty; and they allow conclusions to be
drawn about the authors' literary self-understanding.

No exact data could be found about membership in the
SED. It is known however that five writers, namely Günter
Görlich, Gerhard Holtz-Baumert, Helmut Sakowski, Bernhard
Seeger, and Hermann Kant (elected at the Eleventh Party
Congress, 1986), are members of the Central Committee (ZK)
of the SED. Christa Wolf was a candidate for membership for
several years in the 1960s. Helmut Baierl, Hermann Kant,
Dieter Noll, Helmut Preißler, Max Walter Schulz, and Harry
Thürk have or have had important Party functions on the
district level. Rosemarie Schuder is a member of the executive committee of the CDU. In the 1950s Franz Fühmann was
a member of the presidium and executive committee of the
NDPD.[12] Several of these writers hold important state offices
outside the cultural and literary sphere as well. Kant is a
delegate and member of the presidium of the Nationalrat of
the Nationale Front. Schuder is likewise a member of the
presidium of the Nationalrat. Görlich was for many years a
member of the Zentralrat of the FDJ.

If one takes membership on the executive committee
(Vorstand) of the Writers' Union as indicative of the official
esteem in which an author is held and of his influence, then
the following differentiations based on length of membership
and position result:[13] the longest serving members of the

[12] This information is taken above all from Günther Buch, *Namen und
Daten wichtiger Personen der DDR*, 3rd ed. (Berlin/Bonn-Bad Godesberg:
Dietz, 1982).

[13] The following information is taken from the published documentations
of the Writers' Congresses (Berlin, 1956 ff.). No publisher is listed for the
documentations of the 1956 and 1983 congresses; the remaining (1962 to
1978) were published by Aufbau.

executive committee are Jurij Brězan, Rosemarie Schuder, and Bernhard Seeger, all of whom have served since 1956; Brězan has held the position of vice-president since 1969; Schuder was elected into the presidium in 1983. Helmut Sakowski has been a member of the executive committee since 1969; he later moved up into the presidium, to which he belonged until 1983. Hermann Kant and Max Walter Schulz became members of the executive committee in 1969 and served together with Brězan as vice-presidents of the Union. In 1978 Kant replaced Anna Seghers as president of the Writers' Union, an office which he continues to hold - just as Schulz is still vice-president. Günter Görlich has belonged to the executive committee since1969; in1973 he moved up to the presidium where he is to this day. Rainer Kerndl rose quickly in the ranks: having joined the executive committee in 1969, he was elected into the presidium, and, since 1978, has served as one of the vice-presidents.

With the exception of Hermann Kant, no important GDR writers of this generation are presently on the executive committee of the Writers' Union. The cases of Franz Fühmann and Christa Wolf are typical. Fühmann became a member of the executive committee in 1956, left in 1969, was reelected in 1973 and ousted in 1977. Wolf was a member of the executive committee from 1961 to 1977. Her exclusion, like that of Franz Fühmann, was connected with the sanctions leveled against refractory writers in the wake of the Biermann expatriation. While several distinguished representatives of the second generation - Günter de Bruyn, Franz Fühmann, Karl-Heinz Jakobs, Hermann Kant, and Christa Wolf - were elected to the executive committee at the Seventh Writers' Congress in 1973, only Kant remained in 1978.

It appears that the rank an author has in the Party and state apparatus and in the Writers' Union and other important cultural institutions is not without significance for his being awarded prizes. This hypothesis can be confirmed by looking at the names of the National Prize recipients: the most highly decorated prizewinner is Helmut Sakowski with four; Helmut Baierl, Jurij Brězan, Franz Fühmann, Peter Hacks, Hermann Kant, Dieter Noll, Günther Rücker, Max Walter Schulz, Bernhard Seeger, and Harry Thürk (have) each received two National Prizes. The president of the Writers' Union, Hermann Kant, is the second most frequently honored writer after Sakowski: in addition to the two National Prizes, Kant has received the Heinrich Mann Prize, the Literature

Prize of the FDGB, and the Erich Weinert Medallion of the FDJ; he has an honorary doctorate from the University of Greifswald and is bearer of the *Vaterländischer Verdienstorden in Silber.*

In the figures of Kant, Fühmann, and Hacks, writers of significance are included among the most highly honored authors. That loyalty to the state figures more highly than literary niveau can clearly be seen however in the cases of Sakowski and Brĕzan. And one must not overlook the fact that the distinctions Fühmann received were all awarded before 1976, that is, before his signing of the Biermann petition. Peter Hacks, who supported the SED in the Biermann affair, advanced to highly decorated writer in the second half of the 1970s; after receiving the National Prize, 2nd Class in 1974, he was awarded the National Prize, 1st Class in 1977 and the Heinrich Mann Prize in 1981. Other significant writers of this generation to have received the National Prize are Heinar Kipphardt (1953), Christa Wolf (1964), and Heiner Müller (1986). The surprising bestoyal of the National Prize on the internationally acclaimed Müller can perhaps be seen as a sign of renewed relaxation of the cultural policy. Well-known writers such as Johannes Bobrowski, Günter de Bruyn, and Günter Kunert were not or have not been so honored, although they did receive the Heinrich Mann Prize. It appears as if this latter distinction, which is given by the Akademie der Künste, is more strongly determined by actual literary achievement than the National Prize.

The involvement of the writer in the cultural apparatus through the holding of Party and Union offices and the receiving of highly endowed literary prizes is certainly not without significance for the shaping and strengthening of the writer's literary and political self-image. The question of a negative or positive correlation between literary quality and position in the hierarchy cannot be investigated in detail here. Kant is clearly not a bad writer although he is closely connected with the SED. Still, his literary elbow-room is probably more limited than that of colleagues who maintain a greater distance from political power. It would be a great oversimplification to label writers as "Partei-Schriftsteller" simply because they are high-ranking Union functionaries. This designation may make sense if it is used to denote writers who share a certain concept of literature and whose loyalty to the politics of the SED includes their acceptance of the official literary doctrine of socialist realism and its ideological implications such as partiality, closeness to the people, "scientific" world view, and socialist perspective. Helmut Sakowski and Harry Thürk, for example, can be considered typical writers of this kind. In their view, GDR authors are a team that must adhere to the watchwords and decisions of the Party in their writing; politics and literature are inseparable. Sakowski and Thürk want to have a consciousness-changing effect as writers by supporting views they have gained and constantly regain in their work as functionaries.[14]

Decisive for the drifting apart of this "team" that started out with a common literary concept is the differing evaluation and assimilation of the societal development of the GDR. A fairly large number of writers of the second group gradually distanced themselves from the officially proclaimed partiality and countered this view of reality with their own claim to truth and authenticity in literature. It is a matter here of authors such as Fühmann, Kunert, and Wolf, who in the 1950s and 1960s - like Sakowski and Thürk - had fulfilled functions in the cultural and Party sphere until these activities were spoiled for them or until they realized the irreconcilability of carrying out official functions and realizing their self-imposed literary goals.

The change in literary self-understanding that has been underway since the 1960s is not limited to this generation alone. As mentioned above, Arendt and Hermlin of the older generation emphasized the independence of literature vis-à-vis all official instructions. Their differing lives notwithstanding, the members of the first and second generations have one thing in common: with few exceptions, they consider themselves obligated to Marxist thinking and see themselves as socialists, even though the literary form this commitment takes can vary greatly. A serious break in the political and literary self-image is not evident in the next generation either; it can be seen for the first time in the transition to the youngest generation of GDR writers.

The Third Generation (Born 1931-1945)

The third generation comprises the age group that was scarcely touched by fascism, since its childhood years fell in

---

[14] "Werkstattgespräch mit Helmut Sakowski," *Neues Deutschland,* 20 March 1981; and "Werkstattgespräch mit Harry Thürk," *Neues Deutschland,* 2 April 1981.

the period 1933 to 1945. This generation was shaped essentially by the postwar period and the construction of socialism in the GDR, without having been involved however in the political turmoil of the 1950s. Only partially affected by the enthusiasm of the *Aufbau* years, this generation reached intellectual maturity in the 1960s - in the period of the New Economic Policy and the Scientific-Technical Revolution with its belief in progress. The Vietnam War, Prague Spring, and the student movement in the West were important, consciousness-forming events, especially for those born after 1940. This generation too tends to come from (skilled) working-class and middle-class backgrounds. It has a higher level of education - a larger number of writers have a university education. Approximately one-fifth of the authors of this generation have several years experience in the labor force, either as workers or as low-level employees - some of the better known of these are Kurt Bartsch, Volker Braun, Paul Gratzik, Rainer Kirsch, and Martin Stade. Once again journalistic experience plays an important role in the writers' career before their literary debut. Only a few writers of this generation succeeded, like Brigitte Reimann, in establishing themselves as free-lance writers without the intermediary step of working as a journalist or in the cultural apparatus. Since the majority of these writers don't perceive their profession as a social advancement, their basic attitude is not so much one of gratitude to the state but rather the expectation of being allowed to help shape the socialist state and realize their individual potential.

For a small number of these writers the path to literature via a career conducive to the change-over to free-lance writer remained closed or consciously was not taken. Uwe Greßmann, Wolfgang Hilbig, and Gert Neumann are examples of the type of author who came to writing neither by way of university studies nor a job in journalism or publishing. Greßmann, forced into the role of outsider by a difficult childhood and physical illness, was a special case. Neumann and Hilbig were (and still are) forced to take on unskilled jobs since they have found no or very little official recognition in the GDR and thus have no income from their writing other than royalties from works published in the West.

It is striking in this generation too that for the more significant writers Party and state functions lose their attraction in the course of time and the "Partei-Schriftsteller" is replaced by the critically committed socialist. Writers with official functions outside the cultural sphere include: Erik Neutsch, who has been part of the district SED leadership (Bezirksleitung) in Halle since 1964; Rolf Floß, who is a member of the district Party leadership in Dresden, and Walter Flegel, who serves on the local council (Stadtverordnetenversammlung) in Potsdam and is president of the local Kulturbund. As a member of the executive council, Benito Wogatzki also has an important function in the Kulturbund. On the other side, Jurek Becker, Wolf Biermann, Siegmar Faust, Rainer Kirsch, and Gert Neumann were excluded from the Party.

A rather large number of writers of this generation are on the executive committee of the Writers' Union: Neutsch, Wogatzki, and Hans Weber have been members since 1969; Volker Braun, Joachim Nowotny, Eberhard Panitz, Gisela Steineckert, and Rudi Strahl, since 1973; Flegel, Floß, and Irmtraud Morgner, since 1978. For the most part, these are party-liners with only average literary credentials. Braun and Morgner are exceptions. One must keep in mind, to be sure, that a number of the more important writers of this generation (Jurek Becker, Wolf Biermann, Thomas Brasch, Sarah Kirsch, Hartmut Lange, Stefan Schütz, among others) no longer live in the GDR. Still, other representative authors who were not caught up in the *Ausreisewelle* of recent years - for example, Heinz Czechowski, Elke Erb, Christoph Hein, Rainer Kirsch, Karl Mickel, and Ulrich Plenzdorf are not on the executive committee.

Eight of the twelve National Prize laureates in this generation are members of the executive committee or the presidium of the Writers' Union: Flegel, Neutsch, Nowotny, Panitz, Steineckert, Strahl, Wogatzki, and Morgner. Erik Neutsch enjoys highest official esteem, having received in addition to his two National Prizes the Heinrich Mann Prize, the Erich Weinert Medallion, and - thrice - the Art Prize of the FDGB. Three first-rate authors - Becker, Mickel, and Morgner - as recipients of the National Prize and the Heinrich Mann Prize - are included in the circle of highly acclaimed writers.

The question arises whether or not a new self-image of the writer has been articulated by this generation and how it is expressed. A new literary-artistic pretension is clearly recognizable among the poets who were born between 1933 and 1940 and who debuted as a group at the beginning of the

1960s. Since many of them were from Saxony, Adolf Endler found cause to speak of a "Sächsische Dichterschule."[15] To it belonged Karl Mickel, Volker Braun, Heinz Czechowski, Rainer Kirsch, Klaus B. Tragelehn, Richard Leising, Rainer Kunze, Bernd Jentzsch, and Wulf Kirsten. Artistically related to the group were Uwe Greßmann, Wolf Biermann, Kurt Bartsch, Sarah Kirsch, Elke Erb, and Adolf Endler. What they had in common was the striving for an individual language and an emphatically subjective approach.

Although one can describe the majority of the poets named here as critically committed socialists who, while not relinquishing the free play of their own individuality, still concede that literature has a practical purpose, signs of a transition to an individualistic, solitary posture are visible in this generation. The self-oriented writer who strives for subjective expression gains significance with writers such as Hilbig, Neumann, Schütz, and Brasch, who were all born after 1940 and who form a sort of intermediary generation. This type of writer is more prevalent in the next generation.

The Fourth Generation (Born after 1945)

This generation of writers, whose knowledge of fascism stems solely from history books and who scarcely consciously experienced the social change of the 1940s and 1950s, faces entirely different problems. They were born into socialism and, as Heiner Müller has noted, no longer experienced it as anticipation of "das Andere," but rather as deformed reality.[16]

If one considers the social background and development of these authors, an increased academization and alienation from the sphere of material production can be seen. They come from working-class backgrounds, but partially also from the new intelligentsia. As a rule, they earned the *Abitur* - often in connection with a skilled-worker's certificate, attended the university - whereby education ranks highest as field of study, and came to literature by way of jobs in journalism, the artistic sphere, or other white-collar professions. This picture of high professional qualifications is not insignificantly affected by a second trend in this generation:

15 Wolfgang Emmerich, *Kleine Literaturgeschichte der DDR* (Darmstadt/ Neuwied: Luchterhand, 1981), p. 169.
16 Heiner Müller, "Wie es bleibt, ist es nicht," *Der Spiegel*, 12 September 1977, p. 215.

namely, the tendency of a number of young authors to renounce a career in academic or other highly qualified professions and to either establish themselves as free-lance writers shortly after their literary debut or earn their living with part-time, unskilled jobs.

Two groups, differing in their career development, can thus be ascertained in this generation, although it is debatable whether one can use the term "group" in the sense of smaller social unit or whether the contours are not too vague to infer a group identity. The one group uses the traditional channels for their literary careers. They show themselves as politically loyal and, in regard to their writing, stay within the borders of that which is prescribed by cultural policy and deemed permissible by the majority of critics. They ordinarily come from the FDJ poetry movement, receive *Förderpreise* as young talent, publish their first works in magazines and anthologies, and then their first book. The careers of Hans Brinkmann, Gabriele Eckart, Uta Mauersberger, Steffen Mensching, and Kathrin Schmidt follow this pattern. That young writers who profit from state support are not always willing to fulfill the expectations of the state can be seen in the case of Gabriele Eckart and Uwe Kolbe. Interview documents treating undesirable subjects; encoded, satirical poems; contacts with Western media easily transgress the tolerance levels of the cultural functionaries, so that well-meaning young poets find themselves culturally/politically offside.[17] And in this way they move closer to the second group of writers, who from the beginning considered it a matter of honor not to be recognized by the cultural establishment.

In this connection, a type of poet should be mentioned that can be found above all in the big cities - Berlin, Leipzig, Dresden - now and that seeks a complete break with the conventional GDR literary-artistic self-understanding. These authors reject the path of official support (FDJ and the cultural institutions) and withdraw into private quarters and literary circles where they communicate with one another and create for themselves a public that is limited to their circle of friends. In the older generations there were solitary figures, too, non-conformists whose writing didn't fit the

---

[17] Cf. Gabriele Eckart, *So sehe ick die Sache. Protokolle aus der DDR* (Cologne: Kiepenheuer, 1984); Uwe Kolbe, "Kern meines Romans," in *Bestandsaufnahme 2. Debütanten 1976-1980* (Halle/Leipzig: Mitteldeutscher Verlag, 1981), pp. 82 f.

concept of a politically committed, socialist-realist literature - Arendt, Bobrowski, Greßmann, and, in the third generation, Hilbig, for example. However they were the exception. The development that began at the end of the 1970s aims at nothing less than the rehabilitation of autonomous art, and a large number of young writers have been caught up in it.[18]

Several of these writers have received support from well-known older authors. Franz Fühmann, for example, came to the aid of Kolbe, Hilbig, and Frank-Wolf Matthies. Elke Erb helped a number of young writers to become known in the West with the anthology she published together with Sascha Anderson, *Berührung ist nur eine Randerscheinung. Neue Literatur aus der DDR*.[19] (Sascha Anderson was, until his recent move to West Berlin, one of the spokesmen of this new "beat generation.")

Twenty-nine writers are represented in the Erb/Anderson anthology. Several of them - Christa Moog, Georg Reichenau, Andreas Röhler, Michael Rom, Katja Lange, Cornelia Schleime, and Volker Palme - emigrated to the Federal Republic in 1984. Uwe Kolbe is the only writer in the anthology to have published books of his own in the GDR. Anderson, Moog, Bert Papenfuß, Lutz Rathenow, and Rüdiger Rosenthal have published books in the West. Like the other writers, they have found little recognition in the GDR. Only one GDR poetry anthology, *Vogelbühne*, edited by Dorothea von Törne,[20] has poems by several of the writers included in *Berührung ist nur eine Randerscheinung*: Rathenow, Rosenthal, Anderson, Uwe Hübner, and Stefan Döring. Works by Jan Faktor appeared in *Auswahl 84*, published by Verlag Neues Leben.

Most of these young authors do not only write but are artists, musicians, or filmmakers at the same time or collab-

---

[18] See Anneli Hartmann, "Der Generationswechsel - ein ästhetischer Wechsel? Schreibweise und Traditionsbezüge in der jüngsten DDR-Lyrik," in *Jahrbuch zur Literatur in der DDR*, Vol. 4, ed. Gerhard Klussmann and Heinrich Mohr (Bonn: Bouvier, 1985), 109-34; and my article, "Zum Selbstverständnis junger DDR-Lyriker," in *Studies in GDR Culture and Society 4*, ed. Margy Gerber (Lanham/London/New York: University Press of America, 1984), 171-85.

[19] *Berührung ist nur eine Randerscheinung. Neue Literatur aus der DDR* , ed. Elke Erb and Sascha Anderson (Cologne: Kiepenheuer, 1985).

[20] *Vogelbühne. Gedichte im Dialog*, ed. Dorothea von Törne (Berlin: Verlag der Nation, 1983).

orate with artists in other fields. A few years ago these young writers appeared to be solitary figures;[21] today one has a very different impression. In her introduction to *Berührung ist nur eine Randerscheinung*, Elke Erb corrects the superficial view that they are copying a Western fashion with a few years delay; she sees the reasons for their literary rebellion as lying deeper: "Das Entscheidende ist: Die Jugend in der DDR hat wie die Jugend westlicher Länder die automatisierten und anonymisierten Vollzüge der gegenwärtigen Zivilisation zu bestehen und steht wie diese in der Tradition der europäischen Moderne."[22]

Elke Erb is pointing here to a process which the cultural functionaries in the GDR can only view with suspicion: the renouncing of the understanding of art and literature - considered binding until now - that entails enlisting art as a political force and creating a socialist art that differs from bourgeois art in its content and values. The sensibility of the younger authors for the stuff of literature - language - is replacing the conventional orientation of GDR literature toward content and regaining for literature some of its traditional autonomy. However, even when it is experimental, this literature is drawn into the social debate, in which it has participated throughout the generations and whose most important organ it is.

Transl. Margy Gerber

---

21 Harald Hartung, "Die ästhetische und soziale Kritik der Lyrik," in *Hansers Sozialgeschichte der deutschen Literatur. Bd. 11: Die Literatur der DDR* (Munich: Hanser, 1983), p. 302.

22 Elke Erb, "Vorwort," *Berührung ist nur eine Randerscheinung*, p. 13.

Volker Brauns Essay
"Rimbaud. Ein Psalm der Aktualität" im Kontext seiner Lyrik

Christine Cosentino

Im Jahre 1984 hielt Volker Braun vor der Akademie der Wissenschaften und Literatur in Mainz einen Vortrag mit dem Titel "Rimbaud. Ein Psalm der Aktualität."[1] Brauns Auseinandersetzung mit diesem Vorläufer des französischen Symbolismus scheint mir gewichtig, denn sie fällt in eine Zeit, wo sich eine neue Autorengeneration profiliert,[2] mit neuen Themen, neuen Schreibweisen und neuen neoavantgardistischen, vorrangig expressionistisch-dadaistischen Traditionsbezügen. Die kürzlich erschienene Lyrikanthologie *Berührung ist nur eine Randerscheinung*[3] legt davon Zeugnis ab.

Das Anderssein dieser neuen Literatur der Jüngsten wurde 1984 überzeugend von Anneli Hartmann hervorgehoben, die die Frage stellte: "Der Generationswechsel - ein ästhetischer Wechsel?"[4] Die Antwort schien klar, bis zu jener Aktualisierung Rimbauds jedenfalls, die nun überraschenderweise ausgerechnet von einem Älteren, von einem Sprecher

---

[1] Volker Braun, *Rimbaud. Ein Psalm der Aktualität*, Akademie der Wissenschaften und der Literatur, Abhandlungen der Klasse der Literatur, Jg. 1984, Nr. 4 (Stuttgart: Franz Steiner Verlag, 1985); ebenfalls gedruckt in *Sinn und Form*, 37, Nr. 5 (1985), 978-98. Zitate aus Brauns Essay, inklusive die von Braun zitierten Rimbaud-Passagen, sind *Sinn und Form* entnommen. Der Essay wird im Text der Arbeit mit den Buchstaben *RPA* abgekürzt.

[2] Siegfried Rönisch, "Notizen über eine neue Autorengeneration," *Weimarer Beiträge*, 25, Nr. 7 (1979), 5-10.

[3] Sascha Anderson und Elke Erb (Hrsg.), *Berührung ist nur eine Randerscheinung* (Köln: Kiepenheuer und Witsch, 1985).

[4] Anneli Hartmann, "Der Generationswechsel - ein ästhetischer Wechsel?" in *Jahrbuch zur Literatur in der DDR*, Bd. 4, hrsg. von Gerhard Klussmann und Heinrich Mohr (Bonn: Bouvier, 1985), 109-34.

der Vorgängergeneration, ausging: Volker Braun, auf den sich die Aggressionen und der Identifizierungsunwille der problemlos in den DDR-Staat "hineingeborenen" Jüngsten bisher am intensivsten konzentriert hatte. Man erinnere sich an Uwe Kolbes berühmtes Bonmot: "Meine Generation hat die Hände im Schoß was engagiertes (!) Handeln anbetrifft. Kein früher Braun heute";[5] oder an Fritz-Hendrik Melles salopplässige Glossierung: "Volker Braun? - Da kann ich nur sagen, der Junge quält sich. Dazu habe ich keine Beziehung mehr."[6]

Der so Geschmähte verhielt sich konzilianter. "Rimbaud. Ein Psalm der Aktualität" ist u.a. eine Auseinandersetzung mit der jüngsten Autorengeneration, eine Bilanzziehung über die gegenwärtige Literaturszene, über das eigene Schaffen, thematische Prioritäten und die Suche nach neuen künstlerischen Ausdrucksformen. Braun bilanziert auf dem Hintergrund der Biographie des französischen enfant terrible Rimbaud, zu dem er rote Wahlverwandtschaften entdeckt und dessen ästhetische Ideen er für marxistische Zwecke radikalisiert und aktiviert. Hier sei nebenbei erwähnt, daß Rimbaud bereits 1979 in Rolf Schneiders Sensationsroman *November* Untersuchungsobjekt war, und zwar vom Aspekt der "Nichtrevolution" als Sprachlosigkeit.[7] Erwähnt sei ebenfalls, daß psychoanalytische, auf Jacques Lacan orientierte Sekundärliteratur über die Erschütterung der Instanz "Ich" im Werke Christa Wolfs sich auf Rimbaud beruft, im besonderen auf dessen Maxime: "Das Ich ist ein anderer."[8]

Braun setzt sich mit Rimbaud auseinander, indem er ihn zitiert. Die in seine Abhandlung einmontierten Rimbaud-Zitate mit den von Rimbaud selbst vorgenommenen Kursivierungen sind dessen Briefwechsel mit Freunden entnommen. Hinzu kommen durch Sperrdruck identifizierte Einsprengsel aus verschiedenen Gedichten. Braun setzt dort an, wo der Ältere, scheinbar so Ungleiche, aufgehört hat. Prophe-

---

5 "Ohne den Leser geht es nicht. Ursula Heukenkamp im Gespräch mit Gerd Adloff, Gabriele Eckart, Uwe Kolbe, Bernd Wagner," *Weimarer Beiträge,* 25, Nr. 7 (1979), 46.

6 "Notizen aus einem Gespräch mit F.-H. Melle," in *Berührung ist nur eine Randerscheinung,* S. 147.

7 Rolf Schneider, *November* (Hamburg: Albrecht Knaus, 1979).

8 Zum Beispiel Bernhard Greiner, "'Mit der Erzählung geh ich in den Tod': Kontinuität und Wandel des Erzählens im Schaffen von Christa Wolf," in *Erinnerte Zukunft. 11 Studien zum Werk Christa Wolfs,* hrsg. v. Wolfram Mauser (Würzburg: Königshausen und Neumann, 1985), 107-40.

tisch heißt es bei Rimbaud am Ende des zweiten "Seher"-Briefes, wie Braun berichtet:

> [Der Dichter] *kommt im Unbekannten an, und wenn er schließlich, gestörten Geistes, seine Visionen nicht mehr begreift, so hat er sie doch gesehen! Mag er in seinem Sprung zu den unerhörten und unnennbaren Dingen auch umkommen: es wird neue schreckliche Arbeiter geben. Sie werden an jenen Horizonten beginnen, wo er hinsank!* (RPA, S. 985)

Der vom Politfrust gebeutelte, aber weiterhin fest in den DDR-Staat eingebettete Nachfahre Braun erscheint hier im Lichte des "schrecklichen Arbeiters," der in den Mühen der real-sozialistischen Ebenen nicht die Waffen streckt, sondern weiterhin zäh am "Sehen" des Sozialismus festhält - ein schwierig gewordenes Sehen allerdings, dessen Schwierigkeit an der Komplexität des poetischen Gebildes sichtbar wird.

Lotet nun Braun die Biographie des "Außenseiters" Rimbaud aus, um Exemplarisch-Neues für die Literaturlandschaft der 80er Jahre ins Visier zu nehmen? Werfen wir einen schnellen Blick auf den Lebenslauf des französischen "voyant" oder "Seher"-Dichters, dessen Dichtersein ganze drei Jahre dauerte, vom 17. bis 19. Lebensjahr, der aber innerhalb dieser kurzen Zeitspanne durch Entfesselung aller Sinne, Drogen und Vagabundendasein eine neue, alle Traditionen sprengende Gegensprache, Gegenästhetik, Gegenethik und Veränderung der Verhältnisse suchte. "Aus der bewußten Zerrüttung aller Sinne und Verhaltensweisen" - so Hans Mayer über Rimbaud - "sollte die neue Existenz aufscheinen: als Negation der Negation."[9]

Rimbaud wurde 1854 in der Provinz in Charlesville geboren. Vom Musterschüler entwickelte er sich im Alter von 16 bis 17 Jahren zum Bürgerschreck, rebellierte gegen die autoritär strenge Mutter, gegen die Schule, den Kleinstadtmief, rannte verschiedene Male von zu Hause weg und begeisterte sich für die Pariser Kommune. Ob er aktiv in der Kommune engagiert war, ist unklar. Während des Aufstandes schrieb er jedoch jene zwei von Braun zitierten "Seher"-Briefe, in denen er Ausgangspunkt und Ziel der neuen Gegen-

---

9 Hans Mayer, *Außenseiter* (Frankfurt/M.: Suhrkamp, 1975), S. 243.

ästhetik skizziert: "*Es ist falsch, wenn einer sagt: ich denke.*
Man sollte sagen: es denkt mich" *(RPA,* S. 984), heißt es in
Orientierung auf kollektive Tiefenschichten; visionäres Sehen
des Unbekannten sei - so berichtet Braun weiter - Resultat
maximaler

> *... E n t g r e n z u n g a l l e r S i n n e. Alle*
> *Formen der Liebe und des Leidens, des Wahn-*
> *sinns;* der Dichter *durchforsche sich selbst, er*
> *schöpfe alle Gifte seines Wesens aus und be-*
> *wahre nur ihre Quintessenz für sich. Unsagbare*
> *Folter, für die er seinen ganzen Glauben*
> *braucht, seine ganze übermenschliche Kraft,*
> *und durch die er unter allen Wesen der große*
> *Kranke, der große Verbrecher, der große Ver-*
> *dammte - und der Allwissende wird! - Denn er*
> *kommt an im U n b e k a n n t e n!*
> *(RPA,* S. 984-85)

Innerhalb von drei Jahren schrieb Rimbaud neben vielen
Gedichten seine zwei größeren Werke: die "Erleuchtungen"
("Illuminations") und "Eine Zeit in der Hölle" ("Une saison en
enfer"), wobei letzteres ein halluzinatorisches Durchleben
seines "infernalischen" Verhältnisses zu Verlaine war, aber
auch eine Absage an eine in das Leben eingreifende Gegen-
kunst; letzteres, nachdem der sich gottähnlich fühlende
lyrische Sprecher erkannt hatte, daß Absinth, Drogen,
Skandale und hoffnungsloses Träumen die Zündkraft seiner
Visionen waren - oder, wie einige Kritiker meinen,[10]
nachdem er sich bewußt wurde, daß seine "Illuminations"
nichts anderes als Halluzinationen waren. Als er entdeckte,
daß die Poesie nicht der Zauberschlüssel war, für den er sie
gehalten und nicht das Ideal verwirklichte, nach dem er
gedürstet hatte, gab er sie auf. Er drehte Europa den Rücken
und drang in das innerste Afrika vor, arbeitete für
Exportfirmen, eine Kolonialarmee, wurde Waffenhändler,
vielleicht auch Sklaven-händler. 1891, im Alter von 37
Jahren, starb er in Marseille an Krebs.

Nichts könnte bei oberflächlicher Betrachtung polarisier-
ter sein als die Lebensläufe der beiden Autoren Rimbaud und
Braun. Und doch werden durch vergleichende Querbezüge
(z.B. Er - Rimbaud, Ich - Braun, Wir - die DDR-Zeitgenossen

---

[10] Z.B. Enid Starkie, *Arthur Rimbaud,* 2. Aufl. (Norfolk/CT: New Directions,
1961), S. 17.

oder das globale Wir, Sie - die Jüngsten) Gemeinsamkeiten sichtbar. Rimbauds Grundhaltung der Unruhe, vom rastlosen Suchen über provokatives Sprengen zum visionären Sehen, enthüllt sich im Lichte marxistischer Analyse mutatis mutandis als der weltanschauliche Kern dieser eigenartigen und doch so wenig überraschenden Wahlverwandtschaft. Braun verifiziert: "Er [Rimbaud] blieb ein Gewährsmann meiner Erfahrungen" (*RPA*, S. 978). Braun distanziert sich aber auch: "Dieses unsichere Kind, diesen wilden Toren können wir nicht umarmen, oder nur, um uns mit seinem Dämon auf dem Boden zu wälzen" (*RPA*, S. 992).

In vier literarischen Schlüsselbegriffen erkennt man die Grundpfeiler der Brücke, die sich von Rimbaud zu Braun schlägt: in den Begriffen der Provinz, des Vagabunden, der Formel, des Themengeflechts "Grenze-Entgrenzung-das Offene." Die offensichtlichste Affinität ist die Allergie gegen die "Provinz," die als Metapher für einschnürende Zwänge zu verstehen ist. Im Falle Rimbauds weist sie auf die autoritäre Mutter, die "Pfütze" (*RPA*, S. 988), die Gängelei; im Falle Brauns auf Verschleiß der Illusionen in der sich festfahrenden Revolution: "Provinz, das ist der leere Augenblick. Geschichte auf dem Abstellgleis. Status quo" (*RPA*, S. 982). Den Gestus des Suchens nach Gleisen politischer Bewegung komprimiert Braun, auf den Spuren Rimbauds, in der Metapher des Vagabunden oder Landstreichers, d.h. des Unruhigen, Sicht-nicht-Festlegenden. Für Rimbaud bedeutete Vagabundendasein in den "Illuminations" die Suche nach dem Ort, der die "Formel" für ein menschlicheres Dasein enthält, die er in der Pariser Kommune zu sehen geglaubt hatte, wie seine "Seher"-Briefe bezeugen, jene Formel der Schönheit und des Hoffens, die Braun zu der pauschal apodiktischen Behauptung führt: "Er hat den Kommunismus, der mit Militärgewalt vertagt wurde, nicht aufgegeben, solange er schrieb. Aber er schrieb nur mehr drei Jahre" (*RPA*, S. 987).

Brauns eigene Formel vom Kommunismus, wie seine letzten Gedichte oder der Lyrikband *Training des aufrechten Gangs* beweisen,[11] ist im Prozeß fortschreitender Desillusionierung obskurer und diffuser geworden und deutet sich letztlich nur noch vage im unverbindlichen Neutrum des Pronomens "es" an: "Woher soll ich es nehmen / Wonach ich

---

11 Volker Braun, *Training des aufrechten Gangs* (Halle/Leipzig: Mitteldeutscher Verlag, 1979). Der Band erscheint im Text der Arbeit mit dem Buchstaben *T* abgekürzt.

verlange. . .? (*T*, S. 43) bzw. in der ratlosen Fragestellung: "die langsame Formel, die mit Leben zu füllen ist womit womit womit? oder vom Tod" (*T*, S. 59). Die Aktualisierung des "Sehers" Rimbaud und seiner Visionen kann somit auf dem Hintergrund krisenhafter politischer Erfahrungen als Akt hartnäckiger Selbstermunterung und Herausforderung verstanden werden, als erneutes Heraufbeschwören von "Hinze und Kunze, in fester Umarmung" (*RPA*, S. 993), wenn auch nur an allerfernsten utopischen Horizonten.

Im häufigen schlaglichtartigen Aufleuchten der Schlüsselwörter "Grenze," "Entgrenzung" und "das Offene" auf der Folie der Rimbaudschen "Entgrenzung aller Sinne" erkennt man folglich ein Grundthema Volker Brauns schlechthin: die Sprengung des real existierenden Sozialismus, jenes in der Not angefertigten politischen Behelfes, den man - so heißt es im *Hinze-Kunze-Roman* - nicht so "schmackhaft machen [soll], sonst halten sich die Leute daran fest."[12] Andererseits werden mit dem poetologischen Begriff der "Entgrenzung" Denkanstöße und Gesprächsangebote zum Thema neuer künstlerischer Ausdrucksformen geliefert. Letzteres bedarf einer Untersuchung der in Rimbauds "Seher"-Briefen konzipierten Gegensprache, die Braun fasziniert, die er sich kritisch aneignet, deren Möglichkeiten er in einigen kürzlich erschienenen Gedichten durchzuspielen versucht. Auf einige dieser Gedichte soll im folgenden eingegangen werden. Brauns Diskussion der Rimbaudschen Gegensprache im Sog allgemeiner neoavantgardistischer oder modernistischer Tendenzen in der Literaturszene der DDR ist somit politisch-künstlerischer Ausdruck dessen, daß Berührung mit den Jüngsten letztlich durchaus nicht nur eine Randerscheinung ist, sondern Auseinandersetzung, Prozeß, Offenheit.

Das Thema der Dichtung als Gegensprache zur ideologisch eingefärbten, vergesellschafteten Zeitungssprache bewegte die Gemüter der 1979 in den *Weimarer Beiträgen* interviewten jüngsten Autoren, die den Generationswechsel mit ästhetischem Wechsel einläuteten. Sascha Andersons lakonische Feststellung z.B. - "und manchmal nicht wissen / wessen sprache wir denken / das kleinhirn des riesen / das grosshirn des zwerges"[13] - kreuzt sich hier mit Brauns abschätzigen Etiketten von "gestanzter Festtagskunst," "Ord-

---

[12] Braun, *Hinze-Kunze-Roman* (Frankfurt/M.: Suhrkamp, 1985), S. 95.

[13] Sascha Anderson, "es sind so viele brücken," in ders., *Jeder Satellit hat einen Killersatelliten* (Berlin: Rotbuch Verlag, 1982), S. 72.

nungssprache" und "Rotationsdruck" (*RPA*, S. 990). Brauns Allergie gegen Gestanztes führt ihn zu jener "Seher"-Sprache aus den "Seher"-Briefen Rimbauds, die in ihrer Aktivierung des Unterbewußten - Braun selbst spricht von kalkuliertem Chaos (*RPA*, S. 997) - in sich selbst zwar nichts wirklich Originelles ist, deren Potential Rimbaud jedoch auf dem Hintergrund der griechischen Antike und der Romantik neu untersuchte und radikalisierte. Dichtung - in Anlehnung an Rimbauds "Seher"-Briefe - als Sichtbarmachung des Unsichtbaren in seiner Form oder Formlosigkeit, mit verdichteter Sprache, Dichtung, die der Tat vorauseilt (*RPA*, S. 985), indem sie in Form von Träumen und Gefühlen im Unterbewußtsein abgelagertes Gewußtes aktiviert und zur Utopie steigert, eine solche Dichtung, in der "*jedes Wort ein Gedanke*" ist (*RPA*, S. 986), liefert für den Braun der 80er Jahre einen Fundus von neuen künstlerischen Möglichkeiten, die er seinem marxistischen Weltbild nicht als konträr, sondern als komplementär empfindet.

Die Entzauberung des Unbewußten in Funktionalisiertes destilliert Braun in den von ihm selbst geprägten Begriff der "decouvrierende[n]," "sehende[n]" (*RPA*, S. 986) Metapher, jenes Bildmaterial in den "Illuminations," das er für rezipierbar und aufschlüsselbar hält. Rimbaud selbst benützte den Begriff der "sehenden" Metapher nicht. Braun jedoch, der Brecht-Schüler, nimmt ihn für sich und Rimbaud in Anspruch, indem er sich auf jene dem Gedanklich-Funktionalen gewidmeten Textpassagen in den "Seher"-Briefen konzentriert, die seinem marxistischen Weltbild entgegenkommen. Das kalkulierte Chaos - diese provozierende Nebeneinanderstellung in einer poetologisch politischen Schrift Volker Brauns - scheint mir neu, beinahe programmatisch. Allerdings weit über Rimbaud hinausgehend, der vor der Gesellschaft und der Poesie kapitulierte und sich ins innerste Afrika abwandte, konzentriert sich nun Braun, in deutlicher Abkehr von der jüngsten Autorengeneration, auf jene engagierte Funktion der Dichtung, die Rimbaud als der Tat vorauseilend (*RPA*, S. 985) charakterisiert hatte. Damit ist Gegensprache für Braun Fürsprache, d.h. operative Mitsprache. Rimbauds "innerstes Afrika" der Abkehr wird bei Braun zum erneuten Aufbruch ins "innerste Afrika" hier, am Ort, in der DDR.

Sprachlich anspruchsvoll war Brauns Lyrik von jeher. Aber es scheint, daß sie jetzt noch verdichteter und fragmentarischer ist als zuvor, ja, im Grunde genommen nur dann rezi-

pierbar, wenn man jenen anspruchsvollen Kriterien folgt, die
Braun für die Rezeption der als unergründlich geltenden
Rimbaudschen "Illuminations" empfiehlt (*RPA*, S. 997): durch
mühevolles Abklopfen der tragenden Einzelteile im poetischen Sprachlaboratorium, um dann, durch die Entdeckung
aufschlüsselnder Brüche, Widersprüche, Muster und Strate-
gien in die Helle des kalkulierten Chaos vorzudringen. Brauns
neuer Lyrikband mit dem geplanten Titel *Langsamer*
knirschender Morgen liegt seit Jahren im Lektorat des
Mitteldeutschen Verlags und kann uns folglich nicht weiter-
helfen. Splitterhaft eingeblendet jedoch erscheinen in
seinem Essay Titel oder Themen einiger Gedichte, die in den
letzten Jahren in Anthologien und Zeitschriften erschienen
sind: "Gebremstes Leben," "Der Frieden," "Die Mummelfälle,"
"Burghammer" und - am gewichtigsten - das Gedicht "Das
innerste Afrika."

Letzteres Gedicht, da es explizit durch den Titel auf
Rimbaud Bezug nimmt, verdient besondere Beachtung, denn
es birgt zerreißende Spannungen von Krise und Hoffnung,
von Sein und Utopie, ja, es vermittelt sich geradezu als etwas
zerrissen Chaotisches und wird dann letztlich doch wieder
durch den politischen Imperativ zum synthetisierend
fragmentarischen Gebilde: "DU MUßT DIE GRENZE ÜBER-
SCHREITEN."[14] Das kalkulierte Chaos dieses Gedichtes und
die Erhellung des "es," der obskur gewordenen Formel vom
Kommunismus, schöpft aus einer verwirrend komplizierten
Montage identifizierter oder nicht-identifizierter Versatz-
stücke oder Zitate von Rimbaud, Hölderlin und Kunert. Neu
ist, daß Nichtausgesprochenes, Verdecktes vom Leser selbst
ausgegraben und erhellt werden muß, und zwar durch eine
präzise Untersuchung der geborgten Sprache selbst und
ihres Stellenwertes im Originaltext, ihrer spezifischen Anbe-
raumung zwischen einer vorausgehenden und einer folgenden
Aussage.

Das Gedicht "Das innerste Afrika" beginnt mit einer
Aufforderung zu unverbindlichen politischen Höhenflügen ins
Offene, "in ein wärmeres Land / . . . / Wo unverkleidete
Männer / Deine Genossen sind." "*Dahin! Dahin! / Möcht ich*
mit dir, Geliebter" heißt es auf der Folie des Goetheschen

---

[14] Braun, "Das innerste Afrika," in *Luchterhand Jahrbuch der Lyrik 1984* ,
hrsg. v. Christoph Buchwald und Gregor Laschen (Darmstadt/Neuwied:
Luchterhand, 1984), S. 28. Die im Text der Arbeit erwähnten Seitenzahlen,
die sich auf dieses Gedicht beziehen, sind dem *Luchterhand Jahrbuch* entnommen.

"Mignon"-Liedes. Zwischen dem Sehnsüchtigen und seinem Ziel erhebt sich eine trennende Wand der Ferne, wird Sehnsucht zur unerfüllten Sehnsucht. Wohin orientiert sich nun aber die Sehnsucht des Nachfahren Braun, sein Sehen utopischen Potentials? Zunächst, mit Hilfe eines nichtidentifizierten Versatzstückes aus Rimbauds "Soir historique"[15] - "En quelque soir, par exemple, le touriste naïf" - auf die vierte Welt, das innerste Afrika:

> En quelque soir, par exemple, le touriste naïf EUROPA
> SACKBAHNHOF die verdunkelten Züge aus der vierten
> Welt vor Hunger berstend / hinter der Zeitmauer
> Getöse unverständliche Schreie / Blut sickert aus den
> Nähten der Niederlage / Zukunftsgraupel und fast will /
> Mir es scheinen, es sei, als in der bleiernen Zeit . . .
>
> (S. 27)

Letzterer Satz "und fast will / Mir es scheinen, es sei, als in der bleiernen Zeit," mit dem Braun auf hiesiges Territorium umschwenkt, ist ein geborgtes, nichtidentifiziertes Zitat aus Hölderlins Elegie "Der Gang aufs Land."[16] Kenntnis der literarischen Quelle ist wichtig, denn, wie sich jetzt zeigt, gerade von Braun Nichteinmontiertes hat verweisenden Verfremdungscharakter. Was Braun nicht zitiert, sind die in der Hölderlin-Elegie diesen Zeilen folgenden Zeilen: "Dennoch gelinget der Wunsch, Rechtglaubige / zweifeln an Einer / Stunde nicht und der Lust bleibe geweihet der Tag." Mit Lust also, sich dem Pessimismus der Stunde nicht beugend - so darf man dem Nichtzitierten indirekt entnehmen - zieht Braun mit Hilfe eines markierten Direktzitats, der Anfangsworte aus oben erwähnter Elegie, die optimistische Konsequenz: "*Komm! ins Offene, Freund!* " (S. 27). Das Offene als Sinnbild des Sehens, des "es," wird jetzt mit den eigenen Worten des lyrischen Sprechers auf das Inland - "das innerste Land" - projiziert: "Nicht im Süden liegt es, Ausland nicht / Wo unverkleidete Männer / Wo der Regen" (S. 27), sondern, implizit, *hier*, wobei das eigene Land und das ihm zugemessene utopische Potential durch ein weiteres, ebenfalls nicht präzis identifiziertes Versatzstück aus Hölderlins Elegie

---

[15] Arthur Rimbaud, "Soir historique," *Rimbaud. Sämtliche Dichtungen*, hrsg. und übertr. von Walther Küchler, 6. Aufl. (Heidelberg: Verlag Lambert Schneider, 1982), S. 236. Braun selbst benützte folgende Übersetzung, die mir nicht zugänglich war: *Rimbaud. Sämtliche Werke. Französisch und Deutsch*, übertr. von Sigmar Löffler und Dieter Tauchmann (Leipzig, 1976).

[16] Friedrich Hölderlin, "Der Gang aufs Land," in *Hölderlin. Sämtliche Werke*, hrsg. von Friedrich Beißner (Frankfurt/M.: Insel, 1965), S. 289.

in den Rahmen einer literatur-philosophischen Erbetradition gesetzt wird: "Denn nicht Mächtiges ists, zum Leben aber gehört es / Was wir wollen" (S. 27). Interessant wieder ist das von Braun Nichterwähnte, die im Hölderlin-Gedicht diesen Zeilen vorangehenden Zeilen:

Darum hoff ich sogar, es werde, wenn das Gewünschte
Wir beginnen und erst unsere Zunge gelöst,
Und gefunden das Wort, und aufgegangen das Herz ist,
Und von trunkener Stirn höher Besinnen entspringt,
Mit der unsern zugleich des Himmels Blüte beginnen,
Und dem offenen Blick offen der Leuchtende sein.

Das Leuchtende führt nun im deutlichen Kontrast zum Politpessimismus Günter Kunerts, des "Mann[es] in Itzehoe" (S. 28), auf den Braun anspielt - "Wir befinden uns, sagte er, auf einer schiefen Ebne" (S. 27) - wieder zu den "Illuminations," den Erleuchtungen Rimbauds, nämlich zu dem Ausschnitt "Ouvrier." Braun montiert daraus eine nichtidentifizierte Zeile in sein Gedicht: "Non! wir werden den Sommer nicht mehr in diesem / geizigen Land verbringen, wo wir immer nur einander / versprochene Waisen sind" (S. 28). Darauf folgt Brauns eigener Imperativ "Komm." Blickt man auf das Eingebettetsein des Rimbaud-Zitats in der Originalquelle, nämlich zwischen den Aussagen: "O die andere Welt, die vom Himmel gesegnete Behausung und die schattigen Gründe!" und "Ich will, daß dieser verhärtete Arm nicht mehr ein teures Bild ["chére image"] hinter sich herschleppt,"[17] so hat man es wieder mit dem Sehen des "es," der "chére image," und politischer Sehnsucht zu tun. Die Versalien der Braunschen Schlußzeile "DU MUßT DIE GRENZE ÜBERSCHREITEN!" deuten auf die Sprengung des Politfrusts und unerschrockenes, sich keine Grenzen setzendes Mitsprechen, um das "Gesehene" wieder allgemein sichtbar zu machen. Wieweit jedoch die komplizierte Entgrenzung literarischen Geländes, die Verschachtelung identifizierter und nichtidentifizierter Montagestücke und das kalkulierte Spiel mit Formuliertem und vom Leser erst zu Formulierendem überhaupt rezipierbar ist, ist eine offene Frage in diesem offenen Gedicht.

Neben diesem anspruchsvollen Gebilde wirkt ein Gedicht wie "Der Frieden" beinahe konventionell. Ein markiertes Zitat

---

17 Rimbaud, "Ouvrier," *Rimbaud. Sämtliche Dichtungen*, hrsg. u. übertr. v. Walther Küchler, S. 209.

aus Klopstocks Ode "Die Frühlingsfeier" ("Langsam wandelt die schwarze Wolke") zielt in diesem Prosagedicht auf das Thema globalen Wettrüstens und macht durch ironisches Zersplittern des Kampfliedtextes "Vorwärts und nicht vergessen" klar, daß politisch parteiliches Sprechen innerhalb ideologisch eindeutig abgegrenzter Lager in den 80er Jahren nicht mehr möglich ist. "Wenn wir noch für uns sprechen wollen," heißt es im Rimbaud-Essay, "müssen wir für die Welt sprechen" (*RPA*, S. 994). Ins poetische Gebilde umgesetzt erscheint dieser Gedanke in der Aufweichung des sinnentleerten Begriffs "Solidarität" im typografischen Schriftbild des Textes folgendermaßen:

> VORWÄRTS UND NICHT VER
> VER
> vergammeln/blöden/raten
> Vorwärts und sehn wo du bleibst
> BRÜDER ZUR
> ZUR SONNE
> ja wohin?
> Vorwärts und nicht vergessen anzustellen
> Brüder zum Posten empor!
> Vorwärts an Geschütze und Gewehre
> Vorwärts marsch!
> Brüder zur Kasse
> VORWÄRTS UND NICHT VERGESSEN
> BRÜDER
> Die Solidität
> DIE SOLIDARI
> TÄTERÄTÄH[18]

Weitaus schwerer rezipierbar sind Gedichte, die aus "grünem" Protest schöpfen, ein Thema, das im Rimbaud-Essay wiederholt angeschlagen wird und das in Gedichten wie "Die Mummelfälle" und "Burghammer" poetische Gestaltung findet. Das gestörte Verhältnis zwischen Mensch und Umwelt wird in diesen Gedichten durch das Chaos der Gedichtstruktur selbst ins Bild gesetzt. "Burghammer" ist geradezu ein Musterbeispiel für jene im Rimbaud-Essay akzentuierte fürsprechende Gegensprache. "Burghammer" präsentiert Form in der Formlosigkeit, ist funktionalisierte Entzauberung der Umwelt und kalkuliertes Spiel mit unverbundener, gekappter Sprache, um bei der Diskussion des

---

[18] Braun, "Der Frieden," *Luchterhand Jahrbuch der Lyrik 1984*, S. 33.

zerstörten Verhältnisses von Mensch und Umwelt verantwortliches Mitspracherecht anzumelden:

Mitteldeutsches Loch Ausgekohlte Metapher
Keiner Mutter Boden Loser Satz
Aus dem Zusammen FROHE ZUKUNFT
Hang gerissen.[19]

Neben nun schon obligatorisch gewordener Montage von Zitatmaterialien setzt jetzt eine neue, ebenfalls im Rimbaud-Essay demonstrierte Methode des Negierens, buchstäblichen Ausstreichens von Tradiertem oder Vorgeprägtem ein, um Ungültig-Gewordenes ins Licht zu rücken: "Im Genick / das NEUE LEBEN / Wo sein banges Gesicht hinwandte ~~der ängstliche Phineus~~ Albert . . ." (S. 39).

Rückblickend gewinnt man den Eindruck, daß Brauns "Rimbaud. Ein Psalm der Aktualität" zu einer neuen Saison für Lyrik beiträgt, die einem gewandelten, komplexeren, oft unüberschaubaren Realitätsbegriff gerecht wird. Der Ausdrucksgestus anspruchsvoller Vieldeutigkeit, der Braun seit Anfang seiner dichterischen Laufbahn eigen war, erfährt jetzt eine Erweiterung oder Entgrenzung auf splitterhafte Form im Formlosen. Das scheint auf die Wiederentdeckung einer größeren Kunstautonomie zu weisen, auf Wirklichkeitsrepräsentation durch Sprachpräsentation, auf - Braun benützt den Begriff des poetischen "Laboratoriums" (*RPA*, S. 997) - "vers aus der retorte."[20]

"vers aus der retorte" ist ein Versatzstück aus einem Gedicht Sascha Andersons. Hier allerdings, bei der Sprachpräsentation, sind die "neuen" Töne Brauns von denen der von ihm als "Neutöner" bezeichneten jüngsten Autoren der DDR zu unterscheiden. Zwar wird den Jüngsten das Recht auf künstlerische Entgrenzung durchaus zugestanden: "Aber auch . . . in dem bedeutenden Wortmüll sind verschwiegene Gefühle und Gedanken deponiert, die uns, *selbstredend*, mehr zu sagen haben als die gestanzte Festtagskunst" (*RPA*, S. 990). Zu Müll wird das Wort in dem Augenblick, wo es im Reservat einer reinen Poesie steckenbleibt, wo Gegensprache aufhört, vermittelnde Fürsprache zu sein und zum Selbstzweck degeneriert. So ist dann Brauns Einschätzen der Jüngsten auch kein pauschales Abkanzeln, sondern eher ein

---

[19] Braun, "Burghammer," *Neue Deutsche Literatur*, 31, Nr. 5 (1983), 38.
[20] Sascha Anderson, "es sind so viele brücken," S. 72.

kritisches Wahrnehmen und vorsichtiges Bestätigen von deren künstlerischen Alternativen, solange letztere nicht vom Grundbefinden des gesellschaftlichen Ausstiegs und politischer Gleichgültigkeit getragen werden. Gegensprache, selbst die chaotischste, ist für Braun Mitsprache.

Die Nebeneinanderstellung von Bewußtem und Unbewußtem und die jetzt unverhohlene Befürwortung ehemals als dekadent verpönter bürgerlicher Stilelemente scheint mir neu in der DDR-Lyrikszene. Das Echo ließ nicht auf sich warten. In seinen "Notaten" zu Brauns Rimbaud-Essay, genannt "Sehen," resümiert Max Walter Schulz:

> Nein, ofte geschieht's nicht, daß sich einer von uns solche Art Text leistet. Sich leistet im mehrfachen Sinn des Wortes - als Credo, als Selbstverständigung, als Herausforderung, als Stilprobe, als Versuch (und Versuchung), aus progressivem Erbe Tradition zu stiften, damit Schule gestiftet sei - oder auch nur ein Satyrspiel probiert.[21]

In der Tat endet Braun seinen "Psalm der Aktualität" im Stil eines Satyrspiels:

> Wir müssen jeden Groschen unseres Verstandes dreimal umdrehen und fragen, ob wir ihn ausgeben können und wofür, wir müssen die Ideen einsparen und uns nicht an Experimente verschwenden, und vor allem kommt es jetzt darauf an, die eigene Ungereimtheit einmal beiseite zu lassen und uns auf den Hauptfeind zu konzentrieren, die unbeschreibliche Hochrüstung, mit der wir vollauf zu tun haben, endigte der Satyr. (RPA, S. 998)

Das erinnert an die 1975 in den *Notaten* veröffentlichten Betrachtungen über Kunst und Wirklichkeit, denen ein "Vorwort" beigegeben ist, in dem Braun sich ebenfalls, in ähnlich augenzwinkernder clownesker Manier selbst in Frage stellt: "Diese Notate enthalten selbstverständlich nicht die Meinungen des Verfassers, sondern seine Überlegungen. Er besteht doch nicht auf Worten! . . . Die lichten Momente

---

[21] Max Walter Schulz, "Sehen. Notate zu Volker Brauns Rimbaud-Essay," *Sinn und Form*, 37, Nr. 5 (1985), 1000.

liegen vermutlich dort, wo nach den Handlungen gefragt wird."[22]

Handelt es sich also bei den Schlußworten des Rimbaud-Essays um Brechtsche List, die so aktuellen "lichten Momente" auf dem Hintergrund der Rimbaudschen "Illuminations" vor den Augen des Zensors zu verdunkeln bzw. dem Vorwurf des Abrutschens ins Anarchistische vorzubeugen? Braun hatte bereits in einem ganz frühen Gedicht, "Meine Damen und Herrn" (1964), das Vielseitige und Changierende seiner Dichtung prophezeit:

> Noch ist mir die Maske nicht ins Fleisch gewachsen
> Ich kann nicht mehr abtreten, aber ich hab viele
>   Schlüsse
> Meine Damen und Herren
> Es ist vieles möglich
> Ich kann mich verhüllen oder entblößen, wie Sie
>   wollen
> Ich kann auf den Haaren laufen oder noch besser
> Auf zwei Beinen wie ein Clown.
> Entscheiden Sie sich.[23]

Es scheint, daß "Rimbaud. Ein Psalm der Aktualität" den Schlüssel für einen weiteren politisch dichterischen Schluß innerhalb der vielen Schlüsse enthält. Der neue Lyrikband, *Langsamer knirschender Morgen*, der zu erwarten ist, wird Aufschluß geben.

---

[22] Braun, "Vorwort," in ders., *Es genügt nicht die einfache Wahrheit. Notate* (Frankfurt/M.: Suhrkamp, 1976), S. 7.

[23] Braun, "Meine Damen und Herrn," in *Es genügt nicht die einfache Wahrheit*, S. 16.

The Power of the Oppressed:
The Evolution of the Black Character in Anna Seghers' Caribbean Fiction

Carolyn R. Hodges

When Anna Seghers fled the growing fascism in her country, she began a long period of exile which was to profoundly effect the focus of much of her writing and to provide the vital spark for the genesis of her Caribbean fiction. During that period, in 1941, she spent a brief time in Santo Domingo while waiting for a visa which would allow her and her family to enter Mexico. Her impressions then and subsequent intense study of the history of the Antilles - an interest inspired largely by a biography of Toussaint L'Ouverture she read - led her upon her return to Germany to begin work on the stories which were to focus on the black struggle against oppression and the fight for independence in colonial Haiti, Guadaloupe, and Jamaica. Seghers' Caribbean fiction is spread out over a period of roughly three decades, beginning with two novellas written in 1948, *Die Hochzeit von Haiti* and *Wiedereinführung der Sklaverei in Guadeloupe* ; a third work, *Das Licht auf dem Galgen* (1961), completed the cycle she referred to as her Antilles novellas.[1] Twenty years later, in a trio of stories entitled *Drei Frauen aus Haiti*, she returned to the familiar setting and themes of the earlier cycle, presenting them in a new light.[2]

The novellas and stories of both cycles, which, taken together, cut across several generations, portray the history

---

[1] Subsequent references appear parenthetically in the text and are to Anna Seghers, *Erzählungen* (Neuwied/Berlin: Luchterhand, 1963), Vol. 2. All translations are my own.

[2] Anna Seghers, *Drei Frauen aus Haiti* (Berlin/Weimar: Aufbau, 1982). Subsequent references appear parenthetically in the text.

of the struggle for freedom from slavery and oppression in the Antilles, in particular, of the black proletariat that was all but hopelessly confined to a powerless social position. Critics who have examined Seghers' treatment of the themes of class conflict and revolution have touched upon her image of the black character with respect to race-class issues involved in that struggle: the strife between white overlords and black slaves; the implications of relationships between whites and various minorities, such as Jews, mulattoes, and blacks; and the political and economic forces which pitted mulattoes against blacks.[3] Without ignoring the complex relationships depicted among those racial groups, this study attempts to focus strictly on Seghers' characterization of the black figure, that is, to examine the profile of the black character which emerges over the thirty years spanned by the works. In her images of blacks and her treatment of the various conflicts in which they are involved, Seghers addresses questions concerning their role not only as individuals in a group seeking independence and self-determination but also as members of the human community in pursuit of harmony and equality born of a just social order.

Although the novellas in the first cycle contrast sharply with one another in structure and perspective, all three are firmly grounded in historical fact and are linked by a common theme: abolition of slavery and pursuit of the *liberté, égalité, fraternité* proclaimed as reality for all by the leaders of the French Revolution but denied - or at best gravely limited - in the colonies by those acting on behalf of their leader Napoleon. The stories are also linked by a common figure, the black revolutionary leader Toussaint L'Ouverture, who attempted to bring unity and strength to the Haitians' meager but determined hope for emancipation. However, Toussaint's ascension to power as governor-general of the island in 1801 was followed soon after by betrayal by his French superiors

---

[3] Studies of Seghers' earlier cycle compare her portraiture of the black character to the image presented by Kleist in *Die Verlobung in St. Domingo*. See, for instance, Willfried Feuser, "Slave to Proletarian: Images of the Black in German Literature," in *German Life & Letters*, 32 (1978-79), 122-34. More recent works which refer to this theme may be found in a collection of essays by Sander Gilman, *On Blackness without Blacks: Essays on the Image of the Black in Germany* (Boston: G.K. Hall, 1982) and in a volume edited by Reinhold Grimm and Jost Hermand, *Blacks and German Culture* (Madison: The University of Wisconsin Press, 1986). Of particular interest in the latter collection with respect to Seghers' Caribbean fiction is the essay by Grimm, "Germans, Blacks, and Jews; Or Is There a German Blackness of Its Own?" (pp. 150-78).

and a sudden thrust into ignominy, a course of events which not only bespoke the overwhelming, long-armed power wielded by Napoleon from afar but also very poignantly accentuated the plight of the oppressed black proletariat woefully unable to preserve its hard-won freedom.[4]

Thus, the black characters of the early novellas are portrayed as battered, powerless individuals whose pursuit of freedom is soon reduced to desperate efforts to survive. Yet Seghers does not merely present weak, stereotyped figures locked in a battle of good versus evil. She shows, rather, that their defenseless state is a result of complicated, larger issues: the problematic role of the revolutionary whose lone rise to power leaves him remote from and unattainable to the masses; the complex race-class conflict in which a hierarchy of whites, mulattoes, and blacks are both at odds with and bound to each other in the struggle against social injustice; the web of imperialism and dictatorial power under which blacks are forced to build an economy that only exploits them. As a consequence, their efforts to obtain independence are aborted by powerful forces from without as well as by problems among themselves.

In her later cycle of stories the black characters develop into more resolute figures who manage to prevail against their tormentors not merely by surviving but by taking determined and effective, albeit small, steps toward emancipation. The stories in *Drei Frauen aus Haiti* relate the dilemmas of three women - each representing a different generation and a critical point in Haitian history - whose fates are suddenly altered by their country's upheaval. Although the heroines are removed from one another by several centuries and are immersed in radically different socio-political situations, they are very closely linked as victims of oppression fighting for a common cause. From within this broader historical scope emerge black figures whose roles augment the vision of a

---

[4] In a discussion of the genesis of the Antilles novellas, Seghers mentions how her first acquaintance with the facts of Toussaint's life and Haitian history grew into an interest which occupied her while in Mexico and many years after her return to Europe. Along with the biographical material she found in Mexico, she later studied histories and travel books (many descriptions from which she included in her works) and had a brief interview with the French West Indian poet Aimé Césaire. See Anna Seghers, "Entstehung der Antilles-Novellen," in her *Über Kunstwerk und Wirklichkeit* (Berlin: Akademie, 1971), II, 29-33.

gradually developing and firmly sustained process of revolution and final emancipation.

In *Hochzeit*, which is set in Haiti in 1791, shortly before the slave rebellion led by Toussaint, Seghers introduces the image of house slaves who, beyond the physical labor they perform, are perceived by their masters as little more than shadows, silent "chair backs" standing behind and waiting to serve, while their aristocratic superiors dine and discuss world events crucial to the lives of the slaves. During a visit to Count Evremont to present the precious jewels he has for purchase, Samuel Nathan mockingly tells his son Michael not to be concerned about the thoughts which the free talk about the revolution in France might instill in the minds of the blacks present, for, he states, "Gedankenmachen, das ist eine Beschäftigung für die Weißen. Die Schwarzen stehen hinter den Stühlen, die Stuhllehnen machen sich keine Gedanken über die Tischgespräche" (p. 34). Literally and figuratively they live a caged existence in which freedom and self-determination are considered the most remote of possibilities for all but a few.

In this, as well as in Seghers' later Caribbean fiction, slaves and "free" blacks relate stories of beatings and suffocating confinement which, while sometimes triggered by disobedience, are as often imposed as a consequence of a forgotten errand or an unintentional slip of the foot or hand. Veronika, housekeeper on the Evremont estate, vividly recalls what happened many years earlier when she neglected to change a vase of wilted flowers. Her mistress "machte . . . mir einen Kranz aus den welken Blumen und knüpfte mich an den Pfahl in der prallen Sonne. Ich lag wie tot, als man endlich abends die Stricke durchschnitt" (p. 25). Similarly, in Seghers' later story "Der Schlüssel," Claudine looks back on the harsh punishment she endured for the accidental breaking of a vase, when "die Herrin ließ mich in ein Wandgefängnis einsperren, das man von der Festtafel aus sehen konnte. . . . Ich konnte kaum ein Glied in dem Loch bewegen" (pp. 38-39). The pain and fear suffered in these small, individual cages are further heightened by the all-encompassing cage of fear which surrounds all blacks on each island, for their fates are subject to the whims of the colonial governors and their superiors abroad. The pervasiveness of this invisible net of fear is repeatedly suggested in the description of the estate masters and mistresses alike, whose skin retains, despite hours under the burning sun, its perplexing "unerklärliche weiße Weiß" (*Hochzeit*, p. 24).[5]

The talk of freedom and citizens' rights, however, does spark hope and soon grows into an irrevocable, urgent hunger for emancipation from oppression. A source of release appears in the powerful leadership of Toussaint, characterized by the whites who feared him as the "black Satan" (p. 52). The clever Toussaint, in whom - as one critic has put it - "Züge eines charismatischen Führers" are mixed "mit denen eines politisch interpretierten Heilands,"[6] provided his followers with the reality of a freedom about which they had previously only dared dream. Guided by a firm vision born of a strong sense of self and insight into human behavior, he had realized through his observation of the whites, mulattoes, and blacks surrounding him, "wie wenig die Hautfarbe über den Mann besagt" (p. 52).

In her characterization of Toussaint, Seghers reminds us, though, that his vision was not without its flaws, for his rise to power seemed to remove him further rather than bring him closer in spirit to those whom he helped to free. In contrast to the lives of many slaves held sharply in check by fierce owners whose terrifying whiteness made them seem all the more threatening, Toussaint's stable and less punitive environment, in which he was taught to read and write and allowed to go to school, caused him to view "die weiße Kultur als ein strahlendes, unermeßliches Schloß. . . . Man durfte sie nie geringschätzen, weil sie von den Weißen ausgedacht war. In einem besseren Leben mußte man alle Menschen daran teilnehmen lassen" (p. 52). Thus, rising alone to power, he ultimately adopts the middle-class values and life-style of his former owners. Toussaint becomes an individual who, "lacking class solidarity . . . cannot lead a successful revolt against the aristocracy, because he allows himself to become an aristocrat."[7] Shortly thereafter, fully trusting Napoleon's emissary, Toussaint naively falls into the trap of betrayal.

---

[5] Seghers' untraditional use of the color white as a negative symbol is strikingly similar to that of the Afro-American writer Richard Wright in his short stories and novels about black life in America written in the 1940s.

[6] Erika Haas, "Dauer als Durchhalten der Person. Zur Identitätsproblematik in *Transit*," in *Anna Seghers: Materialienbuch*, ed. Peter Roos and Friederike J. Hassauer-Roos (Darmstadt/Neuwied: Luchterhand, 1977), p. 57.

[7] Lowell Bangerter, *The Bourgeois Proletarian: A Study of Anna Seghers* (Bonn: Bouvier, 1980), p. 107.

The Haitian Toussaint's downfall and death in a desolate prison foretoken the sad turn of events following the insurrections in Guadaloupe and Jamaica. The black revolutionary leaders Paul Rohan (Guadaloupe) and Cuffee (Jamaica), although aided by European outsiders who attempt to help them protect their rights, neither attain the stature of Toussaint nor succeed in any measure in their struggle. In *Wiedereinführung* Paul Rohan commands an imposing presence which exudes strength and beauty and evokes the image of a "black centaur" (p. 75), yet, barely able to read and filled with terror of reenslavement, he is but a shadow of Toussaint and poorly prepared for his task as a leader. He intuitively suspects the intentions of the newly appointed officials who have been ordered to reinstate slavery, yet he remains powerless, for Toussaint's deportation and the lack of strong support by his black allies rapidly seal the fate of the blacks on the island. Forced into hopeless resignation, Paul and his family, afraid to risk escape and almost certain death, return to work on the estate.

While the suffering and persecution of the black inhabitants of the island set the tone for *Das Licht*, the black figures are essentially minor characters of a story within a story: the sailor Malbec arrives in Paris to deliver a letter to Antoine and to tell him the details of the mission to Jamaica as they were related to him by Galloudec, an ally of Sasportas. Here, the black characters have even less control over the course of events. The revolutionary leader Cuffee, who refuses to be enslaved and exists in the woods more or less as a bandit, is hardly known by the blacks who have heard about his efforts and want to aid him. Because he mistrusts all whites, including Sasportas and his superior Debuisson, he lacks the advantage of an organized insurrection. The impetus for an organized fight comes from Sasportas. He is, however, betrayed by Debuisson and suffers a martyr's death on the gallows, as a victim of "unmenschlicher, noch nicht völlig getilgter Macht."[8]

As a consequence of the disappointing results of their efforts, all three black leaders are surrounded by followers who are confused, ambivalent, and, in some cases, thoroughly disheartened over the strangely bitter taste of freedom, which, in principle, they desperately want but for which, in

8 Heinz Neugebauer, *Anna Seghers: Ihr Leben und Werk* (Berlin: Volk und Wissen, 1970), p. 121.

reality, many are inadequately prepared. In *Wiedereinführung*, Seghers demonstrates that without strong black leaders and independence from European control, the free blacks in Guadaloupe exercise little control over their lives, for along with facing unceasingly harsh treatment and discrimination, they must somehow take on the added burden of self-sufficiency. They are unable to cope effectively with freedom not only because of the dishonest governors but also because "they cannot understand that they must freely do the work which they formerly did under the threat of force. Nor can they cope with the responsibility for their own destiny."[9] The option of self-determination suddenly seems, especially for many of the older blacks who have served family members spanning three generations, much more threatening than the certain provisions and occasional kindness of even the severest of masters. Thus, in *Hochzeit*, at the outbreak of the uprising, Veronika hastily leaves with the family which she has served for so many years, and in *Licht*, old Douglas is baffled by all the talk of revolution: "Von Freisein und Freiwerden verstand er gar nichts" (p. 278). He remains adoring and protective of Debuisson, whom he remembers as a child crawling about at his feet.

Despite the negative outcome of each novella, the seeds of change are nevertheless sown, and the light which shines from the gallows where Sasportas dies symbolizes the hope and struggle which are not easily extinguished. When Sasportas refuses to betray and abandon the planned insurrection, he tells Debuisson, "Man kann vielleicht einen Auftrag zurück-ziehen, einen einzelnen kann man zurückberufen. Man kann keine Bewegung ungeschehen machen" (p. 241). This idea becomes the central focus of the stories in *Drei Frauen aus Haiti*.

As with the Antilles novellas, much of the action and details of these later stories are based on historical fact. The main characters, though, are neither prominent historical figures nor representatives of distant colonial powers, but are, instead, "little people," members of the proletariat whose sacrifices are seen as the essential force in the process of change. Models for the three women protagonists are present in minor characters in the earlier cycle. In *Hochzeit* the slave girl Margot takes a risk to bring together Toussaint and Michael Nathan, who, despite the long association between

---

[9] Bangerter, p. 108.

his father (the jeweler Samuel) and the island aristocrats, shows sympathy for the revolutionary movement. Later Margot lives with Michael, his sister Mali, and the mulatto woman Angela in a happy, peaceful coexistence. Similarly, old Manon (Berenger's black servant) in *Wiedereinführung* provides sustenance and emotional nurturing for Paul Rohan (black), Beauvais (French), and Berenger (mulatto), and in *Licht*, Ann, a slave in the household of Debuisson's grandfather, risks her life to help Sasportas, for she senses his deep commitment to the blacks' cause and returns it with her unconditional love. This "unauslöschbare Liebe" ("Schlüssel," p. 36) is the prominent quality in the spirit of the main characters of *Drei Frauen*, wherein all three women demonstrate:

> Zuverlässigkeit, Beharrlichkeit, Treue, die es ihnen ermöglichen, die Härte ihres Alltags durchzustehen. Der Beschreibung der Schönheit der Frauen wird breiter Raum zugemessen, sie wird symbolhaft zum Kraftquell im Kampf. Schließlich kann nicht übersehen werden, daß alle drei das Leben anderer bewahren.[10]

"Das Versteck," set during the fifteenth century, portrays the legendary Indian beauty Toaliina. While she does not share the African descent of the black characters of the other stories and novellas, the suffering which she and her fellow Indians experience is part of the same long history of enslavement and oppression in the New World. Particularly significant is her legendary beauty, which symbolizes the unspoiled, natural state in which she exists and for which (in order to remain on the island) she risks death. She and several other young women sold into slavery by their tribal chief jump from the ship which is to take them to Spain. With difficulty, she reaches a hiding place where she clings to an old tree stump long ripped from its trunk but which, like Toaliina, who has successfully escaped, "wieder Wurzeln geschlagen hatte" (p. 14). Thereafter, she is forced, paradoxically, to live a life of freedom in seclusion, while others around her are victimized by the European intruders. Several individuals, old and young alike, join together - some dying as a result - to protect her, and she remains hidden among the rocks, at one with nature, from whence new roots may spring.

---

[10] Werner Lüder, "Historische Dimensionen im Unscheinbaren," *Weimarer Beiträge*, 29, No. 2 (1983), 315.

In "Der Schlüssel," which takes place three hundred years later in France, the key which Claudine buries with her husband Amédée, a devoted follower of the exiled Toussaint, is the symbol of her continued fight for independence. Shortly before Toussaint's death she looks back on the day of the uprising and remembers when, at the moment slaves were claiming and celebrating their freedom all over the island, she was freed by Amédée from the stockade in which her mistress had locked her. In the mad frenzy of excitement, the blacks overrunning the estate had overlooked her. The key which Amédée miraculously finds in the tumult binds her to him forever, just as he feels forever bound to Toussaint and all others with whom he fought. Thus, Claudine fights to carry out Amédée's wish to be buried with the key around his neck, for he will wear it "bis zur Auferstehung aller Sklaven der Welt" (p. 55).

In the third story, "Die Trennung," Seghers concentrates on contemporary Haitian society, wherein the protagonist, Luisa, becomes a victim of her country's internal conflict between the terrorist police of the Duvalier regime and their resistors. The forces of evil come from among the Haitians themselves, and, as if to underscore this most grotesque of injustices, Luisa is brutally beaten and left to die in jail, because she refuses to betray her former lover Cristobal, one of the organizers of a revolutionary library. The scarred, long-suffering woman not only offers herself up by protecting Cristobal but also later finds happiness in Cristobal's marriage to Susanna, daughter of her friend Juan. Her actions and the consequences suggest at once the pain of her fellow-countrymen who have become prisoners of themselves and the possibility for renewal and wholeness in their divided community. In contrast to Toaliina's inextinguishable, radiant beauty, Luisa's face has become a "verzerrte Maske" (p. 92). Yet she exudes an inner peace and determined spirit which begins to take root in others around her. Seghers writes, "Sie bekam einen stolzen Begräbniszug, an dem alle teilnahmen, die ihre Gedanken geteilt hatten, und solche, in denen beim Mitgehen diese Gedanken zu keimen begannen" (p. 99).

The raging, life-threatening storm at the end of "Das Versteck" and the death and burial scenes at the closing of the other two stories might seem to suggest man's utter helplessness and insignificance in the course of his fate. Seghers, however, makes it quite clear that the vital point in each of these circumstances is, in the words of a critic, "das

Durchhalten, die Kraft, die das kostet, manchmal über das Menschenmögliche hinaus."[11] This "holding on" not only enables the heroines to survive the worst oppression but is an example for others around them who must also prevail. Their ability to stand the test of genuine commitment and thereby preserve and protect their dream is important not only in their time but also for successive generations. A major symbol in each story serves to highlight the important connection between the generations: roots of a stump which, despite detachment from the trunk, do not die ("Das Versteck"); a key that shall be worn until the final uprising against and banishment of all slavery ("Der Schlüssel"); scars which heal external wounds and protect the less easily violated, more lasting internal strength ("Die Trennung").

Thus, in "Das Versteck" Toaliina is left alone and imperiled, ironically, by the very forces of nature from which she had sought and received protection. Although she is filled with despair about the fate of her children and loved ones who worked hard to survive and remain independent, she is nevertheless not disheartened and, at the most perilous of moments, "fühlte bei aller Gefahr, daß das Meer ihr half, mit dem sie von klein auf vertraut war. . . . Sie wußte, ihre Flucht war geglückt" (p. 27). In "Der Schlüssel" Seghers adeptly makes a link between the present and the past through Claudine's memories of her life when she was enslaved and suffered beatings or suffocating confinement. Although she and Amédée have lived to experience freedom, only to have it all too quickly taken away after the demise of Toussaint, they are bound together and with all people before and after them through the key which Amédée wears at his burial: "Wer bei der Beerdigung eine Handvoll Sand in das Grab warf, fühlte sich mit dem Toten verbunden" (p. 55). In "Die Trennung," because Cristobal is proud of Luisa's scars, which represent the ultimate sacrifice and commitment to their goal of revolution, he immediately rejects Juan's suggestion of plastic surgery. Luisa's sacrifice and the unity of Cristobal, Susanna, and Luisa become symbolic of the important solidarity, not only in the present but also in the future, which will enable them to finally gain control of their lives.

On the one hand, the combined episodes represent the history of Haiti's struggle for emancipation, and the lives of

11 Frank Wagner, "Selbstbehauptung und ihr geschichtliches Maß," *Zeitschrift für Germanistik*, 2, No. 1 (1981), 44.

the women portrayed are a metaphor for the slowly evolving process. On a larger scale, the figures represent a progression in terms of Seghers' own experience of and ideas on the possibilities for revolution and rebuilding of a humanistic society. Several critics have pointed to the implicit and explicit connections Seghers seems to be making between the long and difficult revolution against the oppressive social order which existed in the islands and events in her own country which ended in internal catastrophe and division. Thus, Klaus Sauer maintains that, in the earlier cycle, she attempts to show that the "napoleonische Macht-Ideologie" anticipated the fascism from which she was forced to flee.[12] In addition, John Milfull, suggesting a relationship with Seghers' feelings upon her return to the newly formed German Democratic Republic, notes that her portrayal of those tottering republics, along with stressing the need for a realistic revolutionary strategy, "sollte . . . als Warnung davor dienen, die Schwierigkeiten des sozialistischen Aufbaus in der DDR zu verharmlosen."[13] Although Seghers once declared that in writing *Hochzeit* she did not intend to draw a historical parallel, her continued preoccupation with the subject and the more comprehensive, broad historical approach she uses in the later work allow not only a comparison of past and present events and problems associated with emancipation but also provide something of a *"Blueprint* für die weitere Entwicklung der Befreiungsbewegung in der dritten Welt. . . ."[14]

While the events related in *Drei Frauen* in a sense repeat the failed attempts at revolution as portrayed in the earlier Antilles novellas, a more positive viewpoint and ideas about the possibilities for future success are nevertheless suggested in the image of the black character, who begins to look beyond the immediate state of oppression to the final, slowly won goal. Even though they are not more immediately successful in their struggle, the black characters represent a firmer stance whereby one may gradually move forward, for despite the often complex political and social issues by which they are victimized, they are portrayed as better understand-

---

12 Klaus Sauer, *Anna Seghers* (Munich: C.H. Beck, 1978), p. 126.

13 John Milfull, "Juden, Frauen, Mulatten, Neger. Probleme der Emanzipation in Anna Seghers' 'Karibische Erzählungen,'" in *Frauenliteratur. Autorinnen - Perspektiven - Konzepte,* ed. Manfred Jurgensen (Bern/Frankfurt/M.: Peter Lang, 1983), p. 50.

14 Milfull, p. 50.

ing what must come from within - from *each* individual - not only to withstand the pressure but also to react to it. Thus, Wagner notes that in the fate of these women from three different centuries Seghers has emphatically pointed to the necessity of individual contribution, however small, to a cause and to the importance of the long-term impact of that contribution, for the uncompromising stand which each takes provides a model for successive generations.[15]

In "Die Trennung," in answer to Luisa's question about when things will change, Jean is unable to assure her that the terrorism will disappear or even abate with the demise of Bebe Doc Duvalier; he is, however, more certain of what she must do, namely, to remain the same in her pure, unconditional love and willingness to sacrifice. Although he speaks of this in terms of her relationship to Cristobal, his words take on a much larger meaning and point directly to the fight for freedom in which they are all involved. In her inner strength, which seems to grow in proportion to her complete physical debilitation, she represents Claudine's concept of the revolution as "eine überaus mächtige Frau, um die wir singend tanzten" ("Schlüssel," p. 44).

This image of revolution as a powerful black woman adds an interesting light to Seghers' fiction, for critics analyzing her fiction written before *Drei Frauen* have generally characterized the women as being passive, silent, and highly traditional, thereby rendering her work empty of any true "feminist" discourse.[16] Their speechlessness, however, need not be strictly interpreted as representing a lack of self-assuredness or hesitancy to actively participate in the same sense as a Toussaint or Cristobal. Rather it might be seen as a sign of infinite commitment which may not be reduced to words; they do not simply talk about or draw up plans for revolution, they *live* their ideals as true revolutionaries who need "keine philosophischen Aussprachen über Sinn und Ziel der Revolution."[17] Through the manner in which the characters accept and meet the challenges put to them, Seghers not only makes a statement about the complexity of their identities as members of a race and as individuals in a larger

---

[15] Wagner, p. 46.

[16] Erika Haas, "Der männliche Blick der Anna Seghers. Das Frauenbild einer kommunistischen Schriftstellerin," in *Notizbuch*, 2 (1980), 134-38, as quoted in Milfull, "Juden, Frauen, Mulatten, Neger," p. 46.

[17] Milfull, p. 53.

human community striving for a meaningful existence but also offers her own vision concerning the possibility for revolution, emancipation, and renewal in our modern-day world.

Concepts of Socialist Construction and the National Question: The SED's Claims to Legitimacy (1945-1949)

Sigrid Meuschel

The concept of legitimacy to be used in this investigation is Max Weber's notion of *Legitimitätsglaube*. It is a means of analyzing the chances that a given political system's self-conception and self-justification have of being accepted as legitimate by its subjects, and thus of achieving central aspects of social integration.[1] The material and sources utilized in this study are Party documents, periodicals such as *Aufbau* and *Einheit*,[2] and brochures written for purposes of political education. Attention will be focused on the Communist and Socialist Unity Party's concepts of democratic, socialist, and national reconstruction of German postwar society. Other aspects, such as the socio-economic and political reforms and reconstruction - and their effect on these concepts - and differences between the four Allied occupation powers cannot be discussed here.

---

[1] For the theoretical framework, see Sigrid Meuschel, "Integration durch Legitimation? Zum Problem der Sozialintegration in der DDR," in *Ideologie und gesellschaftliche Entwicklung in der DDR. 18. Tagung zum Stand der DDR-Forschung in der Bundesrepublik Deutschland 28. bis 31. Mai 1985*, Edition Deutschland Archiv (Cologne: Wissenschaft und Politik, 1985), pp. 15-29.

[2] The first three issues of *Einheit* were published before the unification of the SPD and KPD with the subtitle "Monatsschrift zur Vorbereitung der Sozialistischen Einheitspartei." These issues are quoted by number, month, and year (1946). After the SED was founded, *Einheit*, edited by the SED *Parteivorstand*, became the "Theoretische Monatsschrift für Sozialismus." The issues are quoted by volume, number, and year (1946 ff.).

General Considerations

In regard to general political attitudes in Germany in 1945 and the years immediately thereafter, I would like to argue that all politically interested individuals, groups, and parties from the center to the left criticized not only capitalism's mode of functioning but also the form of democracy that had allowed and tolerated the political dominance of economic elites, and the political culture that had not prevented but rather alleviated the rise to power of National Socialism. Politicians, however, faced a dilemma: a large part of the German population had complied with or supported the Nazi regime; and since Germans had not liberated themselves, the country was deprived of its political sovereignty and no state institutions existed. The chances of statebuilding presupposed *both* socio-economic reconstruction and moral and political reeducation - be it authoritarian or democratic - *and* the support and approval of the Allied military governments. Thus politicians ran the risk either of successfully politicizing the populace and thereby possibly inducing conflicts with the Allied forces, or of cooperating with the latter and thus diminishing the chance of involving the German political addressees. The SED, from the start, acted in accordance with the second alternative.

Moreover, not only the social, economic, and political spheres needed to be reconstructed but problems of national organization had to be solved as well. The social question - to put it in Marxist terms - refers to the precarious balance of socialism and democracy. The national question, in 1945 and thereafter, embraced three aspects: political (national) culture, nation-state building, and state sovereignty. One may plausibly argue, and plausibly not only within a Marxist approach, that the first two aspects are part and parcel of any solution to the social question, too. The third aspect, however, national sovereignty, is independent of such concerns.

In regard to the SED's chances of gaining legitimacy, my hypothesis will be the following: as a solution to the social and national questions, the Party at first - that is, in 1945-1946 - favored the concept of an antifascist-democratic order, on the one hand, and the notion of an independent, specifically German road to socialism, on the other. After 1947, the proclaimed particularity inherent in both concepts fell victim to the Cold War and the changed Soviet politics which rendered references to specifically German circumstances and to political independence illusory. Like the parties in the people's democracies of East and Central Europe, the SED too had to adapt to the Soviet Union's anti-imperialist and internationalist self-definition and to its obligatory prescription of the road to and mode of socialism. The new argumentative device implicitly asserted the identity of the social and national questions - an implication which had been made, to be sure, at least subliminally, in the preceding years as well. Since the new concepts were unlikely to carry high legitimatory potential, the SED combined them with patriotic campaigns for national unity. The emotional force of patriotism provided the legitimacy and social integration which rational commitment to the construction of Soviet-type socialism, void of national sovereignty, could not offer to a sufficient degree.

Particular German Road to Socialism

In 1945 political deliberations inevitably reflected the experience of National Socialism. Although the immediate past was eminent, most of the ideas on how to reconstruct Germany were not primarily informed by analyses of Nazism. The KPD/SED for instance continued to follow the definition of the Comintern of 1933 and interpreted German fascism as the "most reactionary," "openly terroristic" dictatorship of monopoly capitalism's "most imperialistic" and "wildest" elements.[3] Even though the Party recognized the responsibility and guilt of the German population as well as the fact that millions of Germans were still captives of the Nazi ideology,[4] the orientation of postwar politics relied primarily on diagnoses of National Socialism's origins: i.e., the historical weakness of the German bourgeoisie after 1848, the "mistakes of 1918," and the failure of the Weimar Republic. According to this view, Weimar had failed mainly for two reasons: because in 1918 a "real" democracy had not been fought for - and the bourgeois-democratic revolution thus not "completed"; and because during the Weimar period the organizational split of the labor movement had prevented the building of an

---

[3] "Der Klassencharakter des Faschismus und die Probleme der Einheits- und Volksfront," *Vortragsdisposition*, 1, No. 2 (1945), pp. 1-4. The *Vortragsdis - positionen*, edited by Verlag Neuer Weg in Berlin, are brochures for political education. Translations of quotations here and throughout are my own.

[4] "Aufruf an das deutsche Volk zum Aufbau eines antifaschistisch-demokratischen Deutschlands," in *Um ein antifaschistisch-demokratisches Deutschland* (Berlin: Staatsverlag der DDR, 1968), p. 58. See also "Kommunique über die Bildung des Blocks der antifaschistisch-demokratischen Parteien" in this volume, pp. 91 ff.

antifascist united front.[5] The KPD/SED declared the completion of the bourgeois-democratic revolution to be on the postwar agenda, i.e., the building of an "antifascist-democratic order," the antifascist aspect of which soon was reduced to anti-imperialism and to the appeal for unity.

Beyond serving as a basis for such important political reforms as denazification, expropriation, demilitarization, and so forth, the Party's justification of the antifascist-democratic solution to the social question was intended to prove the continuity of its prewar commitment to the cause of a "new democratic republic."[6] Moreover, the KPD put special emphasis on political and organizational unity: on the unity of the four antifascist parties within the United Front, on the unity of the SPD and KPD within the Socialist Unity Party, and on the unity of the nation.[7] The Party's claim to its leading role - be it within the party bloc, within the working class, or within the nation as a whole - complemented the threefold pleading for unity.[8]

Individual rights could be only of minor importance in a concept which conceived of them as "non-essential" ("das nicht Wesentliche") and as depending on the essential, i.e., the rule of the people. In the period of "transition to a better, more progressive form of democracy" than the bourgeois "formal" democracy had been, individual rights were viewed as reactionary, favoring solely the expropriators' interests and hampering the "dictatorship of the overwhelming majority" of the working people.[9] The SED, responsible to "all of the people" and vanguard of the "laboring masses," informed and guided by the theory of "consequent Marxism," would lead the democratic struggle. Majority rule was regarded as a qualitative principle and defined according to class interests,

---

[5] "Aufruf an das deutsche Volk," p. 59.

[6] "Der Klassencharakter des Faschismus und die Probleme der Einheits- und Volksfront," pp. 13-14.

[7] Wilhelm Pieck, "Die Einheit der Arbeiterklasse und die Einheit der Nation," Einheit, 1 (Feb. 1946), pp. 1 ff; "Grundsätze und Ziele der SED," Einheit, 2 (March 1946), pp. 2 ff.

[8] "Aufruf an das deutsche Volk," p. 63; "Grundsätze und Ziele der SED," pp. 2-3; "Der Weg des Wiederaufbaus Deutschlands," Vortragsdisposition, 1, No. 4 (1945), 6.

[9] "Was ist Demokratie?" Einheit, 1, No. 3 (1946), 216 ff.

which the vanguard party claimed to know and identify appropriately in all social and political spheres.[10]

In contrast to the merely procedural, "formal" bourgeois democracy, the antifascist-democratic order was to be a "real" democracy, an "antifascist-democratic republic" which would eliminate the economic foundations of class power and guarantee the power of the people by abolishing the separation of powers.[11] Democracy was to be more than the "freedom to vote" ("Freiheit der Abstimmung"),[12] namely, people's power, a form of government securing power for and representing the interests of "the overwhelming majority of the people."[13] The "government of all the progressive and responsible forces of the nation," the "rebirth of our people," should be based upon three principles: on the will of the people as the "supreme law," on an economic organization according to the people's interests, and on the creation of a new and democratic culture.[14] These principles would imply parliamentary democracy, "daily cooperation" of the people in the process of social construction and "co-determination of the antifascist-democratic forces" in the economy and state, the unity of powers and control over the executive.[15] The Party declared the building of a "real" democracy as its immediate goal ("Gegenwartsforderung"). This would bring about the destruction of Nazism and militarism, and the reeducation of the populace, and - last but not least - build the foundation for the struggle for socialism. The antifascist-democratic order would learn from Weimar's failure in that it would unite all "progressive" forces, punish those guilty of war, liquidate imperialist monopolies and the reactionary state bureaucracy, construct the "truly democratic" state, and reform the education and legal systems. An "immediate realization of socialism" was seen as inhibited by the Nazi devastation of class

10 Walter Ulbricht, *Der Plan des demokratischen Neuaufbaus* (Berlin: Neuer Weg, 1946), p. 40; "Das Wesen der Sozialistischen Einheitspartei," *Sozialistische Bildungshefte*, 1, No. 1 (1946), pp. 1-2.

11 "Grundsätze und Ziele der SED," pp. 3-4.

12 Otto Grotewohl, "Im Kampf um unsere Zukunft," *Einheit*, 1, No. 4 (1946), 199 ff.

13 "Die antifaschistisch-demokratische Republik," *Sozialistische Bildungshefte*, 1, No. 2 (1946), p. 2.

14 Ulbricht, *Der Plan des demokratischen Aufbaus*, pp. 6-7, 13.

15 "Die antifaschistisch-demokratische Republik," pp. 7-8.

consciousness and by the long experience of working-class disunity.[16]

If we regard the antifascist-democratic order, the construction of a real - albeit not yet socialist - democracy as the SED's device to solve the social tasks, we may ask how the Party conceived of the national question. As for its social content, the struggle for national unity and the attempt to implement the antifascist-democratic model in all the occupied zones were put on one and the same level. If the liberation of the working class is identical with the liberation of the people, if the working class in all capitalist countries pursues the same interests, if the party of the masses leads the struggle of the whole nation, then the Party could conclude that fighting for national unity means fighting for an all-German antifascist order.[17]

The polemic against the separatism of the Western zones was based on this argument, and the SED's antifederalism was aimed at achieving centralist structures not only in the East.[18] The remaining aspect of the national question, the problem of national sovereignty, was discussed indirectly, i.e., in terms of independence of the Party vis-à-vis the Soviet Union. In this respect the notion of a "particular German road to socialism" deserves attention.[19] The notion *per se* was not unique to the SED: the other East European parties under Soviet influence also claimed to be following particular roads to socialism. The particularity of the road was seen in its nonrevolutionary, peaceful, and democratic character, on the one hand, and in the refusal to adopt the Soviet system under the

---

[16] Walter Ulbricht, "Thesen über den Hitlerfaschismus," *Einheit*, 1 (Feb. 1946), pp. 10 ff.

[17] "Grundsätze und Ziele der SED," p. 4; "Das Wesen der sozialistischen Einheitspartei," pp. 5 f., 7.

[18] Walter Ulbricht, *Der Plan des demokratischen Aufbaus*, pp. 36 ff; "Der nationale Kampf der KPD und die Einheit Deutschlands," *Vortragsdisposition*, 2, No. 3 (1946), 16; "Grundrechte des deutschen Volkes," in *Dokumente der SED* (Berlin: Dietz, 1951), I, 91 ff.

[19] "Wir sind der Auffassung, daß der Weg, Deutschland das Sowjetsystem aufzuzwingen, falsch wäre, denn dieser Weg entspricht nicht gegenwärtigen Entwicklungsbedingungen Deutschlands" ("Aufruf an das deutsche Volk," p. 60); similar formulations for instance in Walter Ulbricht, "Strategie und Taktik der SED," *Einheit*, 1, No. 5 (1946), 263 f., and "Grundsätze und Ziele der SED," p. 4; Wilhelm Pieck, "Die Bedeutung der Prinzipienerklärung," *Einheit*, 2 (March 1946), pp. 9 ff. For the concept of the particular German road to socialism, see especially Anton Ackermann, "Gibt es einen besonderen deutschen Weg zum Sozialismus?" *Einheit*, 1 (Feb. 1946), pp. 22 ff.

contemporary circumstances, on the other. Whether the asserted independence of party action referred to the (peaceful) road alone or the socialist goal as well remained open; the goal was left undefined. The "peculiarities of the German situation" indicated no other national specificity than the fact that socialism could be achieved peacefully because war and occupation had destroyed Germany's state apparatus and military potential. The road to socialism would thus depend upon the opportunity to extend the antifascist-democratic order to the rest of Germany. In other words, the solution of both the national and the social question was in principle identical. The sovereignty aspect of the national question was ultimately reduced to and determined by the mode in which the social question was solved.[20]

Toward Sovietization

When in 1947/48 the international situation changed (beginning of the Cold War, theory of the two camps, founding of the Cominform, conflict with Yugoslavia) and - as a result - the East German domestic political conditions as well, the SED did not abandon the concept of an antifascist-democratic order. It was superseded, however, by the notion of a "democracy of a new type" ("Demokratie neuen Typs"). As for the definition of the national question, the perspective of a particular and peaceful road to socialism was explicitly refuted and replaced by the prognosis of increasing internal and international class struggle. The new conceptions of social and national construction acknowledged the Soviet type of socialism as the model which ought to be accomplished; and the acceptance of the Soviet Union's leading role within the anti-imperialist camp was no longer denied. Such political alterations affected the analysis of the Weimar Republic's failure, too. Had hitherto the lack of democracy and of proletarian antifascist unity been blamed, now the Party maintained that socialist revolution had already been on the agenda in 1918. In 1947, therefore, the SED - like all the East European Communist parties - could not pretend to concentrate its efforts on the "completion" of the bourgeois

---

[20] In discussing goal perspectives or problems of the contemporary situation, the SED used the attributes "social" and "national" synonymously, and both covered a broad spectrum: antifascist-democratic construction, unity of the labor movement or of all democratic forces or of the nation, abolition of misery and distress, of shame and disgrace, regeneration of German culture, and so forth. See "Manifest an das deutsche Volk," in *Dokumente der SED* (Berlin: Dietz, 1951), I, 24 ff.

revolution, i.e., on the construction of an antifascist-democratic order.[21]

The concept of the "democracy of a new type" laid emphasis on the importance of building a "party of a new type,"[22] and was itself regarded as part of a general historical evolution of democracy and socialism which distinguished three forms of democracy: the formal-bourgeois one, the new-type or people's democracy, and the Soviet form of democracy. The new-type democracy was to be a form of the dictatorship of the proletariat, a dictatorship in the developing phase of socialist transformation.[23] In that the Soviet model, as the highest form, became the proclaimed aim of all roads to socialism, even the allusion to national or party independence was lost.

Within this newly stated, obligatory developmental concept, the SED kept asserting a German particularity: in contrast to the people's democracies of Eastern Europe, the new-type democracy could not yet be firmly installed in the Soviet-occupied zone because the Nazi ideology still affected class consciousness, because the new-type party was only slowly coming into being, and because the nation was divided to the effect that in the Western zones monopoly capitalism and political reaction were being restored.[24] Such reformulations of a national particularity, however, neither indicated independent party action nor sovereignty of a future German state. On the contrary, the struggle for German unity was justified in terms of revolutionary internationalism, which refuted the "'theory' of a 'particular German road to social-

---

[21] Walter Ulbricht, "Die Hauptlehre von 1918," *Einheit*, 3, No. 10 (1948), 892 ff; Erich W. Gniffke, "Der November 1918 und das Schicksal der deutschen Nation," *Einheit*, 3, No. 10 (1948), 937 f.

[22] For the characterization of the new-type party, see Walter Ulbricht, "Die große Lehre," *Einheit*, 2, No. 11 (1947), 1068 ff., and the complete issue of *Einheit*, 3, No. 9 (1948).

[23] The concept is very clearly formulated in Fred Oelßner, "Die Diktatur des Proletariats - Hauptfrage im Leninismus," *Einheit*, 4, No. 8 (1949), 723 ff; also Paul Merker, "Über die Sowjetdemokratie," *Einheit*, 2, No. 11 (1947), 1038 ff.

[24] Kurt Hager, "Antifaschistisch-demokratische Ordnung," *Einheit*, 4, No. 4 (1949), 209 ff., 302 ff; Klaus Zweiling, "Intelligenz und Arbeiterklasse," *Einheit*, 4, No. 5 (1949), 385 ff.

ism'" as expression of "petty-bourgeois nationalist tendencies."[25]

As was the case during the earlier phase, the Party's definition of the national question was dependent on the conceptualization of the social question. The First Party Conference of the SED (1949) discerned three "main tasks" "closely related to one another and affecting Germany as a whole":[26] the SED's development into a new-type party, the strengthening of the antifascist-democratic order, and the struggle for "democratic unity and a just peace."[27] The Soviet party congratulated the SED on being the true "bearer of the German people's national interests," and on having recognized the "inseparable unity" of international and national tasks, and having acknowledged the Soviet Union's leading role in the world-wide anti-imperialist fight; the "friendship between the German people and the SU" would be "decisive for the national fate of Germany."[28]

Patriotism - A Legitimatory Device?

Pondering the question whom this orthodox Marxist-Leninist reformulation of the social and national problematic can have convinced, it may be useful to briefly mention alternative views of construction as discussed, for example, by the East German Social Democratic Party or in the Communist periodical *Aufbau*, the journal of the Kulturbund zur demokratischen Erneuerung Deutschlands, which reflected the SED's *Bündnispolitik* and its politics toward Germany as a whole.

Taking into consideration the failure of the Weimar Republic, the traumatic experience of Nazism, and the compliance of the majority of Germans, the Social Democrats likewise stressed the importance of achieving proletarian unity; they regarded some sort of educational dictatorship as

---

[25] Rudolf Herrnstadt ("Einige Lehren aus den Fehlern der KP Jugoslawiens," *Einheit*, 3, No. 9 [1948], 799) completely denied and destroyed the notion of a particular road in general, and of a German one in particular. See also Walter Ulbricht, "Die Bedeutung des deutschen Planes," *Einheit*, 3, No. 8 (1948), 678.

[26] Wilhelm Pieck, "Lehren der Parteikonferenz," *Einheit*, 4, No. 3 (1949), 204.

[27] Peace here refers to a peace treaty and to the fight against a new imperialist war (Pieck, "Lehren der Parteikonferenz," p. 198).

[28] Quoted from the Soviet address, in Franz Dahlem, "Lebendiger proletarischer Internationalismus," *Einheit*, 4, No. 4 (1949), 294, 295.

inevitable, and favored centralist state institutions and a planned economy. To be sure, such state-oriented ideas of socialism, its authoritarian conceptualization of politics, economy, and culture, is but one variant of learning from "the lessons" of Nazism, or of Weimar respectively.[29] As is well-known, the SPD - earlier than Communist officials - advocated the reunification of the labor movement, but by no means all of its members envisioned a fusion of the parties which had failed in Weimar and during the period of resistance. Especially trade unionists preferred the British model of a labor party. Others, as for instance Herrmann Brill or Gustav Dahrendorf, aimed at a completely new party which would be temporarily assigned the function of leading and educating the subjects of an authoritarian democracy; authoritarianism was to be moderated once Nazism lost its influence and the occupying forces left. Otto Grotewohl and the *Zentralausschuß* of the Berlin SPD followed still another line. They demanded "democracy in the state and commune, socialism in the economy and society,"[30] and wanted the unification of SPD and KPD to be achieved from below and as a result, not as the starting point, of common politics. Grotewohl expected that the Soviet Union would respect the Social Democrats' freedom of action within the SED. In his view such social-democratization would be the only German guarantee of Soviet security interests.[31]

In its very first years of existence the journal *Aufbau* stimulated a broad discussion on how the long process of the distortion of reason became dominant in German politics and culture. The contributors did not reduce the Nazi problematic

---

[29] There was also a minority which rejected the rebuilding of a strong national state - for precisely the reason that in Germany it had never had a positive effect - and favored federalism and plurality in order to exclude any further excess of power. Such points of view were published primarily in the West, for instance in the journal *Frankfurter Hefte*, which was edited by Eugen Kogon and Walter Dirks. As another example, Kurt Schumacher, who became the leader of the West German SPD, regarded proletarian and national unity as less important than the building of a Western-type democracy within the Western zones.

[30] "Aufruf des ZA der SPD zum Aufbau eines antifaschistisch-demokratischen Deutschland," in *Um ein antifaschistisch-demokratisches Deutschland* (Berlin: Staatsverlag der DDR, 1968), pp. 67-68.

[31] For social-democratic concepts discussed above, see Albrecht Kaden, *Einheit oder Freiheit* (Hannover: Dietz, 1964); Frank Moraw, *Die Parole der "Einheit" und die Sozialdemokratie* (Bonn/Bad Godesberg: Neue Gesellschaft, 1973); Frank Thomas Stößel, *Positionen in der KPD/SED 1945-1954* (Cologne: Wissenschaft und Politik, 1985).

to Weimar or to general imperialist conditions; they used instead differentiated approaches to explain or describe the genesis of the German *Untertanengeist*, Prussian militarism, Protestant state orientation, and Hegelian state fetishism. Authors of divergent political and theoretical leanings such as Ernst Niekisch, Willy Huhn, or - most prominently - Georg Lukács scrutinized the development of irrationalism; and scholars such as Arnold Bauer and Victor Klemperer discussed the character of Nazism, distinguishing it from both racism and fascism.

The journal's approach, however, neither excluded a basic loyalty to the Party and its course of socialist construction, nor a rather exalted attitude towards the German *Vaterland* - as expressed for instance in Johannes R. Becher's patriotic commitment. When the general line of the Party changed in 1947, *Aufbau* too displayed a disinclination to interpret German historical development as a catastrophic, not easily dissolved synthesis;[32] in a quite undialectical manner, the "good" and "evil" aspects of German culture were singled out and regarded separately. During the late forties, such duality alleviated an almost chauvinistic juxtaposition of German humanism and classicism, on the one hand, and of Western imperialism's culturally destructive ("kulturzersetzend") cosmopolitism, on the other.[33]

I should like to argue that anti-cosmopolitism and nationalist-patriotic campaigns may have achieved some degree of legitimacy and of social integration when alternative views of the past and future became politically blocked. As long as the notions of a particular road to socialism and of an antifascist-democratic order officially prevailed, many of the politically interested could assume that their own ideas had a chance of being realized. Party theorists left altogether unanswered how the antifascist "completion" of the bourgeois-democratic revolution related to a future socialist society, the structures of which remained undefined. In that the socio-economic and political reforms of the very first years both overcame the

---

[32] See the valuable analysis of Alexander Abusch, *Der Irrweg einer Nation* (Berlin: Aufbau, 1946).

[33] In regard to the friendship with the Soviet Union and its consequences for art and literature, see *Aufbau*, 3, No. 11 (1947); for the renunciation of the journal's impartial ("überparteilich") orientation, see Klaus Gysi, "Neue Entwicklungen," *Aufbau*, 4, No. 7 (1948), 545 ff., and "Symptom," *Aufbau*, 4, No. 8 (1948), 639 ff; for the attacks on cosmopolitism, for patriotism, and finally frank Stalinism, see *Aufbau*, 5, No. 11 and No. 12 (1949).

Nazi and capitalist past and pointed to a socialist future, either the one or the other aspect could find support.[34] Also, the notion of particularity said little about the road to and nothing about the aim of socialism; and the two-phase model of development did not discern the differences between an antifascist-democratic order and a socialist-proletarian dictatorship.[35] The "particular road to socialism" permitted divergent interpretations and suggested the chance of internal and exterior political independence. Exactly this ambivalence, underlined by the fact that Soviet politics vis-à-vis Germany embraced several options, was likely to integrate protagonists of different political conceptions.[36]

When in 1947 the road to and mode of socialism were explicitly defined and independence was discarded as an illusion, the only specificity remaining was that aspect of the national question which referred to German unity. The SED initiated several campaigns, the most important having been the People's Congress for Unity and Just Peace (Volkskongreß für Einheit und gerechten Frieden).[37] The campaigns intentionally cut across all social groups and political or ethical convictions in the name of a national goal. The Party mobilized sentiments and ressentiments which allowed the mass of the population to identify with the regime's political line for patriotic reasons.[38] Patriotism had more potential to achieve social integration in as much as antifascism was unlikely to convince the bulk of those who had supported Nazism or complied with it and since people rejected being

---

[34] Ernst Richert, *Agitation und Propaganda* (Berlin/Frankfurt: Franz Vahlen, 1958), pp. 37 ff.

[35] The relationship between an antifascist-democratic order and people's or socialist democracy remained unclear: if the antifascist republic deprived the expropriating classes of power, and if it smashed the bourgeois state and militarism, against whom or what would a future dictatorship of the proletariat direct itself? One plausible answer to this question is that from the very beginning the Soviet model had been striven for; see the final passage in "Der Weg zum Sozialismus," *Vortragsdisposition*, 2, No. 5 (1946), p. 15.

[36] Dietrich Staritz, "Funktion, Ausprägung und Schicksal des 'besonderen deutschen Weges' zum Sozialismus," in *Studien und Materialien*, ed. Arbeitsbereich Geschichte und Politik der DDR am Institut für Sozialwissenschaften (University of Mannheim, 1982), I, 224.

[37] For the People's Congress movement, which started in December 1947, see Richard Lukas, *Zehn Jahre Sowjetische Besatzungszone* (Mainz/Wiesbaden/Düsseldorf: Deutscher Fachschriften Verlag, 1955), pp. 24 ff; Hans-Jürgen Grasemann, *Das Blocksystem und die Nationale Front im Verfassungsrecht der DDR*, Diss. University of Göttingen, 1973, pp. 112 ff.

[38] Richert, pp. 53 ff.

constantly reminded of the past. The People's Congress' slogan "Es geht nicht um Parteien, es geht um unser Volk!"[39] didn't mobilize along party lines; the movement explicitly rehabilitated the former nominal members of the National Socialist Party (the so-called "nominelle Pgs") and the former Nazi activists as well - if they had not committed crimes and now participated in the postwar patriotic struggle as patriots of their "Vaterland."[40]

Moreover, the campaigns denounced Western civilization and modernity and thus displayed a well-known syndrome in German culture. A patriotic rhetoric of the anti-rational tradition conjured up *Heimat, Volk, Liebe zum Vaterland* or the *Wiedergeburt der Nation*,[41] and the Party aggressively addressed American imperialism and Western cosmopolitism. Whereas imperialism was regarded as threatening war and physical extinction, cosmopolitism figured as the imminent cultural apocalypse incorporated in the "Dekadenz der amerikanischen Kultur."[42] Such definitions were familiar to the German audience, they completely denied the problems

---

[39] "Aufruf zu einem Deutschen Volkskongreß für Einheit und gerechten Frieden," in *Programmatische Dokumente der Nationalen Front des demokratischen Deutschland*, ed. Helmut Neef (Berlin: Dietz, 1967), pp. 22 f.

[40] "Beschluß des Dritten Deutschen Volkskongresses," in *Programmatische Dokumente*, pp. 57 ff; also Richard Weimann, "Kultur- und Erziehungsaufgaben der SED," *Einheit*, 3 (April 1946), pp. 14 ff.

[41] For such patriotic rhetoric, see Wilhelm Pieck and Otto Grotewohl, "Es lebe die Einheit!" *Einheit*, 3 (April 1946), pp. 1 f; "Offener Brief an alle Sozialdemokraten und Kommunisten Deutschlands," in *Dokumente der SED* (Berlin: Dietz, 1951), I, 31 ff; Walter Ulbricht, "Grundrechte des deutschen Volkes," p. 91; Kurt Hager, "Antifaschistisch-demokratische Ordnung," *Einheit*, 4, No. 4 (1949), 299 ff; Fred Oelßner, "Ein neuer Abschnitt im Befreiungskampf der deutschen Nation," *Einheit*, 4, No. 11 (1949), 961 ff; Ernst Hoffmann, "Die Bedeutung der ideologischen Offensive in der Sowjetunion für Deutschlands Einheit," *Einheit*, 4, No. 9 (1949), 793 ff.

[42] For the "decadence" of American culture, see Hager, "Antifaschistisch-demokratische Ordnung," pp. 305, 306. For the polemics against cosmopolitism, see Otto Grotewohl, "Nationale Front - Antwort auf Deutschlands Zerreißung," *Einheit*, 4, No. 7 (1949), 577 ff., 589 f; Ernst Hoffmann, "Die Stellung des Marxismus zum bürgerlichen Kosmopolitismus," *Einheit*, 4, No. 7 (1949), 606 ff. Its apogee are anticapitalist stereotypes which also figure prominently in anti-semitism: cosmopolitism is attacked as "Theorie vom entwurzelten, artlosen, abstrakten, also unmenschlichen Menschen" (Hoffmann, "Die Stellung des Marxismus," p. 611).

of German culture and history,[43] and they may have helped in the gaining of legitimacy for a regime which could not rely on the social-integrative potential of antifascism and Soviet-socialist construction.

---

[43] According to the SED, German culture, which had been "degraded by Hitler," now was endangered by American cosmopolitism and fascism: "Die Verteidiger der Idee der Weltherrschaft der USA wollen das Nationalgefühl und die Würde des deutschen Volkes in den Schmutz treten, des Volkes, das Luther und Münzer, Schiller und Goethe, Bach und Beethoven, Hegel und Fichte, Humboldt und Virchow, Marx und Engels, Bebel und Thälmann hervorgebracht hat." ". . . [D]er amerikanische Imperialismus . . . hat das Erbe des Hitlerfaschismus im Kampf um die Weltherrschaft angetreten" ("Die Nationale Front des demokratischen Deutschland und die SED," in *Programmatische Dokumente*, pp. 73-74).

German History and National Identity in the GDR

Alfred Loesdau

Historical awareness is an essential component of national consciousness. Thus in shaping the national identity of GDR citizens great importance is attached to the acquisition of German history and the preservation of tradition. The socialist German nation that is evolving in the GDR is a product of the entirety of German history. Its origins reach back centuries; it is linked to the traditions of the progressive classes, in particular the working class, and is allied with the progressive traditions of all nations. The program of the SED states: "Historically, the socialist nation in the German Democratic Republic is rooted in the people's centuries-old struggle for social progress, especially the struggle of the revolutionary German working class for liberation from capitalist exploitation."[1] These political and social aspects find expression in the predominating socialist historical consciousness.

The Socialist German Nation

Socialist national consciousness in the GDR has its objective foundation in the development of the socialist German nation. The objective basis for this process is provided by the conditions of socialist production. Ethnic factors continue to play their special role, i.e., language, traditions, customs, habits, and socio-psychic peculiarities, which, taken together, go to make up nationality. The majority of GDR citizens are of German nationality. The ethnic characteristics of this nationality go back to the early Middle Ages.

---

[1] *Programme of the Socialist Unity Party of Germany* (Dresden: Zeit im Bild, 1976), pp. 62-63.

The foundations of a socialist society having been laid in the GDR, the Eighth Party Congress in 1971 spoke for the first time of a socialist German nation, in contrast to the Federal Republic, where the bourgeois nation continues to exist. The bourgeois German nation which existed from 1871 to 1945 within the framework of a single state belonged to the past; its continued existence was not viable. At the Ninth Party Congress in 1976 new findings about the development of the socialist German nation in conjunction with the emergence of an advanced socialist society were examined and incorporated in the new Party program. Two basic principles of the nation's development under these new conditions were emphasized: that it is a process, and that the nature of this process is complex.[2]

The proclaimed development of an advanced socialist society marked a new period in the consolidation of the socialist nation in the GDR. The continued development of socialism called for an appropriate elaboration of the national framework. The unfolding of economic, social, and political conditions, the consolidation of the socialist state, and the continued advance of national culture furthered socialist nationhood. The Tenth Party Congress in 1981 was able to conclude that the socialist nation had come into being.[3]

Historical Awareness and National Consciousness

However, one must not equate the actual process of national development and the awareness of this development within the population. It is necessary to foster a sense of national identity. Essential to instilling a feeling of nation in the population is the effective dissemination of history and its lessons. Every nation must be made aware of its historical roots. History promotes a sense of nationhood, as expressed in love and commitment to one's country, efforts to achieve top performance in the economy, science, and culture, and the encouragement of positive national characteristics.

The Role of History and Historical Science

New dimensions have thus opened up for the study and teaching of history in the GDR. Along with changes in the

---

[2] *Protokoll der Verhandlungen des IX. Parteitages der Sozialistischen Einheitspartei Deutschlands* (Berlin: Dietz, 1976), I, 42 ff., 62 ff.

[3] *Protokoll der Verhandlungen des X. Parteitages der Sozialistischen Einheitspartei Deutschlands* (Berlin: Dietz, 1981), I, 47.

economic, political, and cultural conditions, there are also new questions to be asked of history, ultimately new objects, and, not infrequently, new methods of historical science. Historical awareness is itself part of a long-term development. It changes and expands in keeping with the current needs of society. The development of the socialist consciousness of history in the GDR is a reflection of the actual, concrete development of the socialist German nation. The evaluation of historical events and processes is ultimately determined by the requirements of society, from which no historian can isolate himself. It is a major responsibility of historical science to meet these requirements as effectively and promptly as possible.

There are three distinct periods in GDR historical science: the first, during the antifascist-democratic transformation in the latter half of the 1940s, the coming to terms with fascism and the reactionary legacy of German history; the second, from the late 1940s to the early 1960s, the assimilation, first and foremost, of the revolutionary traditions of the German labor movement; and the third, the broader and more differentiated approach to German history as a whole, which runs parallel to the development of an advanced socialist society.[4]

Commensurate with the spreading of the understanding of the GDR as a socio-historically new type of nation, the need arose to rethink the attitude toward Germany's history.[5] The purpose of these reflections, which are supported by historical analyses and interpretations, is the acquiring and deepening of a new national identity. A more precise definition of what is meant by heritage (Erbe) and tradition has emerged. It has become clearer that the GDR must deal with the whole of its historical heritage, even though it does not take a positive attitude to each of its parts. It identifies with the revolutionary, democratic, and humanistic traditions of the historical heritage, and rejects the reactionary traditions.[6]

---

4 Cf. Walter Schmidt, "Zur Entwicklung des Erbe- und Traditionsverständnisses," Zeitschrift für Geschichtswissenschaft, 33, No. 3 (1985), pp. 195 ff.

5 Cf. Walter Schmidt, p. 206

6 Cf. Helmut Meier and Walter Schmidt, Was du ererbt von deinen Vätern hast... (Berlin: Dietz, 1980).

Acknowledging the Cultural Heritage

At its Ninth Party Congress in 1976, the SED set as a goal the tapping of the rich cultural heritage. The Party program decided there states:

> The socialist national culture of the German Democratic Republic includes the careful preservation and acquisition of all humanistic and progressive cultural accomplishments of the past. The socialist culture of the German Democratic Republic is indebted to the rich heritage that was created during the entire history of the German people. Everything that is great and noble, humanistic and revolutionary is honored and continued in the German Democratic Republic by making it relevant to the tasks of the present.[7]

This orientation led to new high points in the acquisition of the cultural heritage and preservation of tradition. In 1981, when the permanent exhibit on the history of the German people was opened in the Museum of German History, Kurt Hager, ZK Secretary for Art and Science, pointed out:

> We have chosen to cover *the whole* of German history with its truly checkered course. Even far-off times, events, and personalities which to date have received little attention are given the prominence they objectively deserve - something which derives from our scientific understanding of history, an understanding based on historical materialism. Not a little has been done, but much still remains to be done in order to capture, in their full scope and with all their heterogeneity, the traditions of which our socialist state is the legitimate heir and to make them the intellectual property of a broad public, and the younger generation in particular.[8]

---

[7] *Protokoll der Verhandlungen des IX. Parteitages*, II, 247. My translation here and throughout.

[8] Kurt Hager, "Der Reichtum unserer Traditionen," *Sonntag*, 2 August 1981, p. 8.

The years 1982 to 1984 saw the appearance of the first four volumes of a twelve-volume history of Germany.[9] These volumes cover German history from its beginnings to the emergence of bourgeois society in the late 18th and 19th centuries. They show that the GDR is rooted in German history. New historical facts are included; conceptual questions are clarified; and the evaluation of historical events and processes is made more precise.[10]

In 1983 the GDR marked the 500th anniversary of the birth of Martin Luther. The theses published on this occasion honored Luther as initiator of the Reformation and trailblazer of the early bourgeois revolution in Germany.[11] The Luther anniversary underlined that the Church has a great deal of scope in which to fulfill its mission in socialist society. This kind of awareness is indispensable for the consolidation of the socialist German nation.[12]

Tribute has been paid as well to contradictory figures of Prussian tradition whose activities, though reactionary in nature, were marked by positive achievements. A biography of Frederick II of Prussia by Ingrid Mittenzwei appeared in 1979[13] and was followed in 1985 by a collection of his essays and letters.[14] Discussion of Prussian history was enlivened by the publication of the volume *Preußen - Legende und Wirklichkeit* in 1983.[15] In these works the enlightened absolutism of Frederick is treated in detail: the fact that he fostered not only the militarization of public life but science and the arts as well; that Prussia experienced economic prosperity in the 1770s and 1780s;[16] and that Berlin became one of the

---

[9] *Deutsche Geschichte in zwölf Bänden*, Vols. 1-4 (Berlin: Akademie, 1982-84).

[10] See *Von den Anfängen bis zur Ausbildung des Feudalismus Mitte des 11. Jahrhunderts*, Vol. I of *Deutsche Geschichte in zwölf Bänden*, pp. 5 f.

[11] "Thesen über Martin Luther. Zum 500. Geburtstag," *Einheit*, 36, No. 9 (1981), 890 ff.

[12] Cf. *Die SED und das kulturelle Erbe. Orientierung, Errungenschaften, Probleme* (Berlin: Dietz, 1986), p. 516.

[13] Ingrid Mittenzwei, *Friedrich II. von Preußen. Eine Biographie* (Berlin: Deutscher Verlag der Wissenschaften, 1979).

[14] *Friedrich II. von Preußen. Schriften und Briefe* (Leipzig: Philipp Reclam jun., 1985).

[15] *Preußen - Legende und Wirklichkeit* (Berlin: Dietz, 1983).

[16] Cf. Ingrid Mittenzwei, "Der 'Philosoph von Sanssouci,'" in *Preußen - Legende und Wirklichkeit*, 3rd ed. (Berlin: Dietz, 1985), pp. 59 ff.

intellectual centers of the developing German nation in the last third of the 18th century.

In 1985 a biography of Bismarck, *Bismarck. Urpreuße und Reichsgründer*, by Ernst Engelberg appeared, and a collection of documents dealing with Bismarck's life was published in the following year.[17] In the case of Bismarck, the discussion has centered around his contradictory role in the bourgeois revolution in Germany. The realistic aspects of his foreign policy have been pointed out along with criticism of his anti-worker policies, the *Kulturkampf*, and his politics of Germanization.[18]

The most recent example of the breadth of historical perception in the GDR was the tribute paid to Leopold von Ranke, the founder of bourgeois historical science, on the centenary of his death on May 23, 1986. GDR historians voiced their recognition of his work's international appeal and his humanistic convictions, at the same time indicating that Ranke's historiographic and ideological endeavors bore the mark of conservatism.[19] On the centenary of his death, the GDR Historians' Society laid a wreath at his grave in the churchyard of Berlin's Sophienkirche. The commission of the Historians' Society concerned with the theory, methodology, and history of historical science held a seminar on Ranke and the achievements and limits of idealistic German historicism in December 1986.

This reevaluation of figures from Luther to Bismarck and Ranke is not born of the pragmatic interests of the moment; it is rather, as Erich Honecker has stressed, "a question of our fundamental attitude toward German history."[20] It is crucial that the socialist German nation develop a socialist national culture embodying the humanist heritage of German history.

---

[17] Ernst Engelberg, *Bismarck. Urpreuße und Reichsgründer* (Berlin: Akademie, 1985); *Otto von Bismarck. Dokumente seines Lebens 1815-1898*, ed. Heinz Wolter (Leipzig: Philipp Reclam jun., 1986).

[18] Cf. Kurt Hager, *Gesetzmäßigkeiten unserer Epoche - Triebkräfte und Werte des Sozialismus* (Berlin: Dietz, 1983), pp. 64 f.

[19] Gerhard Lozek and Gerhard Schilfert, "Begründer der bürgerlichen Geschichtswissenschaft. Zum 100. Todestag von Leopold von Ranke," *Neues Deutschland*, 17-18 May 1986, p. 10.

[20] Erich Honecker, *Aus meinem Leben* (Berlin: Dietz, 1980), p. 437.

The development of every nation has its own individual bases, the conscious acquiring and use of which can contribute to the further shaping of national consciousness. In the case of the GDR, the historical components of the GDR's policy of peace have proven to be an effective national identification factor. Antifascism is a constructive element of the socialist German nation. On May 8, 1985 the GDR - like other countries - celebrated the 40th anniversary of the liberation from fascism. Fascism, which plunged the German people into a deep national catastrophe, was subjected to a thorough accounting.

Several progressive aspects of German history were commemorated in the period leading up to the Eleventh Party Congress in 1986. Early in April, the Marx Engels Forum, a memorial adjacent to the Palace of the Republic in Berlin, was inaugurated. At this historic place, from which the Hohenzollern dynasty reigned, a monument to Marx and Engels honors the revolutionary workers' movement, whose advent can now be traced back 140 years. On April 15, to coincide with the centenary of the birth of the German workers' leader Ernst Thälmann, a park bearing his name and housing a new residential area was opened in the traditionally working-class borough of Prenzlauer Berg, and a monument to Thälmann was unveiled.

750 Years Berlin

Finally I would like to point to a celebration of national importance in the GDR, to the 750th anniversary of the founding of Berlin. The chief objective of this extensive celebration is to bring the history of Berlin, rich as it is in humanistic, cultural, and revolutionary traditions, closer to all GDR citizens and thus to develop, as an element of national awareness, the people's awareness of the capital.

Theses on Berlin, written by a group of historians headed by Ernst Diehl, appeared in late 1985.[21] They are an example of the broad approach now being taken toward German history. Outlining the history of Berlin, they illustrate the prominence attached to the city in the Marxist perception of history. So many great events in German history are in some way connected with Berlin. The foundations of many tenets of sci-

---

[21] *750 Jahre Berlin. Thesen* (Berlin: Dietz, 1986). English edition: *750 Years of Berlin. Manifesto* (Berlin: Panorama, n.d.).

entific socialism were laid in Berlin. Acquaintance with the history of Berlin is thus of major importance for deepening the sense of national identity felt by GDR citizens.

Value of Personal and Local History

The Berlin celebration confirms once again the thesis that regional and territorial history is in a specific way capable of deepening the attachment of the people to their *Heimat*. The communicating of historical insights and teachings by mobilizing the wealth of individual experience has proven to be particularly effective as a means of developing historical awareness and strengthening national ties. This explains the special value of memoirs, local chronicles, the history of work sites, and local history in general. For thirty years now, the SED county and district committees as well as large industrial and agricultural undertakings have had their own history divisions. Recognition must be given to the work done by the Committee of Antifascist Resistance Fighters, the heritage commissions, the young historians' interest groups, and the Local History Society attached to the League of Culture. University history departments have subdivisions dealing with local history too.

History is thus not only the business of a few professional historians but also the concern of many interested citizens. The researching and presenting of German history has become a societal need. Publications and anniversary celebrations attest to a multifaceted, differentiated approach to tradition and the cultural heritage. In this way the national history of the GDR has shown itself to be an integrative factor in the development of the socialist German nation.

The GDR and the German Question:
The Unofficial Debate in the Peace Movement

John Sandford

The object of this paper is to examine some of those unofficial voices in GDR society that, by their raising of the German Question, represent a persistent irritant to the process of "nation building" that the state is seeking to accomplish. The official position is familiar enough: it rejects any claims that the "German Question" is still open, and insists that there are now two states on German soil, with two irreconcilably differing social and political orders, integrated into two separate military alliances, and with competing assessments of the German history that led up to them.[1]

This has, of course, not always been the case. Whilst the official Western position has changed little, the official Eastern view of the German Question has changed fundamentally over the three and a half decades of the GDR's existence. Today's insistence on the separateness of the two German states is a result of the reassessment of the German Question that began in the 1960s, was formulated in the 1970s, and is being further elaborated in the 1980s. At an unofficial level, voices have always been heard that were unwilling to keep step with these changes, obstructing the methodical closing of the German Question that was being undertaken by the SED. Today, these unofficial voices are still audible: indeed, there are distinct signs of a reawakened interest in the German Question in the GDR. This is especially the case among certain sections of the "unofficial peace movement," whose statements on the German Question

---

[1] See, for instance, the entry "nationale Frage" in *Kleines Politisches Wörterbuch*, 4th ed. (Berlin: Dietz, 1983), pp. 642-44.

reflect a growing interest similar to that among their counterparts in the West German peace movement.[2]

The peace movement's involvement with the German Question in both German states signals a process of rediscovery. Its participants are largely younger people who have grown up in the postwar years, and who can thus be presumed not to have the same sentimental attachment to ideas of German identity that may still linger among older generations. They have instead reached the German Question via discussions about the perceived current threats to peace in Europe and in the two German states in particular. What they have rediscovered are firstly the debates of the 1950s and 1960s in which the division of Germany was perceived as a crucial factor in the threat to world peace, and secondly the fact that discussion of the German Question is by no means the prerogative of the "revanchist" right, but that rather the right managed to appropriate the terms of the debate in the wake of the *Ostpolitik* of the 1970s, reasserting irredentist notions of "reunification" that warped recollections of an earlier pacific left-wing tradition of discussing Germany.[3]

The unofficial debate on the German Question in the GDR has focused on a number of pertinent issues. Four terms in particular are of special interest: two of them - the bloc-division of Europe and the de jure occupation of the two German states - provide a starting point for the analysis; the other two - calls for a German Peace Treaty and for a German Confederation - posit potential ways out of the present impasse.

The division of Germany is seen as exemplifying the self-perpetuating and perilous division of Europe into two mutually reinforcing blocs, each of which needs the other and the "threat" it (allegedly) poses to ensure cohesion and to justify the disciplined maintenance of the status quo, both domestically and externally. This division of Europe and of Germany is perceived as a function of the interests of the superpowers rather than as a result of the wishes of the Europeans or Germans themselves. The countries of Eastern

---

[2] On the new debate in the Federal Republic see my article "Alternative Approaches to the German Question," *German Life and Letters*, 38, No. 4 (1985), 427-41.

[3] See the invaluable anthology *Die Linke und die nationale Frage*, ed. Peter Brandt and Herbert Ammon (Reinbek: Rowohlt, 1981), which contains numerous examples.

and Western Europe are thus - it is further asserted - in a state of occupation: a de facto occupation in most countries of NATO and the Warsaw Pact; but, above and beyond this, a de jure occupation in the Federal Republic and the GDR resulting from unique legal provisions in the four-power treaties.

Among the long-term proposals for a resolution of this situation, the formulation and implementation of a German Peace Treaty that would provide for a neutralization and demilitarization of Central Europe plays an important part. Once foreign troops were removed from German soil, and the two German states released from their respective pacts, the way would be open to a closer accommodation between them: wary of simplistic notions of "reunification," participants in the new debate have resurrected proposals for a "German Confederation" as a possible model for such an accommodation.

It is in the nature of a system such as the GDR's that hard-and-fast evidence for dissenting or unofficial views is a) limited in quantity, b) virtually impossible to authenticate conclusively, and c) almost impossible to assess in terms of its representativeness for public opinion or for "behind-the-scenes" debate in ruling circles. It is thus readily dismissible by the "authorities."

Notwithstanding these reservations, a number of documents have appeared in recent years that attest persisting interest in the German Question, and whose authenticity has not been denied. The following four are of particular interest: the "Havemann-Brief" (to Leonid Brezhnev) of September 1981; the "Berliner Appell" of January 1982; the "Papiere aus Osteuropa," collated by the West German Greens in the summer of 1984 (the so-called "Perugia-Papiere"); and the statement "An die Unterzeichner des Prager Aufrufs" of June 1985.

The "Havemann-Brief"

Robert Havemann, the last of the older generation of critical Marxists in the GDR, was, in the years leading up to his death in 1982, much concerned with the relationship of the German Question to the constantly threatened and uneasy postwar "peace" in Europe. In December 1979 *Die Zeit* published a piece that Havemann had headed "Wiedervereinigung oder Tod," and which he had written as a response to the then imminent NATO "Nachrüstungsbeschluß." Hailing the Brezhnev initiative of unilaterally withdrawing 20,000 Soviet troops, as well as tanks and other equipment from the GDR, Havemann went on to propose something much more radical: the "Abzug *aller* sowjetischen Truppen, *aller* Panzer und *allen* Kriegsmaterials, das unter sowjetischer Kontrolle steht, aus dem Gebiet der DDR . . . wenn gleichzeitig die USA bereit sind, auch ihrerseits *alle* ihre Truppen, Panzer, Flugzeuge und sonstiges Kriegsmaterial aus der BRD abzuziehen."[4] But this was not simply a military matter: for Havemann, such a move would unlock the frozen German Question and lead to "das Ende der unglückseligen Nachkriegspolitik, die mit der Teilung und Spaltung Deutschlands begann" (p. 27). His conclusion was, to say the least, provocative:

> Deutschland würde wieder den Deutschen gehören. Wie wir dann unsere nationale Frage lösen werden, ist schwer vorauszusehen. Aber wir wären dann endlich dazu gezwungen und nicht, wie bisher, daran gehindert. Die beiden Deutschlands werden es nicht leicht haben, wieder zusammenzuwachsen. In beiden werden große Veränderungen vor sich gehen. Aber ich denke, die gegenwärtigen Zustände in beiden deutschen Staaten, so extrem verschieden sie sind, verdienen es doch nicht, daß man ihnen auch nur eine Träne nachweint. (p. 27)

These ideas were taken up again in a letter that Havemann wrote in June 1981 to Helmut Schmidt in which he called on the Chancellor to act "nicht als ein Kanzler der Amerikaner, sondern als ein Kanzler der Deutschen";[5] now he called for "Abrüstung, schrittweise Entfernung aller atomaren Waffen vom Territorium der beiden deutschen Staaten, Abzug der ausländischen Besatzungstruppen aus beiden Teilen Deutsch-

---

[4] Robert Havemann, "Wiedervereinigung oder Tod," *Die Zeit,* 7 December 1979, p. 27. Havemann's emphasis. *Die Zeit* explicitly distanced itself both from the article and its title, which it prefaced with the statement: "Heute drucken wir ein Manuskript Havemanns zur Diskussion über die Nachrüstung der NATO ab. 'Wiedervereinigung oder Tod' hat er selber darüber geschrieben. Wir stimmen weder mit seiner militärischen Analyse noch mit seiner politischen Zielvorstellung . . . überein."

[5] The text of the letter is reprinted in *Schwerter zu Pflugscharen. Friedensbewegung in der DDR,* ed. Klaus Ehring and Martin Dallwitz (Reinbek: Rowohlt, 1982), pp. 208-09.

lands, Entmilitarisierung und Neutralisierung Deutschlands" (p. 208).

Havemann's most public expression of these sentiments came in an open letter that he addressed to Leonid Brezhnev on the occasion of the Soviet leader's state visit to Bonn in late November 1981. Once again he identified the division of Germany as the crucial factor in Europe's peril: "Die Teilung Deutschlands schuf nicht Sicherheit, sondern wurde Voraussetzung der tödlichsten Bedrohung, die es in Europa jemals gegeben hat."[6] Once again he called for the removal of "occupation forces" from Germany: "36 Jahre nach Ende des Krieges ist es jetzt zur dringenden Notwendigkeit geworden, die Friedensverträge zu schließen und alle Besatzungstruppen aus beiden Teilen Deutschlands abzuziehen." Once again - though now in a mildly more positive form - came the vision of the Germans resuming responsibility for their own future: "Wie wir Deutsche unsere nationale Frage dann lösen werden, muß man uns schon selbst überlassen und niemand sollte sich davor mehr fürchten, als vor dem Atomkrieg" (p. 14).

The "Berliner Appell"

Although, needless to say, it was passed over in official silence in the GDR, Havemann's letter to Brezhnev received wide publicity in the West, where it was taken up and promoted as a "Deutsche Friedensinitiative," with large advertisements in newspapers sponsored by over twenty thousand additional signatories.[7] GDR signatories were inevitably few in number: the document as originally circulated contained twenty-seven names from the GDR. One of these was that of Pastor Rainer Eppelmann. He was now to become prominent himself as the initiator of the "Berliner Appell."

In fact, to talk of this document as "Rainer Eppelmann's 'Berliner Appell,'" as is so often done in the West, is misleading, and nowhere more so than in the case of its

---

[6] "Offener Brief an den Vorsitzenden des Präsidiums des Obersten Sowjets der UdSSR, Leonid Breshnew," *Die Zeit*, 20 November 1981, p. 14. The text of the "Havemann-Brief" is reproduced in part in Ehring and Dallwitz, pp. 212-14. An English translation of the letter is to be found in John Sandford, *The Sword and the Ploughshare. Autonomous Peace Initiatives in East Germany* (London: Merlin Press, 1983), pp. 89-91.

[7] In adition to *Die Zeit*, it appeared, for instance, in the *tageszeitung* on 20 November 1981, and in *Der Tagesspiegel* and the *Süddeutsche Zeitung* on 21 November 1981.

references to the German Question. It was actually put together jointly by Eppelmann and Havemann, with the former responsible for its underlying Christian and pacifist sentiments, and the latter for the by now familiar references to the broader German context. Eppelmann, an East Berlin pastor specializing in youth work whose "alternative" "Blues-Messen" had a considerable following among young people from far beyond his own parish, had already written - without receiving a reply - to Erich Honecker in June 1981, criticizing manifestations of militarization in GDR life, and calling for a nuclear-free zone in Central Europe, the withdrawal of foreign troops, and step-by-step total disarmament.[8]

The "Berliner Appell" was formulated by Havemann and Eppelmann early in 1982, and was launched on 25 January that year, when it began circulating unofficially in the GDR with a request for signatures. Although overall it bore the stamp of Eppelmann rather than that of Havemann, the latter's contributions were clear in the earlier sections - in particular the third:

> Das geteilte Deutschland ist zur Aufmarschbasis der beiden großen Atommächte geworden. Wir schlagen vor, diese lebensgefährdende Konfrontation zu beenden. Die Siegermächte des Zweiten Weltkrieges müssen endlich die Friedensverträge mit den beiden deutschen Staaten schließen, wie es im Potsdamer Abkommen von 1945 beschlossen worden ist. Danach sollten die ehemaligen Alliierten ihre Besatzungstruppen aus Deutschland abziehen und Garantien über Nichteinmischung in die inneren Angelegenheiten der beiden deutschen Staaten vereinbaren.[9]

Although the Church distanced itself from the Appeal - stating amongst other things: "Genauer als es im Appell geschieht, muß die tatsächliche politische und militärische

---

[8] The letter is reprinted in Ehring and Dallwitz, pp. 218-20. English translation in Sandford, pp. 92-94.

[9] The "Berliner Appell" is reprinted in Ehring and Dallwitz, pp. 227-29; quotation, pp. 227-28. English translation of document in Sandford, pp. 95-96, and in Roger Woods, *Opposition in the GDR under Honecker. 1971-85* (London: Macmillan, 1986), pp. 195-97.

Konstellation bedacht werden"[10] - there is no doubt that the loose network of contacts among Christians in the GDR did facilitate its circulation and discussion, whilst the very fact of the Church's official reservations about it inevitably drew attention to the Appeal and raised curiosity about it, as is indicated, for instance, in the applause and excitability of the audience when the Appeal was mentioned - and the shout "Lest den Appell doch vor!" - at the Dresden "Friedensforum" of 13 February 1982.[11]

The "Perugia-Papiere"

In July 1984 representatives from peace movements from all over the world met in Perugia, Italy, for the third European Nuclear Disarmament Convention. The majority came from Western Europe; most East European countries, including the Soviet Union, sent small official delegations, though two - Czechoslovakia and the GDR, the countries chosen for the Soviet "counterdeployments" of nuclear missiles - were notably absent. With the partial exception of Hungary, "unofficial" spokespersons from Eastern Europe were unable to attend, though a number of recent members of the GDR peace scene who had since moved to the West were present. As a contribution to making good this widely regretted absence, the West German Greens presented a set of "Papiere aus Osteuropa." Seven of these ten papers were statements from the "autonomous" peace movement in the GDR, and two of these explicitly addressed the German Question.

The first paper - "Gedanken zur Erreichung einer europäischen Friedensordnung" - raises the issue of the role of the German Question in peace movement discussion; the topic is, it asserts, unavoidable:

> Es ist bisher von Teilen der Friedensbewegung mit Unverständnis zur Kenntnis genommen worden, wenn im Zusammenhang mit friedenspolitischen Diskussionen die Behandlung der

---

[10] "Stellungnahme der Kirchenleitung der Evangelischen Kirche in Berlin Brandenburg (Ost) (13.2.1982)," in *Friedensbewegung in der DDR. Texte 1978-1982*, ed. Wolfgang Büscher, Peter Wensierski, and Klaus Wolschner (Hattingen: Scandica-Verlag, 1982), p. 283.

[11] "Stellungnahme der Kirchenleitung," p. 277. For a more detailed discussion of the "Havemann-Brief," the "Berliner Appell," and the Dresden "Friedensforum," see Sandford, pp. 58-75.

"deutschen Frage" als ein wichtiger Aspekt zur Konfliktverminderung in den Vordergrund gestellt wird. Dieses Unverständnis ist historisch begründet und basiert auf der Sorge um das Wiedererstarken eines geeinten Deutschlands. Wir müssen diese Sorge ernst nehmen. Doch die Analyse des Zustandekommens der gegenwärtigen Situation läßt uns an der Lösung dieses Problems nicht vorbei.[12]

The paper goes on to claim that the division of Europe has placed the two German states "in den Zustand eines besetzten Landes" (p. 2). The way out of the present dilemma lies in the "Abschluß eines Friedensvertrages, der den Abzug der Besatzungsmächte vertraglich sichert und es den beiden Staaten ermöglicht, in freier Selbstbestimmung über ihre Zukunft zu entscheiden" (p. 2). And beyond that peace treaty lies the possibility of even more far-reaching changes: "Ob diese Zukunft sich in einer Konförderation [sic] und der späteren Wiedervereinigung gestaltet, ist notwendiger Bestandteil unserer Diskussion mit allen Europäern" (p. 3).

Paper 6 - "Überlegungen für ein Europa ohne militärische Blockkonfrontation, für eine Gesamteuropäische Friedensordnung" - is the longest and most wide-ranging of the "Perugia-Papiere." It sees the German Question as essentially one of creating "normality" in the relations between the German states; as a solution it too proposes the creation of a German Confederation:

> Aufgrund wirtschaftlicher und kultureller Beziehungen bzw. Traditionen sollte, unter Berufung auf die gleiche Nationalität und gemeinsame nationale Beziehungen miteinander, eine Politik verfolgt werden, die die Realisierung einer Konföderation zum Ziel hat. Im Rahmen einer Konföderation ließen sich die existierenden Unterschiede, allein bedingt durch die verschiedenen und praktizierten Gesellschaftsordnungen beibehalten. (p. 9)

---

[12] The "Papiere aus Osteuropa" are collated in a loose-leaf format consisting of photocopies of the original typescripts. Here: Paper 1, p. 2.

The point is stressed again later in the paper, which, in contradistinction to Paper 1, explicitly rejects notions of "German unity":

> Für die fernere Stufe einer Gesamteuropäischen Friedensordnung stände die Frage, wie werden sich die beiden deutschen Staaten zueinander in Beziehung stellen, auf der Verhandlungsliste und müßte positiv entschieden werden. Positiv hieße, und dies sei ausdrücklich unterstrichen: die Nachkriegsentwicklungen in Fragen der unterschiedlichen Gesellschaftsordnung sind nicht rückgängig zu machen, sind anzuerkennen. Aus diesem Grunde und aus Beachtung europäischer Geschichte kann nicht die Wiedervereinigung Deutschlands das Ziel sein, sondern eine Konföderation beider deutscher Staaten. (p. 10)

"An die Unterzeichner des Prager Aufrufs"

The "Perugia-Papiere" showed that the death of Robert Havemann in April 1982 had not meant the end of the German Question debate within the GDR. They also indicated that participants in the debate were, like Havemann, sensitive to the concern the raising of this issue might arouse among the Germans' European neighbors. Considerable interest was therefore generated when, on 11 March 1985, Charter 77 published a document that it called the "Prague Appeal" - a statement that took the form of a letter to the participants in that year's END Convention, to be held in Amsterdam - in which for the first time in the new debate the German Question was broached in another East European country:

> In pursuit of these aims [of a "democratic and sovereign Europe"] we can no longer avoid those issues which have so far been taboo, one of which is the division of Germany. If our aim is European unification, then no one can be denied the right to self-determination; and this applies equally to the Germans. . . . let us acknowledge openly the right of the Germans freely to decide if or how they wish to unite their two states within their present frontiers. Following Bonn's agreements with its Eastern neighbours and the Helsinki Accords, the sign-

ing of a peace treaty with Germany could become one of the most important levers for a positive transformation of Europe.[13]

In many respects, Charter 77 was thinking along lines that went beyond what was being discussed in the GDR, but the fact that it had, without prompting, raised the centrality of the German Question to visions of a European peace order, struck a resonant chord in the GDR. On 8 June 1985 twenty East Berlin peace activists - Rainer Eppelmann among them - signed an open letter "An die Unterzeichner des Prager Aufrufs," in which they expressed their accord with the sentiments Charter 77 had expressed. Their response to the raising of the German Question came around the middle of their letter, as it had in the original Charter document, and was elaborated in some detail; it was clear that they were deeply grateful that the issue had been made more "respectable" by being raised by non-Germans:

Ein für uns wichtiger Bestandteil Eures Aufrufs ist die Haltung zur deutschen Frage. Wir sind froh, daß gerade Ihr dazu Stellung genommen habt und zur Diskussion auffordert. Ist dies doch ein mit starken Ressentiments verbundenes Thema für viele europäische Staaten. Deutschlands Bedeutung im europäischen Spannungsfeld legt uns eine besondere Verantwortung auf. Wir denken, daß die Lösung der europäischen Frage nicht von der deutschen zu trennen ist. Die deutsche Vergangenheit mahnt uns jedoch zu großer Vorsicht und Rücksichtnahme gegenüber den Befürchtungen der ehemals von Deutschland unterdrückten Länder. Um die Teilung Deutschlands zu überwinden, müssen alle Lösungsmöglichkeiten der deutschen Frage diskutiert werden. Dies sollten die Deutschen gemeinsam mit allen Völkern Europas tun, weil Selbstbestimmung der Völker heute nur mit Rücksichtnahme auf die Interessen aller anderen Völker Europas zur Entspannung und Überwindung der Teilung

---

[13] The English version of the Prague Appeal ("Charter 77 Document No. 5/1985") was made available by Palach Press Agency in London. It was published in, amongst other places, the *END Journal* (London), No. 15 (April-May 1985), p. 34, and *Peace and Democracy News* (New York), 2, No. 1 (1985), 10-11.

unseres Kontinents beitragen kann. Die Lösung der deutschen Frage kann daher nur eingebettet in einem gesamteuropäischen Vertragswerk eine Rolle spielen. Im Rahmen eines solchen Prozesses wird die Frage nach Abschluß eines Friedensvertrages mit den beiden deutschen Staaten von Bedeutung sein. Wichtigste Kernpunkte wäre [sic] die Erfüllung des Potsdamer Abkommens, hinsichtlich der Entmilitarisierung Deutschlands, und die endgültige Festschreibung der deutschen Grenzen, wie sie seit 1945 bestehen.[14]

The Significance of the Debate

It becomes clear when one places the references to the German Question in these four documents alongside one another that a debate is taking place in the GDR that is developing and extending the analysis of this topic. Havemann's initial premise (in the letter to Brezhnev) that answers to the German Question could provide answers to the European Question was obscured to a certain extent by the brusque tone of his indignantly nationalist formulations. The tone of the relevant passages in the "Berliner Appell" is milder, though the focus is still very much on Germany, and the forthright reference to "Besatzungstruppen" remains.

The "Perugia-Papiere" broaden the focus: as their titles indicate, their concern is with a "European Peace Order." Their arguments are more sophisticated and sensitive to the unease of others at the raising of the German Question. In Paper 1 the idea of "occupation" is again raised, though it is discussed in more detail in the context of the overall division of Europe. The significant innovation of both of these papers is their raising of the vision of a German Confederation. In the case of Paper 1, this is done almost in passing, and combined with a reference to a possible later "Wiedervereinigung."

---

[14] Facsimiles of "An die Unterzeichner des Prager Aufrufs" were made available to participants in the Amsterdam END Convention in early July 1985; the quoted passage is on p. 2 of the letter. On 22 November 1984 "unofficial" peace campaigners from Czechoslovakia and the GDR (describing themselves as "Tschechen, Slowaken und Deutsche aus der DDR") had issued a joint declaration expressing their solidarity with one another in the search for a peaceful, just, and democratic Europe. (The declaration was printed in, amongst other places, the *Frankfurter Rundschau* of 26 November 1984, p. 2.)

Paper 6 makes of the confederation a much more definite proposal, but on the other hand expressly envisages this as the end-point of the process: "die Nachkriegsentwicklungen in Fragen der unterschiedlichen Gesellschaftsordnung sind nicht rückgängig zu machen, sind anzuerkennen . . . die Wiedervereinigung Deutschlands [kann] nicht das Ziel sein."

It is noticeable that this more subtle approach to the German Question, which eschews the simplistic notion that "division" can only be rectified by "reunification," is not so evident in the Charter 77 document, which speaks of the "right of the Germans . . . to unite their two states." Charter does, however, add the rider "within their present frontiers" - a point explicitly picked up in the response "An die Unterzeichner des Prager Aufrufs," which lays stress on "die endgültige Festschreibung der deutschen Grenzen, wie sie seit 1945 bestehen."

"Bloc-division," "occupation," "German Peace Treaty," and "German Confederation" seem to have emerged, then, as crucial terms of this "unofficial" debate on the German Question in the GDR. But these are also crucial terms of the debate on Germany within the *Western* peace movement,[15] and inevitably any presentation of this GDR debate is liable to be dismissed with the suggestion that it is derivative and Western-inspired. Clearly such suggestions are, in the final analysis, impossible to prove or disprove. The paternalistic assertion that autonomous peace initiatives in the GDR were "inspired" by the West German "neue Friedensbewegung" is belied by a look both at the dates by which a revival of the peace movement began to manifest itself in the two states, and by the distinctively "home-bred" nature of the issues that first exercised peace activists in the GDR.[16]

What has happened since the early eighties is a re-discovery on both sides of the German-German border of

---

[15] There are many examples of this Western debate, especially in the journal *Deutschland Archiv*. Many of the sources are mentioned in my article "Alternative Approaches to the German Question" (Note 2 above). See also the sixty-page "Denkschrift: Friedensvertrag, Deutsche Konföderation. Europäisches Sicherheitssystem" that appeared in West Berlin in March 1985. (Subsequently published as: Herbert Ammon and Theodor Schweisfurth, *Friedensvertrag, Deutsche Konföderation, Europäisches Sicherheitssystem. Denkschrift zur Verwirklichung einer europäischen Friedensordnung* [Starnberg: ibf-Verlag, 1985].)

[16] See Sandford, *The Sword and the Ploughshare*, pp. 25-47.

earlier premises of Euro-strategic and peace-movement analysis: of the fact that in the 1950s overcoming the division of Germany was widely recognized in both East and West as the key to the establishment of a peaceful order in Europe. And it was not only the voices of "unofficial" peace protesters that raised these issues in the 1950s, as is made clear by the 1952 "Stalin Note" on German reunification, Ulbricht's proposal for a German Confederation of 1957, the Soviet Peace Treaty proposal of 1959, and the "Nationales Dokument," unanimously approved by the GDR's Nationale Front on 17 June 1962. Proceeding from the premise that the concluding of a peace treaty and the forming of a confederation of the two German states was the "safe and less painful path" toward the solving of the German Question, the "Nationales Dokument" went still further in the direction of full reunification. The confederation was conceived of as a temporary measure: "Sie würde also mit der Wiedervereinigung Deutschlands erlöschen. . . . Die Konföderation ist der einzig noch verbliebene reale Weg, die Einheit des deutschen Volkes schrittweise wiederherzustellen."[17]

In fact, arguments about how much, and of what, this debate is "derivative" are red herrings. All ideas come from somewhere: what is important is that the debate is there. But this leads to a much more important reservation, and that concerns the representativeness of this debate in the GDR. Does it really signify an obstacle to official attempts at "nation building"? Is it not rather the expression of an eccentric viewpoint by a handful of malcontents that is not only largely unheard by, but also utterly untypical of, the majority of GDR citizens? In the absence of public opinion polls there is no way of telling.[18] But certainly the views analyzed here are decidedly *not* in tune with the officially voiced approach to the German Question.

Yet it is striking that the official response to this debate has been one of total silence. What has been attacked, and

---

[17] Quoted in Brandt and Ammon, pp. 215-16. This anthology contains many other documents of the SED's "Deutschlandpolitik" prior to the 1970s.

[18] According to Karl Wilhelm Fricke, "Die Einheit der Nation kann als gemeinsamer Nenner noch immer in der übergroßen Mehrheit der Bevölkerung bis hin zu den gut zwei Millionen Mitgliedern der SED unterstellt werden." (*Opposition und Widerstand in der DDR* [Cologne: Verlag Wissenschaft und Politik, 1984], p. 217). Fricke also sees "das Ja zur Einheit der Nation" as the only common denominator of the various oppositional forces in GDR society (p. 217).

vociferously and persistently at that, have been the right-wing, "revanchist" approaches to the German Question that are still current in certain quarters in the Federal Republic, including circles close to the Kohl government itself. It is also striking that contacts between Eastern and Western proponents of a more thoughtful approach to the German Question have been hindered to a quite unprecedented degree by the GDR authorities, as have visits to Czechoslovakia by exponents of such an approach from East Berlin.[19] These facts suggest that the authorities suspect that a discussion of the German Question that explicitly opposes "revanchist" attitudes and that links it with the establishment of a peaceful order in Europe, may well have great potential appeal for the people of the GDR. But perhaps too there is a desire in high quarters to ensure that when the debate *is* conducted openly, its terms and agenda are controlled and determined by the state.

Just how closed *is* discussion of the German Question at the official level in the GDR? On the surface the "Deutsche Frage" has been consigned to history. Yet at the same time the GDR is very busy appropriating that history. It is also, particularly in the person of Erich Honecker, very busy protecting German-German relations from the chill winds of the new Cold War - even at the cost of incurring Soviet displeasure. Just occasionally there are odd glimpses through gaps in the official façade, as in January 1983 when *Neues Deutschland* reprinted a speech by Gert Bastian that called for a "Rückkehr zur Normalität in Europa"[20] and included the words: "es ist ja eigentlich ein unnormaler Zustand, daß

---

[19] See the dossier "'Sie sind unerwünscht . . .' Einreiseverbote in die DDR. Eine Dokumentation," published by the Alternative Liste Berlin, December 1985.

[20] "Die Grünen sind für eine neue Politik der Bundesrepublik Deutschland. Ehemaliger Bundeswehrgeneral Bastian zu Fragen der Gleichheit der Nuklearrüstung," *ND*, 28 January 1983, p. 5. A year later, an editorial in *ND* attacking the Bundestag's acclamation of the "Bericht zur Lage der Nation" picked out precisely this phrase for special scorn: "Dennoch wird hier erneut davon geredet, 'unser Land' sei geteilt. Wessen Land?" (*ND*, 11/12 February 1984, p. 2). Much has been written about the apparent ambivalence of official statements on the German Question in the GDR; see, for instance, Karl-Ernst Jeismann, "Die Einheit der Nation im Geschichtsbild der DDR," *Aus Politik und Zeitgeschichte*, 13 August 1983, pp. 3-16; and Hans-Dieter Schütte, *Zeitgeschichte und Politik. Deutschland- und blockpolitische Perspektiven der SED in den Konzeptionen marxistisch-leninistischer Zeitgeschichte* (Bonn: Verlag Neue Gesellschaft, 1985).

Europa und unser Land auch in zwei sich mißtrauisch belauernde, waffenstarrende Militärblöcke geteilt ist" (p. 5).

Occasionally too accounts of "unofficial" meetings with more or less "official" people in the GDR appear that suggest a more receptive attitude to new approaches to the German Question than more public pronouncements display. A recent case in point is the account by Richard Sperber, a moving force behind the West German "Initiativkreis Friedensvertrag," of a discussion "mit einem prominenten DDR-Journalisten und mit zwei Dozenten des 'Instituts für Internationale Beziehungen' an der 'Akademie für Staats- und Rechtswissenschaften der DDR.'" Sperber explained his ideas for a German Peace Treaty; "Die DDR-Vertreter," he then reported,

> schienen von diesen Ausführungen positiv beeindruckt und brachten keine Einwände gegen unseren Vertragsentwurf vor. Sie ließen auch durchblicken, daß die schroffe Ablehnung bisheriger westdeutscher Friedensvertragswünsche durch die DDR sich nur auf solche Vorschläge bezieht, denen eine revisionistische Grundtendenz anhaftet, wie z.B. den Vorstellungen der westdeutschen Vertriebenenverbände. Da jedoch unser Vertragsentwurf von ganz anderen, nämlich von realistischen, Voraussetzungen ausgeht, sagten die DDR-Vertreter eine sorgfältige wissenschaftliche Prüfung des Vertragstextes im Institut für Internationale Beziehungen der Akademie für Staats- und Rechtswissenschaften in Potsdam zu.[21]

"Ich verließ das Internationale Presse-Zentrum in Ostberlin," Sperber concludes, "mit dem Eindruck, daß die DDR einem deutschen Friedensvertrag nicht mehr grundsätzlich ablehnend gegenübersteht, vorausgesetzt, daß die Sowjetunion zustimmt." Sperber also noted guarded interest in the idea of a German Confederation.

---

[21] "Wie steht die DDR zu einem Friedensvertrag?" in *Rundbrief* No. 7 of the "Initiativkreis Friedensvertrag" (Garbsen, 1 November 1985), pp. 4-5. The "Initiativkreis," which has a largely Green and left-wing constituency, campaigns for the adoption of the peace-treaty issue by the broader peace movement, and has produced its own draft of a possible peace treaty.

Skeptics might argue that these glimpses are glimpses of the past rather than of the future. One thing is undeniable, though, and that is that - be they the tail end of what has gone before, or harbingers of something to come - they *are* glimpses of the present: the German Question debate has not been entirely closed by the GDR's exercise in "nation building." It is thus conceivable that the German Question will after all turn out to be still "open" - though not in the terms of simplistic irredentist notions of "reunification" with which the West gives the East such ready targets for undifferentiated rejection.

Contributors to *Studies in GDR Culture and Society 7*

Authors

Lothar Bisky, Cultural Sociologist, *Rektor*, Hochschule für Film und Fernsehen der DDR "Konrad Wolf," Potsdam-Babelsberg.

Christine Cosentino, Germanist, Professor, Department of German, Rutgers University, Camden, New Jersey.

Günter Erbe, Sociologist, *Dozent*, Researcher at Zentralinstitut für sozialwissenschaftliche Forschung, Freie Universität Berlin.

Wolfgang Ertl, Germanist, Associate Professor, Department of German, University of Iowa.

Gisela Helwig, Political Scientist, Editor, *Deutschland Archiv*, Cologne.

Carolyn R. Hodges, Germanist, Assistant Professor, Department of Germanic and Slavic Languages, University of Tennessee, Knoxville.

Gail P. Hueting, Librarian/Germanist, Assistant Modern Languages Librarian, University of Illinois at Urbana-Champaign.

Fred Klinger, Political Scientist, Researcher and Lecturer, Institut für sozialwissenschaftliche Forschung, Freie Universität Berlin.

Wolfgang Kohlhaase, Author and Screen Writer, DEFA.

Nancy A. Lauckner, Germanist, Associate Professor, Department of Germanic and Slavic Languages, University of Tennessee, Knoxville.

Christiane Lemke, Political Scientist/Sociologist, Researcher and Lecturer, Institut für sozialwissenschaftliche Forschung, Freie Universität Berlin.

Alfred Loesdau, Historian, Professor, Institut für Geschichte der deutschen Arbeiterbewegung, Akademie für Gesellschaftswissenschaften beim ZK der SED.

Sigrid Meuschel, Sociologist, Researcher, Institut für sozialwissenschaftliche Forschung, Freie Universität Berlin.

Rüdiger Pieper, *Diplom Volkswirt*, Paul-Löbe-Institut, Berlin, Institut für Unternehmensführung, Freie Universität Berlin.

John Sandford, Germanist, Reader, Department of German, University of Reading, England.

Rainer Saupe, Economist, Bereich Internationale Finanzen, Sektion Wirtschaftswissenschaften, Humboldt-Universität, Berlin.

H.-J. Schulz, Germanist, Associate Professor, Department of Germanic and Slavic Languages/Comparative Literature Program, Vanderbilt University, Nashville, Tennessee.

Denis M. Sweet, Germanist, Assistant Professor, Department of Foreign Languages and Literatures, Bates College, Lewiston, Maine.

Editors

Margy Gerber, Germanist, Professor, Department of German, Russian, and East Asian Languages, Bowling Green State University, Bowling Green, Ohio.

Christine Cosentino, see above.

Volker Gransow, Political Scientist/Sociologist, *Dozent*, DAAD Professor, University of California, Berkeley.

Nancy A. Lauckner, see above.

Christiane Lemke, see above.

Arthur A. Stahnke, Political Scientist, Professor, Department of Government, Southern Illinois University, Edwardsville.

Alexander Stephan, Germanist, Professor, Department of Germanic and Slavic Languages and Literatures, University of Florida, Gainesville.

W. Christoph Schmauch, ex officio member of editorial board, Pastor, Director of World Fellowship Center, Conway, N.H.